Linking Assessment to Instructional Strategies

A Guide for Teachers

Cathleen G. Spinelli

Saint Joseph's University

PEARSON

Boston Columbus Indianapolis New York San Francisco Upper Saddle River
Amsterdam Cape Town Dubai London Madrid Milan Munich Paris Montreal Toronto
Delhi Mexico City Sao Paulo Sydney Hong Kong Seoul Singapore Taipei Tokyo

Vice President and Editor in Chief: Jeffery W. Johnston
Executive Editor: Ann Castel Davis
Editorial Assistant: Penny Burleson
Senior Managing Editor: Pamela D. Bennett
Project Manager: Kerry J. Rubadue
Senior Operations Supervisor: Matthew Ottenweller
Senior Art Director: Diane Lorenzo
Text Designer: S4Carlisle Publishing Services
Cover Designer: Candace Rowley
Cover Art: Corbis
Full-Service Project Management:
S4Carlisle Publishing Services
Composition: S4Carlisle Publishing Services
Printer/Binder: Bind-Rite
Cover Printer: Lehigh-Phoenix Color/Hagerstown
Text Font: Palatino

Credits and acknowledgments borrowed from other sources and reproduced, with permission, in this textbook appear on appropriate page within text.

Library of Congress Cataloging-in-Publication Data
Spinelli, Cathleen G.
Linking assessment to instructional strategies : a guide for teachers / Cathleen G. Spinelli.
p. cm.
Includes bibliographical references and index.
ISBN 978-0-13-714624-6
1. Individualized instruction. 2. Cognitive styles in children. 3. Mixed ability grouping in education.
I. Title.
LB1031.S675 2011
371.26--dc22

2010013081

17 18

PEARSON

www.pearsonpd.com

ISBN 10: 0-13-714624-8
ISBN 13: 978-0-13-714624-6

Preface

Linking Assessment to Instructional Strategies: A Guide for Teachers is written for preservice and practicing teachers, support staff, and administrators: those school professionals dedicated to working with our increasingly diverse population of students receiving general and special education. It is intended for those who are interested in developing or expanding their assessment skills, monitoring student progress, and using this information to inform instruction, thus improving student performance. This compendium of easy-to-use, authentic, curriculum- and performance-based assessment strategies also includes an array of matching instructional suggestions for students who have either (a) mastered the skills assessed, (b) need additional remediation, or (c) require more intensive intervention.

While most assessment books focus on formal, standardized testing, this book is different. It provides the reader with informal, teacher-friendly, and classroom-relevant methods of measuring achievement, identifying strengths and weaknesses, and monitoring the progress of students with diverse learning needs. The goal of this book is to provide the teacher with the skills necessary to identify and address the needs of the whole child.

This book can also serve as a supplemental text for general and/or special education assessment, educational psychology, tests and measures, consultation, and methods courses. It is also ideal for use in professional development and inservices for school district personnel.

CHAPTER CONTENTS AND ORGANIZATION

Each chapter begins with an introduction to the importance of and the uses for each assessment covered; the particular skills each assessment evaluates; and specific diagnostic questions, so that teachers can match the student's problem to the appropriate assessment. In addition, each assessment description includes the appropriate age and grade range for administration, the amount of time that should be allocated for each assessment, and a step-by-step guide for preparation, including required materials and explicit examples. Consideration is given to accommodations and alternatives for students with special cultural, linguistic, academic, cognitive, emotional, social, medical, and physical needs. A special added feature in the basic skills and content area subject assessment chapters, "Next Step," provides instructional interventions for use once the assessment process is completed.

This book is organized as follows: Chapter 1 provides an introduction to assessment methods with particular focus on early identification, progress monitoring, and the intervention process for students who are at risk for academic and behavior problems.

Chapter 2 covers the initial information-gathering process. It addresses how to obtain, interpret, and use preliminary assessment information, including parent, teacher, and student interviews; observation techniques; record reviews; work-sample analyses; health assessments; textbook and classroom environment analyses; and related supplemental assessments.

Chapters 3, 4, and 5 deal with basic skills and content area subject assessment, including reading, written language, math, science, and social studies subject content. These chapters address how to plan, construct, administer, score, and connect results to appropriate instructional interventions.

Chapter 6 is focused on assessment and the implementation of accommodations for students with special needs, including English language learners, those who have emotional-social problems, and all students who require monitoring and intervention.

Chapter 7 provides an overview of grading, graphing, scoring, and reporting procedures; instruction on how to convert scores to grades; and guidelines for reporting progress to parents.

ACKNOWLEDGMENTS

I am grateful to all those who have encouraged and supported me through this endeavor. Special appreciation to my husband, Michael, for his advice and support; to my mother, Helen, for her endless encouragement; and to our children—Eric, Joan, Julie, Debbie—and a special dedication to our angel, Drew, forever our hero for his faith, determination, and courage.

My sincere gratitude goes to Ann Davis, executive editor, for her guidance, patience, and ongoing enthusiasm for this project. Many thanks also to Penny

Burleson, editorial assistant, and to Kerry Rubadue, project manager, and Tiffany Timmerman, project editor. I also appreciate the efforts of the manuscript reviewers who provided thoughtful and insightful comments: Valerie Dehombreux at Northern Arizona University, and Mark B. Sperling at Indiana University Northwest. Special acknowledgment and appreciation goes to Clare Rachko for her research assistance and to Yvette Prioleau-Bishara for her editorial help.

ABOUT THE AUTHOR

Cathleen G. Spinelli is a professor and chair of the Special Education Department at Saint Joseph's University in Philadelphia, Pennsylvania, where she has spent the last decade teaching undergraduate and graduate classes in diagnosis and teaching techniques. She also has extensive experience working in the public school system, as a special education teacher, school administrator, and as a certified school psychologist and educational diagnostician evaluating students from preschoolers to adults. She is the author of numerous articles dealing with assessment and instruction and another Pearson publication, *Classroom Assessment for Students in Special and General Education*, Third Edition. Readers may contact her at cathleen.spinelli@sju.edu.

Please be sure to visit her text website, *http://www.sju.edu/~cspinell/*.

Contents

Chapter 1

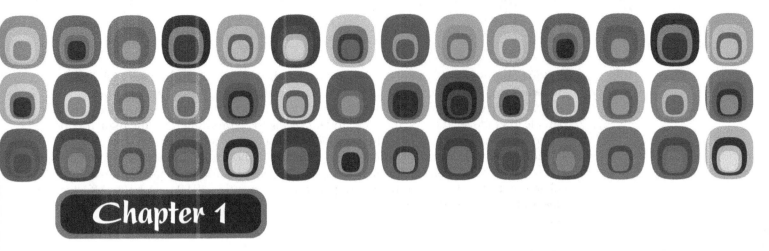

An Introduction to Classroom Assessment

INTRODUCTION

As teachers, we have children in our classes who experience academic or behavioral problems, or both. The educational system and federal law have increasingly emphasized the need for ongoing assessment to determine students' instructional levels, ascertain their specific strengths, identify areas in need of remediation to plan instruction and learning styles, and closely monitor progress to revise educational programs when students are not meeting expected instructional goals. Classroom-based, informal assessment serves all these purposes.

GETTING STARTED WITH ASSESSMENT

As teachers, our initial step in the assessment process is to learn about our students. We must know whether a student's functioning is significantly different from that of their classmates. In an effort to understand the whole child, it is important to determine whether there is a history of school problems; whether the intensity of those problems has increased and, if so, over what period of time; and whether the problems are more evident in particular circumstances or settings, at specific times, or with certain people. It is also important to identify pertinent student interests and special skills, the impact that medical and psychosocial issues have on the student's academic functioning, as well as family expectations. Academic achievement data—such as scores on standardized achievement tests, results from informal evaluation procedures, grades, classroom observations, work-sample analyses, and behavior rating data—can be helpful information to consider.

During this initial assessment it is also important to identify personal and environmental factors that may be inhibiting the student's classroom adjustment and to determine which types of instructional materials and methods seem to be most effective. Refer to Chapter 2 for more information about how to gather this preliminary assessment data.

IDENTIFYING THE PROBLEM

Concerns about a student's progress or adjustment may surface early in the school year, or they may emerge over a period of months. Frequently, we observe that particular students are not adjusting well to class routine and procedures, are unable to complete assignments, perform poorly on tests, or fail to relate appropriately with school staff or peers. Obviously, students have varying experiences and knowledge and do not achieve at the same degree of academic competence. When the learning rate of the identified student is at least comparable to grade level peers, then the student seems to be profiting from the regular education environment. However, when academic or behavioral adjustment problems do not subside after a few weeks or when a student is not demonstrating academic, emotional, and social growth when other students are thriving, special interventions need to be considered. A relatively new initiative, response to intervention (RTI), can be an effective means of identifying the need for intervention.

RESPONSE TO INTERVENTION

At this point in our discussion of assessment, it is necessary to introduce RTI, an early intervention model used for prevention and remediation that relies heavily on assessment and is intended to limit or prevent academic failure. RTI was originally conceptualized not only to identify students who truly require special services but also to provide necessary interventions as early as possible so that struggling students can be successful and maintain their class placement (Mellard & Johnson, 2008). This process is accomplished through evaluation of students' response to high-quality instruction that has been demonstrated to be effective for most students (Batsche, Elliott, Graden, Grimes, Kovaleski, & Prasse, 2005). When it is determined that students are not making adequate yearly progress (AYP), evidence-based interventions need to be initiated. Progress is closely monitored and adjustments are made in a timely manner to ensure that the individual needs of students at risk are addressed.

A fundamental premise of RTI is that poor performance may reflect curriculum disability rather than student disability (Strangman, Hitchcock, Hall, Meo, & Coyne, 2008). RTI is not mandated by federal law so the local education agency (LEA) is not required to implement it; however, a school district would be prudent to use at least some of its basic structure as a model for tracking progress. Such monitoring allows us to know whether our students are benefitting from classroom instruction, to identify students at risk, and to provide documentation on all students for accountability and reporting purposes. Another important aspect of the RTI process is to keep families informed and involved in decision making throughout the intervention process (Learning Disabilities Association of America, 2006). If particular students do not respond to these planned interventions, this may be evidence that they need more support than the typical general education program can provide and that a referral should be made to the multidisciplinary team for testing to determine their eligibility for special education services.

RTI IMPLEMENTATION

Response to intervention emphasizes "student outcomes instead of student deficits" (Kavale, Holdnack, & Mostert, 2005) and makes a clear connection between assessment and instruction (Vaughn & Fuchs, 2003). RTI uses a tiered approach to specialized intervention. The number of levels or tiers is generally three, but may include as many as five, depending on how the LEA decides to group the general format of screening, progress monitoring, and diagnosis. Each tier is designed to provide increasingly intensified and high-quality, research-based individualized instruction, continuous monitoring of progress to calculate gains, and criteria for changing the intensity or type of subsequent interventions through a team decision-making process (Fuchs & Fuchs, 2006; Kavale et al., 2005). The use of evidence-based interventions and progress monitoring, used at all tiers, has shown improved academic outcomes (Stecker, Fuchs, & Fuchs, 2005). The following is a summary of the three-tier model.

Tier 1

At the first tier, the teacher administers screening assessment to the whole class to guide instructional decisions made on behalf of learners with different needs and readiness levels. It is used to determine students' responsiveness to general education instruction and, in the process, to identify students who are not making acceptable progress. Tier 1 screening, is generally based on the classroom curriculum. It should be administered periodically, tracked, and monitored on a regular basis. See Chapters 2 through 6 for assessment guidelines and Chapter 7 for guidelines on scoring, charting, and reporting progress. This initial Tier 1, whole class assessment, referred to as universal screening, is intended to do the following:

- Measure growth over time
- Measure individual student's achievement compared to grade level peers
- Measure progress related to specific benchmarks (e.g., local or national norms)
- Identify students at risk for academic failure
- Ensure that all students are benefitting from instruction

Plan of Action

1. If the results of the whole class screening indicate that students are making adequate progress, then the teacher should keep up the good work and continue to monitor progress through periodic screening assessment.
2. If the results of the whole class screening indicate that the majority of students are not making adequate progress, then the teacher should be concerned that the instructional program is inadequate and the overall program needs to be modified. Once the whole class program is changed (e.g., using research-based curriculum and teaching techniques), the teacher maintains a program of periodic whole class assessment (see subsequent chapters for details).
3. If only a small percentage of students fail to demonstrate adequate progress, then these identified students proceed to the next tier.

Tier 2

Students identified through the initial screening process as being at risk move to Tier 2. At this level, students receive academic supports that are based on high-quality, scientific-based, researched interventions for the targeted area of deficit. These interventions must be provided with fidelity, meaning the intervention curriculum and strategies are delivered consistent with the manner used in the original research studies. In this way, they are proven efficacious with students who have similar characteristics to those identified as requiring the interventions. This does not mean that the teacher must create individualized lesson plans, but that instructional accommodations are provided that address students' specific learning needs with instruction adjusted accordingly to maximize student achievement. At Tier 2, interventions are remedial rather than preventive. Once these interventions are implemented, the teacher must continually monitor student performance on a schedule that will be frequent enough to impact instruction but not take excessive amounts of time (Gurganus, 2007). Assessment results gathered during this monitoring process are referred to as response data. This information should be used to determine how and when to change the intensity or type of subsequent interventions and to provide teachers with the data they need to improve instruction for all students.

Plan of Action

Monitor progress closely, assess students frequently, and, depending on their response to the intervention, choose one of the following:

1. If performance has increased to that of grade level peers, then students return to the traditional program of instruction in the general education classroom, where progress continues to be closely monitored.

2. If students are making progress with Tier 2 interventions but still not functioning at expected grade level norms, then they generally remain at the Tier 2 intervention level with more frequent progress monitoring.
3. If students remain chronically unresponsive, then they require more specialized assistance and are moved to the next level of intervention, Tier 3.

Tier 3

Students who require the most intense form of intervention are moved to Tier 3, where instruction is individually focused. Students receive specific remedial instruction in a small group or on a one-to-one basis.

Plan of Action

1. At this level, the teacher monitors progress closely and more frequently, generally one to two times per week to check on growth toward long-term goals.
2. Failure to respond to the highest tier leads either to referral for multidisciplinary evaluation to determine eligibility for special education or directly to a diagnosis of specific learning disability and special education services, depending on the RTI model used (Fuchs & Fuchs, 2006; Fuchs, Mock, Morgan, & Young, 2003).
3. Although some students may respond to a Tier 3 intervention, referral for special education services may be made if it is not feasible to maintain this more intensive level of intervention in the regular classroom (Batsche et al., 2005).

EARLY INTERVENING SERVICES

Regardless of the teacher's best efforts, some students may fail to thrive. If a learner consistently demonstrates the need for additional support, the classroom teacher can share the results of intervention efforts already undertaken in the classroom and work collaboratively with colleagues to explore additional instructional options. Even school districts following the RTI model generally have a special team of school personnel who work collaboratively to support the teacher and ultimately help the student. This early intervening services (EIS) team (often referred to by other terms, such as the school resource team, the teacher support committee, or the student assistance team) functions as problem solvers. They listen to the teacher's concerns, discuss options for remediation, develop an intervention plan, monitor how the plan is working with the student in the classroom, meet again to discuss progress, and recommend needed adjustments in the intervention plan. If the problem has not been resolved after appropriate intervention, then this team will recommend referring the student for eligibility assessment to determine whether special education services are necessary.

In the process of determining appropriate recommendations, the EIS team will typically consider not only readiness levels and the impact of instructional interventions used in the classroom, but also outside influences that impact student achievement. Are there ongoing family issues? Could vision and hearing screenings be needed? Might a speech or language deficit be a factor? Are there ways outside agencies could support the needs of the student? The EIS team and classroom teacher determine whether the target student requires additional support to the prescriptive instruction already being provided in the classroom by RTI. This supplemental service can be directly aligned with classroom efforts and is generally coordinated with other school-based services and personnel including Title 1, bilingual/English Language Learners (ELL) teachers, special education support staff, remedial and behavioral specialists, and special service therapists.

Steps to Problem Solving

1. *Identify the problem*—Gather information, observe, and record performance and/or behavior.
2. *Define the problem*—Analyze the data; identify the type/severity, quality/quantity of the problem in measurable terms.

3. *Plan the intervention*—Identify specific research-based intervention(s) to remediate the problem(s), set a goal, determine progress monitoring strategies.
4. *Implement the intervention*—Carry out the intervention plan in the prescribed manner; monitor fidelity of implementation.
5. *Assess intervention success*—Use progress monitoring data for decision making; determine the level of response to the intervention.
6. *Determine the next step*—Stay the course, or increase or change the intervention(s).

INITIAL REVIEW PROCESS

Screening is the first step in the overall assessment process. The purpose of the screening is to collect data to determine whether more intensive or additional assessments should be conducted by educational, psychological, or medical specialists (Salvia, Ysseldyke, & Bolt, 2010). Students can be screened individually or as an entire class. Screening individual students requires parental consent, but screening of the whole group does not require consent. Typically, the RTI process starts with an overall academic screening of the whole class, but it is also important to determine particular students' strengths and weaknesses by focusing on the following:

- Class work and homework
- Work-study skills
- Classroom adjustment
- Attention to detail and time on task
- Work pace and work quality

In addition to routine academic and behavioral screening procedures conducted by the teacher, speech, vision, and hearing specialists are routinely involved in the screening process. These screening procedures are informal and therefore do not fall under the strict regulations mandated by the Individuals with Disabilities Education Act (IDEA).

Informal diagnostic assessment for individual students may include teacher-made tests, skill inventories, behavioral checklists, daily observations, and/or student interviews. These assessment measures are used to determine the identified student's ability to function in relation to age and grade norms and the degree to which the student is comprehending and retaining the skills and concepts presented in class. Informal assessment provides the opportunity to analyze the learning process rather than to simply analyze the product (Taylor, 2009).

When tests are used as a screening device, the results are used to determine the current functioning level of the student and to compare the current year's test results with the previous year's results to establish whether progress has been made. A number of criteria may be used for screening purposes, such as the high stakes testing that school districts administer at least once each year to measure academic growth. The administration of a standardized test to all students enables a comparison to be made between each student's performance to that of local district or classroom-based norms, or a benchmark designated to predict end of the year performance on high stakes tests or graduation requirements (Fuchs & Fuchs, 2006).

Schools generally administer standardized group tests (e.g., the California Achievement Test, the Terra Nova, or a specific state department of education test) to their elementary and secondary education students to assess performance in reading, math, written and oral language, science, social studies, and study skills. Test profiles of these screening tools, also referred to as universal screening in the Response to Intervention process, provide national and local (district) percentiles, grade equivalencies, and stanine scores. Most school districts have cutoff scores that serve as criteria for qualification for remedial services, and they may use the results to determine whether further, more comprehensive educational evaluation in all areas of suspected disability is needed.

PROGRESS MONITORING

As teachers we can no longer assume that each student benefits from classroom instruction alone. Progress monitoring is a valid and efficient tool for gauging the effectiveness of instruction. When used effectively as early intervention, preventive services, such as instructional modifications, can be implemented prior to the onset of serious deficits, when instruction is still ongoing and before a student fails (Fuchs, Fuchs, & Hollenbeck, 2007). Over two decades of research indicates that when teachers use progress monitoring for instructional decision making, the benefits include increased student achievement, improved teacher decision making, and enhanced student awareness of their school performance (Batsche et al., 2005; Fletcher, Coulter, Reschly, & Vaughn, 2004; Fuchs & Fuchs, 2006; Fuchs et al., 2003; Marston, 2005).

By closely monitoring student progress, teachers are able to make informed decisions regarding what instructional material and approach is appropriate for each student. This process provides the teacher with data to enable them to be effective with their planning and to use instructional time efficiently by knowing whether students are mastering the curricular content covered, to determine which students need review before covering additional content and which students are ready to move forward. The information gained from progress monitoring assessment allows teachers to create an appropriate instructional plan, which helps students learn and teachers teach.

Steps for Implementing Progress Monitoring

1. Determine student's current level (baseline) performance
2. Identify student's learning goals
3. Establish the teacher's instructional goals
4. Implement the instructional program
5. Measure the student's performance regularly (e.g., biweekly, weekly, monthly)
6. Construct a system for plotting progress points (e.g., a graph)
7. Chart student's progress
8. Use established cutoffs for determining whether the student's performance is improving, decreasing, or staying the same
9. Based on results; plan and implement program and/or instructional modifications
10. Continue with monitoring, charting, and analysis

BENEFITS OF PROGRESS MONITORING

Progress monitoring can make a significant difference for both the student and the teacher. It enables teachers to be aware of students' response to intervention so that instructional decisions are informed and match students' needs; it promotes higher expectations and thus accelerates the learning process. Students can be involved in their educational program, when they participate in tracking and graphing their progress, they tend to be motivated to succeed. Communication between the school and home is more effective when progress reports are based on evidence, such as work samples, rubrics, and performance graphs, which provide parents with documentation. Ultimately, when students' learning problems are identified early and remedial interventions are implemented, teachers make fewer referrals for special education services.

The implementation of progress monitoring and responsive intervention per the RTI model serves as a proactive alternative to the "wait-to-fail" or the aptitude-achievement discrepancy model used in the past. When students fail to respond to tailored interventions of increasing intensity, this serves as the basis for special education referral for comprehensive eligibility evaluation. When this occurs, progress monitoring provides systematic, reliable, and multiple data points that can inform eligibility determination decisions and subsequent development of specially designed instruction. As part of an individualized education program (IEP), progress monitoring also provides information about student progress toward reaching their annual goals.

CONSIDERATIONS WHEN SELECTING AN ASSESSMENT

Some measures for collecting data are more appropriate for a specific age level, skill level, or culture, and teachers often find it beneficial to use multiple assessments when gathering information on student performance (Wren, 2004). According to IDEA (2004), a variety of assessments must be provided in "the language and form most likely to yield accurate information of what the child knows and can do academically, developmentally, and functionally, unless it is not feasible to provide or administer." The National Education Association (NEA) also strongly supports using multiple measures of student achievement versus standardized tests alone. It is important that assessment be instructionally relevant, focused on essential skills, and sensitive to cultural and linguistic differences (Skiba, Simmons, Ritter, Kohler, & Wu, 2003).

Recognizing the value of assessment, its many uses for screening, identification, intervention, monitoring progress, and accountability, you should find this guide to assessment to be a helpful resource.

REFERENCES

Batsche, G., Elliott, J., Graden, J. L., Grimes, J., Kovaleski, J. F., & Prasse, D. (2005). *Response to intervention: Policy considerations and implementation.* Alexandria, VA: National Association of State Directors of Special Education, Inc.

Fletcher, J. M., Coulter, W. A., Reschly, D. J., & Vaughn, S. (2004). Alternative approaches to the definition and identification of learning disabilities: Some questions and answers. *Annals of Dyslexia, 54*(2), 304–331.

Fuchs, D., & Fuchs, L. S. (2006). Introduction to response to intervention: What, why, and how valid is it? *Reading Research Quarterly, 41*(1), 93–99.

Fuchs, L. S., Fuchs, D., & Hollenbeck, K. N. (2007). Extending responsiveness to intervention to mathematics at first and third grades. *Learning Disabilities Research & Practice, 22*(1), 13–24.

Fuchs, D., Mock, D., Morgan, P. L., & Young, C. L. (2003). Responsiveness-to-intervention: Definitions, evidence, and implications for the learning disabilities construct. *Learning Disabilities Research & Practice, 18,* 157–171.

Gurganus, S. (2007). *Math instruction for students with learning problems.* Boston: Pearson.

Individuals with Disabilities Education Act (IDEA) Regulations. (2004). 34 CFR 300.304(c)(1)(ii); 20 U.S.C. 1414(b)(3)(A)(ii).

Kavale, K. A., Holdnack, J. A., & Mostert, M. P. (2005). Responsiveness to intervention and the identification of specific learning disability: A critique and alternative proposal. *Learning Disability Quarterly, 28,* 2.

Learning Disabilities Association of America (LDA). (2006). *Response to intervention: Position paper of the Learning Disabilities Association of America.* Retrieved May 10, 2009, from *http://ldanatl.org/about/position/print_rti.asp*

Marston, D. (2005). Tiers of intervention in responsiveness to intervention: Prevention outcomes and learning disabilities identification patterns. *Journal of Learning Disabilities, 38,* 539–544.

Mellard, D. F., & Johnson, E. (2008). *RTI: A practitioner's guide to implementing response to intervention.* Thousand Oaks, CA: Corwin Press.

Salvia, J., Ysseldyke, J. E., & Bolt, S. (2010). *Assessment in special and inclusive education* (11th ed.). Boston: Houghton Mifflin.

Skiba, R. J., Simmons, A. B., Ritter, S., Kohler, K. R., & Wu, T. C. (2003). The psychology of disproportionality: Minority placement in context. *Multiple Voices for Ethnically Diverse Exceptional Learners, 6*, 1–29.

Stecker, P. M., Fuchs, L. S., & Fuchs, D. (2005). Using curriculum-based measurement to improve student achievement: Review of research. *Psychology in the Schools, 42*, 795–819.

Strangman, N., Hitchcock, C., Hall, T., Meo, G., & Coyne, P. (2008). *Response-to-instruction and universal design for learning: How might they intersect in the general education classroom?* Washington, DC: Access Center.

Taylor, R. L. (2009). *Assessment of exceptional students: Educational and psychological procedures* (8th ed.). Upper Saddle River, NJ: Pearson.

Vaughn, S., & Fuchs, L. S. (2003). Redefining learning disabilities as inadequate response to instruction: The promise and potential problems. *Learning Disabilities Research & Practice, 18*(3), 137–146.

Wren, S. (2004). Descriptions of early reading assessments. Southwest Educational Development Laboratory. Retrieved November 16, 2004, from *http://www.balancedreading.com/assessment/assessment.pdf*

Chapter 2

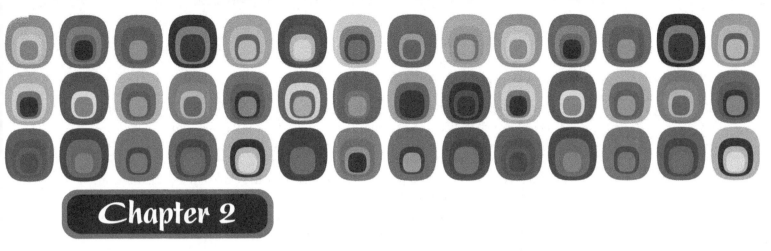

Information Gathering: Evaluating the Student and the Instructional Environment

INTRODUCTION

To truly grasp the factors that could be impacting our students' learning, as teachers, we perform a preliminary investigation of their educational and health history, their current educational status and learning style, their family perspective, the classroom environment, and determine whether text and curricular material fit. Before assessing subject matter, we must understand the learning context and students' performance in relation to the context in which they are expected to learn and perform. Keep in mind that our students' academic problems can be exacerbated or even caused by contextual factors (Lipson & Wixson, 2009).

To obtain contextual information, we need to observe, interview, and analyze. This includes observation of how the student interacts in various subject areas and classroom settings, and how the student functions when working individually, with peers, and in small and large groups. It is necessary to obtain pertinent information from school personnel who work with our students, such as the school nurse, counselor, remedial specialists, and classroom assistants. It is also important to analyze the school environment and classroom setup, as well as the appropriateness of the learning material selected.

OBSERVATIONS AND INTERVIEWS

Assessment Strategy: *Student Observation*

Strategy Description

Many prominent student behaviors can be identified only through direct observation in natural settings. Observations of students provide only a sampling, or snapshot, of their day—a representative sampling of their behavior, observed at a specific time, and in a specific setting and situation. **Systematic observation** can reveal how a student works through different tasks, which tasks seem most and least problematic, and what the student does when faced with difficulties (Vallecorsa, deBettencourt, & Zigmond, 2000).

Implementation

- ✓ Use a guideline form listing various factors to consider while observing (see Figure 2–1).
- ✓ Develop a checklist of curriculum core standards or IEP goals, which includes specific content and skills to be mastered from curriculum scope and sequence. Observe and note progress.
- ✓ Make a detailed list of steps in a performance task to be mastered (e.g., doing an experiment) and observe each step.
- ✓ Move around the classroom and note group progress toward completing an assignment, such as brainstorming ideas or outlining a current events research project (see Figure 2–2).
- ✓ Use a checklist on a clipboard to track personal learning, work-study, or behavioral characteristics, such as "follows oral directions" (see Figure 2–3).
- ✓ Take note as to whether students are applying new skills and concepts in a variety of contexts and in meaningful ways, and are making connections between new learning and personal experiences.

FIGURE 2–1 Factors to Consider When Using Observation as a Method of Assessment

- Student's age, gender, and type of disability ____________________
- Observation setting and structure ____________________
- Day, month, season ____________________
- Subject, period, place of observation ____________________
- Length of observation and types of activities ____________________
- Number and types of distractions during observation ____________________
- Severity (extent of the problem) ____________________
- Intensity (how much the problem interferes with the student's progress) ____________________
- Duration (length of time the problem has been evident) ____________________
- Frequency (how often the problem is occurring) ____________________
- Generality (number and types of situations in which the problem occurs) ____________________
- Consequences (effect the problem has on others) ____________________
- Conditions (factors involved and situation in which student is expected to perform) ____________________
- Intervening factors that precipitated, aggravated, or preceded an incident ____________________
- Atypical occurrences (e.g., appearance of a substitute teacher) ____________________
- Unplanned school events (e.g., an assembly) ____________________
- Disruptions in normal routine (e.g., fire drill, upcoming holidays, unexpected visitors) ____________________
- Any events significant in determining student's ability to cope with a change and transitions ____________________

Special Considerations, Accommodations, Alternatives

- It is important to consider environmental conditions and to compare the child's behavior to that of the "typical" or average student.
- Focusing on group dynamics can alert the teacher to peer preference, influence, dominance, indifference, or antagonism.
- Students may perform differently in large groups versus individually or in small groups.
- Multiple and varied observations are needed to gain a perspective of what works, what does not work, and why.
- Observations should occur in different grouping situations, in the setting(s) in which the target behavior is evident, at different times of the day, and in different subject areas.
- It is important to consider environmental conditions and to compare the child's behavior to that of the "typical" or average student.
- Rather than take note of isolated skills at the end of a lesson or unit of study, effective teachers monitor skills regularly, looking at the full spectrum of students' learning characteristics.

FIGURE 2–2 Sample Forms for Observing Small Group Activities

Checklist of Cooperative Group Activity

Skill	Brad	Ken	Jane	Tess	Ben	Jean	Mary	Tim
Listened to directions								
Had materials to begin								
Contributed ideas								

Checklist of Class Observation

Subject: ______________________ Date: ______________________

Ratings
+ = Completed
X = In progress
O = Not started

Names of Students	Defined Vocabulary	Read Chapter Outline	Drafted Research	Answered Questions
1. ____________				
2. ____________				
3. ____________				
4. ____________				
5. ____________				
6. ____________				

FIGURE 2–3 Observation Focus Points

Does the student:	***Yes***	***No***	***N/A***	***Comment***
Speak in a well-modulated voice, with appropriate volume, pitch, and rate?	___	___	___	______
Express self articulately and thoughtfully?	___	___	___	______
Listen carefully and respond directly to the question asked?	___	___	___	______
Take turns during conversations?	___	___	___	______
Orally participate in class?	___	___	___	______
Appear to note subtle nonverbal gestures and cues?	___	___	___	______
Accurately copy from the chalkboard?	___	___	___	______
Write letters/numbers without reversing or transposing?	___	___	___	______
Seem to be prepared?	___	___	___	______
Begin and complete work on time?	___	___	___	______
Stay on task, appear to be attentive?	___	___	___	______
Work steadily, use time wisely?	___	___	___	______
Persevere in pursuing a difficult assignment?	___	___	___	______
Use consistent strategies to problem solve?	___	___	___	______
Use a different strategy if the first one is unsuccessful?	___	___	___	______
Work well independently?	___	___	___	______
Follow teacher's oral directions?	___	___	___	______
Follow written directions?	___	___	___	______
Follow routine?	___	___	___	______
Interact appropriately with peers?	___	___	___	______
Interact appropriately with teacher?	___	___	___	______
Work cooperatively with peers in problem solving?	___	___	___	______
Participate in a group situation or is he/she a loner?	___	___	___	______
Share and compromise in a group?	___	___	___	______
Disagree in a considerate manner?	___	___	___	______
Share responsibility helping the group get the job done?	___	___	___	______
Seem to be accepted by group members?	___	___	___	______
React appropriately when teacher is not directly supervising the group?	___	___	___	______

Assessment Strategy: *Teacher Interview*

Strategy Description

In addition to the primary teacher, it is often necessary to consult with other teachers and support staff who interact with the student (e.g., teachers of other academic subjects, remedial specialists, guidance counselors, the school nurse, cafeteria and playground aides, case managers for students who are receiving special education services, and administrative personnel). These individuals can provide additional anecdotal information and important insights about students from various perspectives and in settings outside the main classroom. Social service agency, therapeutic, or medical personnel who are or have been working with the student should also be interviewed.

Implementation

✓ Prepare a list of relevant and appropriate questions starting with broad-based queries and move toward specific, probing questions to elicit more elaborate and in-depth responses (see Figure 2–4).

✓ Develop a checklist of work-study skills or competencies for specific subject areas (see Figure 2–5).

✓ Ask open-ended questions rather than questions that require only a yes or no response.

✓ Question in a nonthreatening, relaxed manner using a friendly, nonjudgmental tone.

✓ Listen carefully to responses and be flexible enough to ask for clarification for responses that are unclear.

Special Considerations, Accommodations, Alternatives

- An important consideration is the matter of confidentiality. For ethical, moral, and legal reasons, any personal information about students and their families should only be obtained and shared with others on a need-to-know basis.

FIGURE 2–4 Sample Open-Ended Teacher Academic Interview Guide

What grade level materials are used for instruction in class? ______

Does the student function below grade norms in any subject area? ______ If so, which area? ______

What assessment measures are used to evaluate class work? ______

What is the average class level in reading?______ math?______ language?______ science? ______social studies? ______

What is the student's level in reading?______ math?______ language?______ science?______ social studies? ______

What assessment measures are used to evaluate class work (oral/written, multiple choice, short answer, essay)? ______

______

What are the student's academic strengths? ______ weaknesses? ______

Have accommodations or modifications been used?______ If so, which have been successful? ______

Has the student been receiving any remedial services?______ If so, in which subject(s)? ______

for how long?______ how many times per week? ______

If the student is receiving remedial services, how much improvement has been noted? ______

What strategies have been successful? ______

Does the student seem anxious, frustrated, depressed, lethargic, or unmotivated? ______

What is the student's disposition toward learning and participating in classroom activities? ______

Does the student function better when working independently or with a group of students? ______

Does the student function better in the morning or afternoon? ______

Does the student function better in some subjects than in others?______

Do emotional, health, or social problems interfere with the student's school adjustment and progress?______

______

FIGURE 2–5 Teacher Interview Checklist: Student Work-Study Behaviors

Does this student:	Mastered	Emerging	Undeveloped
Remain on task for appropriate periods of time?			
Follow oral directions?			
Follow written directions?			
Respond appropriately when called upon?			
Listen attentively?			
Recall and retain what he or she hears?			
Raise a hand to be called on before speaking?			
Work independently?			
Work cooperatively during group activities?			
Handle frustration appropriately?			
Complete written classroom work in a timely manner?			
Complete homework assignments?			
Become actively involved in problem solving?			
Follow classroom and school rules?			
Cope with minor distractions?			
Adapt to varied teaching methods?			
Ask for help or clarification when needed?			
Participate in class discussions?			
Copy from the chalkboard?			
Transition from one class to another?			
Transition from subject to subject?			
Transition from activity to activity?			
Transition from idea to idea?			
Complete assignments on time?			
Organize books and school work?			
Organize ideas into a plan of action?			
Use critical thinking and make logical arguments?			
Organize, plan, and carry out long-term assignments?			
Copy adequately with time pressures?			
Adapt to interruptions in the daily schedule?			
Relate appropriately to school staff and peers?			
Work cooperatively with a partner?			
Behave appropriately in unstructured settings?			
Take responsibilities for own actions?			
Willingly participate in activities?			
Retain and recall subject matter information?			
Grasp and apply abstract concepts?			
Analyze and solve problems?			
Apply and generalize new learning?			
Comprehend cause-and-effect relationships?			
Adjust to changes in subject content, format, or mode of response?			

Assessment Strategy: *Student Interview*

Strategy Description

The student interview provides insight into students' ability to communicate, and can be useful in determining how they confront, analyze, and solve a problem. Interviews also provide an opportunity to take note of students' oral language skills, vocabulary development and syntax, information-processing ability, attention to task, and listening skills. When interacting on a one-to-one basis with the teacher, students have the opportunity to explain, in greater detail than with other methods of assessment, what they understand, what problems they are having, and what steps they feel need to be taken to improve their learning. Often, students can give a reasonable explanation for an incident that would otherwise seem unreasonable to the observer.

Implementation

- ✓ Start with broad-based questions and move toward more specific probing questions in order to elicit increasingly more elaborate and in-depth responses.
- ✓ Ask questions in a nonthreatening, relaxed manner using a friendly, nonjudgmental tone.
- ✓ Actively listen and be flexible enough to ask for clarification on responses that are unclear.
- ✓ Structure questions that are open ended, rather than requiring a yes or no response.
- ✓ Allow sufficient time for the response since some students may be slow to process information presented orally.
- ✓ Expand interview questions to gain information about study skill mastery strategy use with specific content subjects (see Figures 2–6 and 2–7).

Special Considerations, Accommodations, Alternatives

- If students struggle to communicate their thoughts clearly, encourage them to demonstrate, draw, sing, use pictures or manipulatives, show an example, or act out their responses.
- If students are reluctant to verbally share in a typical interview situation, they may be more comfortable answering questions as they work on assignments at their desks, at a learning center, or during solitary play.

FIGURE 2–6 Student General Interview Questions

What did you learn today? ____________________

Why was it important to know? ____________________

Did you know anything about it before it was discussed in class today? ____________________

What do you most like to do in school? ____________________

What do you least like to do in school? ____________________

How do you feel about your classes? ____________________

In what subjects are you doing well? ____________________

What makes this your best subject? ____________________

In what subjects are you having difficulty? ____________________

What subject is the most difficult for you? ____________________

Why is this subject hard for you? ____________________

What could be done to make this subject easier for you? ____________________

Are you able to stay focused in class? ____________________

Is there any particular subject(s) that you have difficulty concentrating on? ____________________

Do you usually finish assignments before, after, or with your classmates? ____________________

Do you usually volunteer in class? If not, why not? ____________________

Do you complete homework assignments? If not, why not? ____________________

Do you get along with your classmates? ____________________

Are you involved in any school-related clubs, such as sports activities? ____________________

What do you want to learn next? ____________________

What is the best way for you to learn to do that? ____________________

What does your teacher do to help you learn? ____________________

What do you do when you want to remember something? ____________________

Do you learn best when you read, hear, talk about, or write about what you are learning? ____________________

What things are scary to you? ____________________

What do you worry about? ____________________

What would you like to be learning next year? ____________________

Pick various subject assignments and ask the student the following questions:

What part of this assignment was easiest for you? ____________________

What part of this assignment was most difficult for you? ____________________

FIGURE 2–7 Student Interview Questions for Specific Subjects

Reading:

When you have a word to learn, how do you remember it? ______

When you are reading and come to a word that you don't know, what do you do? ______

Which subject has the hardest words: reading, science, social studies, or math? ______

Can you sound out a word that you do not know? ______

Can you break a word into parts? ______

Can you memorize new vocabulary words? ______

Do you understand what words mean when reading assignments? ______

Can you retell a story in your own words? ______

Can you tell what the main idea is in a story? ______

Can you describe the characters in a story? ______

Can you figure out the problem and the solution in a story? ______

Do you learn better if you read to yourself or if someone reads aloud to you? ______

Assessment Strategy: *Parent Interview*

Strategy Description

Parent contributions are important to help provide a comprehensive assessment of the whole child. To facilitate and maximize information gathering, teachers should contact parents to obtain relevant information about the student including developmental, physical, medical, social, emotional, cultural, ethnic, linguistic, and family issues. Parent involvement in the evaluation process is mandated when students are being tested to determine eligibility for special education services.

Implementation

✓ Talk with the parents at a convenient time and location.

✓ Have a list of questions prepared that will provide a comprehensive view of the child, including a history and current status (see Figure 2–8).

✓ Avoid using educational jargon; provide examples to clarify students' strengths and weaknesses.

✓ Provide parents with a written version of the questions.

Special Considerations, Accommodations, Alternatives

- Provide optional communication modes to accommodate parents with language differences or communication difficulties (e.g., an interpreter for families who do not speak fluent English or are hearing impaired).
- Allow time for reflection or locating information (e.g., medical or early development records).
- Encourage parents to bring a support person or advocate to the interview session.

FIGURE 2–8 Sample Parent Interview Questionnaire

What are your child's strengths, abilities, special talents, and interests? ______

In what areas does your child have difficulty? ______

Do you think your child is progressing satisfactorily in school? ______

Is your child actively involved in extracurricular activities? ______

Does your child have any particular fears or worries? ______

Does your child have friends? Do these friends value education? ______

Do you feel your child speaks in a clear, organized, and fluent manner? ______

Does your child seem to have difficulty sharing ideas? asking questions? ______

Do you feel your child writes in an organized, legible manner? ______

What is your child's basic attitude about oral presentations? writing tasks? ______

Does your child enjoy speaking in a group or prefer one-to-one communication? ______

Does your child enjoy pencil-paper tasks? Drawing? Copying? Composing? Conversing? ______

Does your child have any difficulty with tasks that require eye-hand coordination? ______

Have you noticed fine motor skill delays (e.g., inability to stay within lines when drawing; poor control of pencil, scissors, comb, or knife)? ______

Is there any type of assignment that is stressful or difficult for your child? ______

Is there anything in your child's developmental, educational, or medical history that might affect skill acquisition or school performance and behavior? ______

Has your child had previous diagnostic testing? If so, would you provide a copy of the results? ______

Has your child had any special school services (e.g., remedial reading, therapy, or counseling? ______

What are your goals for your child this year? ______

What questions do you have about helping your child become a better student? ______

How well is your child able to communicate wants and needs? ______

Is your child independent in basic hygiene and grooming skills at home? ______

Does your child behave appropriately at home? ______ If not, how do you deal with misbehavior? ______

How does your child deal with changes in routine at home? ______

Is your child able to follow basic directions at home? ______

Is your child able to focus on stories, puzzles, or quiet activities? ______

How many times has your family moved? ______

Was there a time when your child was unable to attend school? ______ If so, for how long? ______ Why? ______

Did your child attend school in another country? If so: ______

Did your child start school speaking another language? ______

Did your child learn to read before coming to the United States? ______

Does your child have any difficulty reading in his/her native language? ______ If so, what type of problem? ______

Has your child ever been assessed for English language proficiency? ______

Is there information that would be helpful in understanding how your child learns best? ______

Assessment Strategy: *Interest Inventory*

Strategy Description

Interest inventories provide information about students' interests, which will enable the teacher to choose subject matter content and to plan an instructional focus that is personally motivating and will maintain attention.

Implementation

✓ Develop inventory questions to include the following: the student's hobbies, extracurricular activities, and favorite recreational pastime. Information gained from the interest inventory can be useful when selecting material, such as reading passages, to be used for assessment (see Figure 2–9).

✓ Focus interview questions on how students feel about learning; their personal likes and dislikes, preferences for subject matter, reading habits, the kinds of things they most like to do in class.

Special Considerations, Accommodations, Alternatives

- For young readers, the inventory can be administered orally or in an interview format.
- For older students, use questionnaires, conferencing, or incomplete sentence formats.

FIGURE 2–9 Interest Inventory

Ask the student:

What is your favorite subject in school? Why? ____________________

What subject is easiest for you? Why? ____________________

What subject is hardest for you? Why? ____________________

What do you like best and least about school? ____________________

What do you like to do after school? on weekends? during summer vacation? ____________________

What do you know a lot about? ____________________

What would you like to learn about? ____________________

What are your hobbies and special interests? ____________________

What kind of collections do you have? ____________________

What special places have you visited? ____________________

What is your favorite place? ____________________

What is your favorite story? ____________________

Would you rather read a story or listen to a story? ____________________

Would you rather tell a story or write a story? ____________________

What was the last book you have read? ____________________

What kinds of stories do you like to read? ____________________

What is your favorite book? ____________________

Do you borrow books from the public library? the school library? ____________________

Do you read newspapers, magazines, or comic books? ____________________

What do you want to be when you grow up? ____________________

Assessment Strategy: *Student Self and Peer Assessment*

Strategy Description

Self-assessment provides students with an opportunity to analyze their ability and to reflect on their own learning. Checklists can be designed to help students proofread work products before submitting them for grading. This process can give teachers information about what students are thinking and how they feel they are doing while engaged in academic tasks. Peer assessment is a method of evaluation that allows students to compare their work with others and to gain insight into the reasoning and problem-solving abilities of their peers. This process promotes collaborative learning, analysis skills, and reflective skills. In addition, peer assessment fosters respect for the work of others and provides opportunities for positive interaction as students learn to give constructive criticism.

Implementation

✓ Structure the self-assessment process so that, during an instructional activity, students describe aloud or in written form, perceptions of their skills, motivation, confidence level, and how they feel about their academic tasks (see Figure 2–10).

✓ Explain to students that the goal of self and peer assessment is to monitor progress. Be sure they are familiar with the standards and criteria which they are to meet. Students need frequent opportunities to evaluate their own work.

✓ Promote the development of self-assessment skills by encouraging students to talk and write about their reactions to what they have learned; to describe in oral and written form their attitudes about the project; and to explain the problem-solving process they used, why the process did or did not work, and what they would do differently next time.

✓ Provide students who are doing peer assessment with an evaluation guide, such as a rubric or checklist of expected outcomes, as a guide for appraising the work products of classmates (see Figure 2–11).

✓ Supply a list of terms for peer evaluators to use when providing constructive criticism and provide examples of how to be specific yet sensitive in noting areas in need of improvement.

Special Considerations, Accommodations, Alternatives

- To help students think about what they learned and focus on what they need to analyze, teachers may need to provide verbal prompts or visual cues.
- It is helpful for the teacher to model self and peer assessment; it may also be useful to pair students with learning difficulties or language differences with peers to work until a level of comfort in partnership and competency is established.

FIGURE 2–10 Student Self-Report

While doing this assignment, I felt (check one):

_____ Confident that I knew how to solve all of the problems. I felt that I could teach others how to solve similar problems.

_____ Like I knew how to solve some problems, but there were many that I did not feel sure about. Please explain:

____

_____ Like I thought I could solve the problems when I started, but then I got confused and couldn't remember how to solve them. Please explain: ______________________________

_____ Lost from the start. I never understood what the teacher was doing during instruction.
Please explain: ______________________________

FIGURE 2–11 Sample Self and Peer Rating Scale: Research Report Assessment

Rate each category from 1 (poor) to 5 (terrific). Use the "Comments" area to write your reasons.

Self-Assessment	Skill	Peer Assessment
1 2 3 4 5	Followed assignment directions	1 2 3 4 5
1 2 3 4 5	Included all required components	1 2 3 4 5
1 2 3 4 5	Organized thoughts in writing	1 2 3 4 5
1 2 3 4 5	Completed report from outline	1 2 3 4 5
1 2 3 4 5	Included only necessary information	1 2 3 4 5
1 2 3 4 5	Used proper sentence structure	1 2 3 4 5
1 2 3 4 5	Used proper punctuation	1 2 3 4 5
1 2 3 4 5	Used proper grammar and spelling	1 2 3 4 5
1 2 3 4 5	Stated clear introductory statement	1 2 3 4 5
1 2 3 4 5	Included clear concluding statement	1 2 3 4 5
1 2 3 4 5	Submitted report neatly and on time	1 2 3 4 5

Comments

____

____

OBSERVATION RECORDING

Assessment Strategy: *Sample Anecdotal Record*

Strategy Description

Anecdotal records are dated data recordings of student behavior which help the teacher to note whether certain behaviors are chronic or incidental. They help to determine whether the student has made progress, whether behaviors are increasing or decreasing, and to analyze patterns of behavior over time. Besides providing information about students' academic skills, anecdotal records are used to track students' strategy use, work habits, interaction with classmates and teachers, and attitudes toward particular activities and assigned tasks. Records should be kept on a daily, weekly, or monthly basis; and document both successful and unsuccessful efforts.

Implementation

- ✓ Base observation recording on direct teacher observation and provide as much detail as possible to describe the behavior and the incident in which it occurred, including context and setting (see Figure 2–12).
- ✓ Observe and record students in a variety of situations, such as (a) working in discussion or writing conference groups, (b) participating in independent writing activities, (c) interacting in cooperative groups, (d) using strategies in writing, (e) applying strategies when studying informational text, and (f) encountering an unknown word or confusing passage (Gunning, 2010).
- ✓ Develop brief entries as understandable abbreviations for students, actions, and contexts by establishing a key or color-coded system for the data, such as the date, time, description of the setting, context of the situation, and antecedent, including what was said or done by the child(ren) involved. In this way, teachers can rely on a tally sheet or checklist to note, for example, how often the student contributed to the group discussion about the week's current events topic. This is particularly helpful for those teaching young children who require much hands-on involvement, and may find it difficult to take notes during class time.

✓ Review records periodically, summarize, and note developmental trends or patterns.

✓ Make recordings as soon as possible following the incident to reduce the risk of erroneous recordings caused by inaccurate recall and the tendency to generalize negative judgments about more than one behavior.

✓ Be cautious about including interpretations of the observed behavior. When included, interpretation or possible explanations should be clearly identified by placement in brackets or marked in some way to avoid confusing the interpretation of the behavior with the observation of it.

Special Considerations, Accommodations, Alternatives

- Anecdotal records may need to be interpreted cautiously due to reliability issues related to teachers' experience and skill.
- Anecdotal records can be invaluable when considering students' present level of educational performance, when writing progress reports to parents, and when reviewing students' day-to-day progress for projecting the next year's IEP goal.

FIGURE 2–12 Sample Anecdotal Record

Actions, Activities, Behaviors Observed — **Date:** 10/2

Target Student: Betsy

11:00 AM	T tell ss to open bk, & hmwrk nbk, turn to pg 57, do prblms 1–20.
11:01	B looks around rm, then stares out wdo.
11:02	B looks over at other ss.
11:03	T asks for volunteers to read hmwrk answ.
11:04	B's glance returns to wdo.
11:05	T tells B to take out hmwrk nbk and explain 1st prblm.
11:06–11:08	B looking in dsk for hmwrk.
11:09	T asks if she has hmwrk.
11:10	B says she forgot to do it.
11:11	T calls on J.
11:12–11:16	J explains 1st math prblm, writes answ on chlkbd. R looks at his nbk.
11:17	B reverts to staring out wdo.
11:18	T reminds B to check hmwrk.
11:19	B looks at nbk.
11:20	R is asked to explain prblm #2.
11:21–11:25	B picks up pcl and doodles on bk cover.

Key:

B = Betsy	wdo = window	dsk = desk
T = Teacher	pcl = pencil	prblm = problem
R = Roger	bk = book	chlkbd = chalkboard
J = Jill	nbk = notebook	rm = room
ss = student	hmwrk = homework	answ = answer

Assessment Strategy: *Direct Observation Recording*

Strategy Description

Event recording is a method of direct observation in which the observer counts the number of times a target behavior occurs. This can be used when the behavior has a definite beginning and end. Duration recording is a type of direct measurement used to record how long a specific behavior lasts. In some situations, the duration of a certain behavior may be more significant than how often it occurs. For meaningful duration recording, the behavior must have a clear beginning and end. Latency recording is similar to duration recording in that time is a critical factor. This type of assessment is particularly useful for students who are often off task, unfocused, uncooperative, unable to process directions well, or slow to initiate or follow through on an assignment. Latency recording is based not only on how long the behavior occurred, but also on how long it took before the student actually engaged in the targeted behavior. Interval recording is another direct method of observing specific target behaviors. The teacher chooses a specific amount of time for the observation (e.g., 20 minutes) and divides this time period into smaller, equal time segments (e.g., 10-second intervals). During each interval, the teacher carefully watches the student and records whether the target behavior is observed. Time sampling is another type of interval recording method. Using this method, an observation period is divided into equal intervals.

Implementation

✓ *Event recording*—Track behavior by making slash marks on a notepad, by using a handheld counter, or by simply moving a rubber band from one finger to the next to count incidents of specific target behavior (see Figure 2–13).

✓ *Duration recording*—Track behavior by either totalling or averaging the segments of time the behavior occurred during a specific period of time. To obtain the total, add each recorded period of time that the behavior occurred. To obtain an average, divide the total number of minutes that the behavior occurred by the number of times the behavior was observed during the identified period (see Figure 2–14).

✓ *Latency recording*—Track behavior by counting the length of time a particular behavior was observed or how long it took before the student initiated the activity. Results can be calculated in average time or total latency, whichever most clearly defines the issue (see Figure 2–15).

✓ *Interval recording*—Track behavior by dividing an observation period into specific intervals. Mark the prepared rating sheet with a plus sign (+) or some other code to indicate that the behavior was observed. If during that interval the behavior was not observed, then enter a minus sign (−) or a zero (0) on the rating sheet. Three types of interval recordings can be made: (1) Partial interval recording is when the behavior occurs at any time during the interval (e.g., for 2 seconds during the 10-second interval); (2) percentage interval recording is when the observer records the percent of time that the behavior occurs during the interval (e.g., 20% of the 10-second interval); and (3) total interval is when the behavior occurs throughout the complete interval (e.g., 2 out of 10 seconds would be recorded as a minus [−], but 10 seconds out of the 10-second interval would be recorded as a plus [+]). This is also referred to as time sampling (see Figure 2–16).

Special Considerations, Accommodations, Alternatives

- An adaptation of this strategy is to use this activity as a student self-monitoring system. The students can do some of these recordings as a self-monitoring activity (i.e., for interval recording). By giving students a chart and a timer, whenever the timer goes off (or the teacher gives a signal) the students can record what they were doing and how they were doing at that point in time. This activity can increase self-awareness and promote responsibility.
- Be aware of particular disabling conditions that would impact the students' behavior, such as attention deficit disorder (inattentiveness), attention deficit hyperactive disorder (impulsivity), a learning or physical disorder that impacts the ability to follow directions, perform in a timely manner, and so forth.

Additional Resources

Special Connections: An Introduction to Data-Based Decision Making
http://www.specialconnections.ku.edu/cgi-bin/cgiwrap/specconn/main.php?cat=assessment&section=ddm/main

FIGURE 2–13 Sample Event Recording Chart

Name: Nancy Date: 9/10–9/15
Target Behavior: Any inappropriate verbalizations

Day	Observation Period	Frequency	Total for Period
Monday	1:00 PM to 1:45 PM	⁄⁄⁄⁄ IIII	9
Tuesday	12:45 PM to 1:30 PM	⁄⁄⁄⁄ ⁄⁄⁄⁄	10
Wednesday	12:48 PM to 1:33 PM	⁄⁄⁄⁄ II	7
Thursday	1:15 PM to 2:00 PM	⁄⁄⁄⁄ ⁄⁄⁄⁄ II	12
Friday	1:02 PM to 1:47 PM	⁄⁄⁄⁄ ⁄⁄⁄⁄ I	11
TOTAL			49

FIGURE 2–14 Sample Duration Recording Chart

Name: Jesse Date: 11/3
Target Behavior: Thumb sucking

Behavior Began	Behavior Ended	Duration
8:30 AM	8:40 AM	10 minutes
8:45 AM	8:52 AM	7 minutes
8:55 AM	8:58 AM	3 minutes
9:00 AM	9:08 AM	8 minutes
9:18 AM	9:30 AM	12 minutes
TOTAL		40 minutes
AVERAGE DURATION	8 minutes	

FIGURE 2–15 Sample Latency Recording Graph

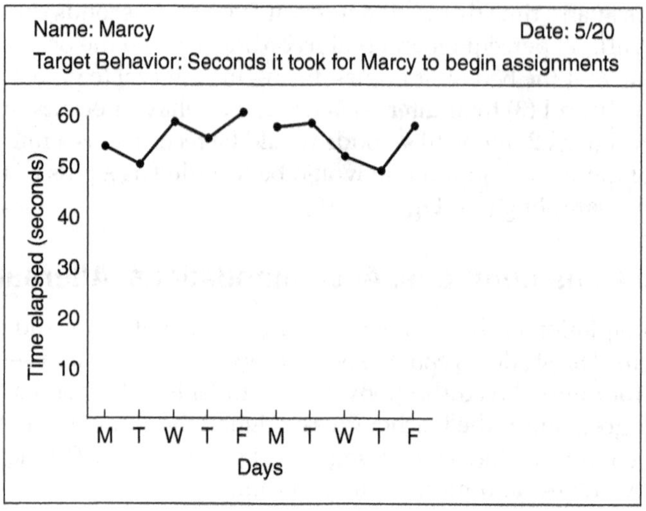

FIGURE 2–16 Sample Interval Recording Graph

Name: Jesse Date: 10/2
Target Behavior: On task

+ 5 min.	– 10 min.	– 15 min.	+ 20 min.	+ 25 min.	– 30 min.
– 35 min.	– 40 min.	– 45 min.	+ 50 min.	– 55 min.	– 60 min.

SUPPLEMENTAL ASSESSMENTS

Assessment Strategy: *Visual/Auditory Acuity/Perceptual Development*

Strategy Description

Students can have varying degrees of vision or hearing loss, inefficiency, or perceptual dysfunction, and not be diagnosed until they enter school. Teachers are often the first to identify these deficiencies. Teachers need to identify visual and auditory symptoms of dysfunctions that impact the learning process, such as intermittent hearing loss often due to the residual effects of an ear infection, visual inefficiency that impacts the ability to see and take in information for sustained periods of time, or processing disorders that affect the ability to analyze and interpret incoming visual and/or auditory information.

Implementation

✓ Know the symptoms of vision and hearing acuity and perceptual deficits in order to recognize even subtle changes that may suggest the need to refer the student for diagnostic testing.

✓ Monitor students' visual and auditory skill development using a proficiency checklist (see Figure 2–17).

Special Considerations, Accommodations, Alternatives

- Prior to assessing for visual or auditory inefficiency or perceptual processing, it is important to have visual and auditory acuity evaluated. The school nurse can administer this basic evaluation.
- Visual efficiency problems often do not begin to surface until the upper elementary or junior high grades, when students are required to cover a significant amount of reading material.
- Visual and auditory perceptual problems, which can begin in kindergarten and impact early learning, occur in approximately 15% to 20% of all children who have learning problems.

FIGURE 2–17 Visual/Auditory Acuity/Perceptual Screening Checklist

Teachers should be cognizant of the following characteristics that may indicate vision efficiency problems.

The student:

_____ Squints, blinks, frowns, or rubs or covers one eye when doing close visual work or copying from the board

_____ Holds printed material too close, at an unusual angle, or far away

_____ Tilts or turns the head forward while reading and writing

_____ Complains of headache, nausea, or eyestrain after reading

_____ Tires easily or avoids doing visual work

_____ Has difficulty staying on lines when writing or within lines when coloring

_____ Inaccurately spaces letters or words when writing

_____ Has difficulty copying from the board

_____ Omits words, skips, or rereads lines

_____ Loses place, uses finger to track when reading

_____ Has difficulty judging distances

_____ Exhibits poor eye–hand coordination

Teachers can play an important role in the diagnosis of auditory acuity problems by noting the following behaviors.

The student:

_____ Lacks normal response to sound, or an inappropriate or unrelated response to sound

_____ Fails to respond to his or her name when called or spoken to

_____ Constantly requests repetition of directions and questions

_____ Turns up the volume of the radio, tape player, or television

_____ Appears confused when oral directions are given

_____ Watches what others do, then imitates their actions

Assessment Strategy: *Class and School Environmental Assessment*

Strategy Description

Environmental factors can significantly affect students' interest, motivation, and perseverance in the classroom. The teacher plays a major role in providing an environment conducive to learning. Teachers, too, can benefit from regular self-checks to ensure that they are providing a challenging yet supportive and accommodating environment that promotes maximum student performance.

Implementation

✓ Use an environmental checklist to monitor how the classroom is organized and whether it is safe and conducive to learning (see Figure 2–18).

✓ Check the classroom environment and the school climate; schedule regular teacher self-checks as well.

FIGURE 2–18 Class/School Environmental Checklist

Is the classroom:

_____ Structured so that there is a free flow around the room?

_____ Well lit?

_____ Free from chemicals (e.g., toxic cleaning products), pollutants (e.g., insect repellents)?

_____ Maintained with a comfortable temperature?

_____ Arranged so that desks allow good communication, grouping, peer partners?

_____ Set up so that the students have easy access to supplies, classroom tools?

_____ Bright, colorful, and student friendly?

_____ Designed with student learning centers?

_____ Equipped with sufficient technological supports?

As teacher, do I:

_____ Check to determine whether students are paying attention before giving instruction?

_____ Monitor to be sure students understand the material being taught?

_____ Make expectations for appropriate student performance very clear (e.g., classroom rules)?

_____ Use preassessments to guide instruction?

_____ Typically use one summative assessment, or can students demonstrate mastery of new concepts and skills in more than one way?

_____ Involve students in regular self-assessment? If so, how?

_____ Attempt to meet individual needs by grouping? altering content? changing tasks? providing different level of supports? differentiating instruction?

_____ Teach in ways that address students' learning styles and preferences?

_____ Consistently offer multiple strategies through which students can master essential content and skills and demonstrate their learning?

_____ Adjust my presentation style to meet the information processing and learning style of all students?

_____ Place students in small groups based on their different interests, levels of readiness, or learning preferences?

_____ Make appropriate accommodations and modifications for students with special learning needs?

_____ Ensure that my lessons involve structure, the appropriate pace, and maximum engagement through appropriate questioning?

_____ Develop lesson plan formats that reflect responsive teaching?

_____ Provide specific feedback that includes cultural affirmations for success?

_____ Provide instruction that is standards based, student centered, and monitored by regular assessment?

_____ Ensure that there is consistent use of best instructional practices and materials that are grounded in research?

_____ Maintain a strength-based teaching style to sustain a culturally responsive learning community?

_____ Provide an intellectually stimulating classroom environment; infuse culture in the curriculum?

_____ Provide students with immediate, specific, positive feedback about their behavior or academic performance?

_____ Monitor the general noise level and behavior of students that can impact group instruction or independent seat work?

_____ Manage to immediately and consistently manage or prevent classroom disruptions?

Special Considerations, Accommodations, Alternatives

- Be aware of the need for classroom accommodations for specific disabilities (e.g., structural considerations for students in wheelchairs and those with mobility issues; special desk arrangements for students with ADHD who are easily distracted or for students with limited vision or hearing impairments who need to be seated near the teacher, close to the chalkboard, near an interpreter or peer partner).

Assessment Strategy: *Readability Evaluation Assessment*

Strategy Description

A readability formula or graph is used to determine the reading level of students' texts, reading material, or trade books.

Implementation

✓ Randomly select three sample passages. If using a book, select a passage from the beginning, the middle, and the end of the book. If using a single written piece, such as a newspaper article, select a section from the beginning, the middle, and the end of the article.

✓ For each passage, do the following:

Count out exactly 100 words starting with the beginning of a sentence. Count proper nouns, numerals, and initials (e.g., St.) as words.

Count the number of sentences estimating the length of the last sentence to the nearest tenth.

Count the total number of syllables in each 100-word passage. Count one syllable for each numeral or initial or symbol, for example, 1990 is one word and four syllables. LD is one word and two syllables, and "&" is one word and one syllable.

Average the number of sentences and number of syllables across the three samples.

Enter on the graph the average sentence length and average number of syllables; put a dot where these two lines intersect. The area where the dot is plotted will provide an approximate estimate of readability (grade level). See the following example.

✓ Recount using different 100 word sample passages from same material, if there is a great deal of variability found in the syllable count or sentence count (Fry, 1977).

Example	*Syllables*	*Sentences*
First Hundred Words	124	6.6
Second Hundred Words	141	5.5
Third Hundred Words	158	6.8
Total	423	18.9

To get the averages divide the syllables total by 3, which equals 141, and divide the sentences total by 3, equaling 6.3. Plot the average number of syllables (i.e., 141) and the average number of sentences (i.e., 6.3). This example yields an approximate seventh-grade readability level.

Special Considerations, Accommodations, Alternatives

- Figure 2–19 can be used with reading matter from levels first grade through college.
- Once the teacher identifies appropriate grade level material using a readability analysis, comprehension ability can be determined by using techniques such as the cloze procedure or oral reading sample.
- Readability graphs are approximations; they can vary by as much as 1.5 grade levels.

FIGURE 2–19 Fry Readability Graph

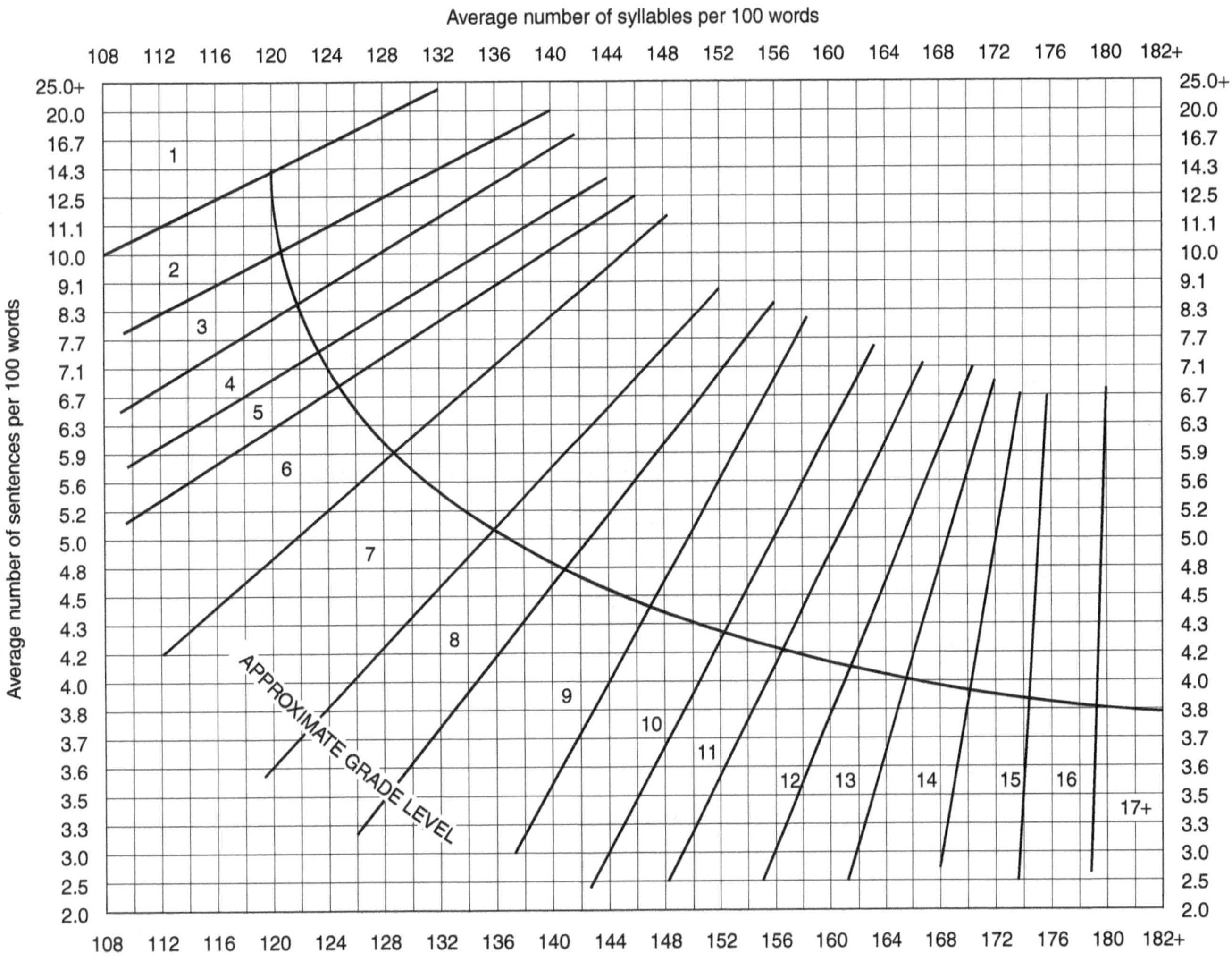

Source: "Fry's Readability Graph; Clarifications, Validity, and Extension to Level 17," by Edward Fry © 1977 International Reading Association. Reprinted with permission.

Assessment Strategy: *Textbook Evaluation*

Strategy Description

Textbooks are used for a significant amount of in-class curriculum content and homework assignments. However, many textbooks are not written with text *considerateness*, meaning that they are not designed with the needs of the diverse learner in mind. Texts are often written at an advanced readability level. The organization and writing format is often unfamiliar to students, based on patterns of problem and solution, cause and effect, classification, definition, and example. The concepts, theories, and language used tend to be complex, detailed, and technical.

Implementation

✓ All textbooks and curriculum materials need to be carefully previewed.

✓ Use specific criteria to determine textbook considerateness (see Figure 2–20 for guidelines).

FIGURE 2–20 Textbook Evaluation Guidelines

Readability

_____ Is the reading level appropriate?

_____ Is the vocabulary and language understandable, not too advanced or too "sophisticated"?

_____ Are the complex terms or vocabulary defined with examples?

_____ Are new concepts clearly explained with sufficient examples or visual aids?

_____ Are there sufficient illustrations, color, and so forth to maintain interest and motivation?

Content Coverage

_____ Is the content appropriate and current?

_____ Is the material in each lesson too detailed? too limited?

_____ Does the content cover the scope and sequence of district, state, and national guidelines?

_____ Is the material presented in a manner that promotes critical analysis and higher order thinking?

_____ Are chapter objectives and a summary statement provided?

_____ Are application problems, reinforcement activities, and critical thinking supplements included?

_____ Does the text address diversity issues, cultural perspectives, and cross-cultural differences?

Text Structure

_____ Is the topic clearly introduced?

_____ Is the content presented in an organized form, following a logical, sequential, consistent order of presentation?

_____ Is there a relationship between and among concepts, headings/subheadings, difficult vocabulary highlighted or underlined?

_____ Is the font size appropriate for readability?

_____ Are there transition words that illustrate time and order (*before, next, later*), enumeration (*first, next*), compare and contrast (*similarly, in contrast*), cause and effect (*therefore, because, resulted in*), sequence (*first, second*), and classification (*type of, group of*)?

Evaluation Procedures

_____ Is there a match between course objectives and assessment focus?

_____ Is there an assortment of informal assessment procedures (curriculum based, performance based, portfolio based)?

_____ Are directions for the evaluation procedures explicit and easy to follow?

_____ Is there a match between the order of questions and the order of concepts presented in the text?

_____ Are study guides or strategies incorporated into the chapters?

_____ Is the format of the questions appropriate (multiple choice, true-false, fill in the blank, essay, open ended)?

_____ Do evaluation measures address varying cognitive thinking processes (e.g., using Bloom's taxonomy)?

_____ Are end of section, chapter, or unit questions provided for self-assessment?

Special Considerations, Accommodations, Alternatives

- Textbooks for exceptional learners need to be carefully reviewed to determine text content, layout, format, and readability. When texts are universally designed, traditional text format and test question format are sufficiently adaptable or can be modified to meet the needs of all learners, including students with various special learning needs.
- Check the textbook's teacher manual for suggested adaptations.
- Consult with text publishers for supplemental materials, such as audiotaped versions.
- Often textbooks are available in adapted form by the Commission for the Blind and the Library of Congress.

REFERENCES

Fry, E. B. (1977). Fry's readability graph: Clarification, validity, and extension to level 17. *Journal of Reading, 21*, 242–252.

Gunning, T. G. (2010). *Assessing and correcting reading and writing difficulties* (4th ed.). Needham Heights, MA: Allyn & Bacon.

Lipson, M. Y., & Wixson, K. K. (2009). *Assessment and instruction of reading and writing difficulties: An interactive approach* (4th ed.). Boston: Allyn & Bacon/Pearson.

Vallecorsa, A. L., deBettencourt, L. U., & Zigmond, N. (2000). *Students with mild disabilities in general education setting: A guide for special educators*. Upper Saddle River, NJ: Merrill/Prentice Hall.

Chapter 3

Reading Assessment

INTRODUCTION

Most students progress through the normal reading process smoothly, but some do not. There are various degrees of reading disability, ranging from first graders who have not mastered sound-symbol association to high school students who drop out of school after enduring years of anguish and embarrassment about their inability to read fluently and comprehend required reading material. An estimated 7% to 9% of the school age population have reading disabilities (Gersten, Fuchs, Williams, & Baker, 2001; Riddle-Buly & Valencia, 2002). The reasons for reading disability are numerous, and frequently many factors interact to affect students' inability to master the fundamentals of reading.

Although more instructional time is dedicated to the teaching of reading than any other school subject, more students experience problems in this subject than any other. According to the National Reading Panel (2005), approximately 1 million children, more than 17.5% of our nation's students, encounter reading problems during the crucial first 3 years of schooling. In addition to these staggering statistics, longitudinal data indicate that the consequences of poor reading do not stop at high school; children who are poor readers early on are 3 to 4 times more likely to become teen parents and 3 times more likely to become unemployed adults (Torgesen et al., 1999).

It is critical to identify reading problems early so that appropriate intervention can begin. The facts speak for themselves; it takes 4 times as long to improve the skills of a struggling reader in the fourth grade as it does between mid-kindergarten and first grade. It takes 2 hours of intervention in fourth grade to have the same impact as 30 minutes per day in first grade (Lyon, 1997). The National Assessment of Educational Progress (NAEP) continues to find that as many as 40% of our nation's fourth graders read too poorly to understand or learn from grade level texts; and in high poverty neighborhoods, this statistic rises above 60% (National Center for Educational Statistics, 2005). At least 20 million school age children suffer from reading failure, and of these, only about 2.3 million meet the criteria to receive special education services under the category of learning disabilities. The remaining 17.7 million poor readers either receive some form of compensatory education or are overlooked all together (Lyon, 2003). Children do not outgrow reading problems. There are devastating consequences for many young children, particularly those from poverty, when they are not identified early so that they can receive systematic focused intervention, prevention services, and progress monitoring (Lyon, 2001).

Teachers need to be skilled not only in instructional methods, but also in informal, classroom-based assessment strategies, so that they can identify students' specific strengths and areas in need of reinforcement or remediation and monitor progress in an effective and timely manner. This is especially true with the increasing numbers of students who are at risk for reading problems due to medical, nutritional, social-emotional, cultural, environmental, and/or socioeconomic problems, and for those who are classified as having a disability and are included in general education classes. This chapter provides a variety of reading assessments for screening, diagnosis, progress monitoring, and accountability purposes.

EMERGENT LITERACY SKILLS

Assessment Strategy: *Oral Language Assessment*

Strategy Description

Competency in oral language is necessary for development of basic literacy skills such as reading, writing, and spelling. Oral language assessment is used to determine whether students have adequately developed vocabulary, and the ability to use and understand complex sentence structure and correct grammatical form. It is important to assess students with delayed oral language who may not have adequate understanding of what is said (receptive language) and those who have difficulty expressing themselves verbally (expressive language). This assessment is appropriate for students at the emergent literacy stage, ranging from pre-kindergarten through the early primary grades. Allow generally 10 to 15 minutes to assess this skill.

Questions to Ask

Is the student able to:

- Respond in detail, or are verbal responses limited to one- or two-word phrases?
- Retell a story in sequential order?
- Complete a sentence in his or her own words?
- Ask for help when confused by directions or concepts?
- Directly answer "wh" questions (why, when, what, where)?
- Respond to questions without excessive delay, or require considerable time to process questions before responding?

Assessment Preparation

- Review the cumulative file for a history of language-related problems.
- Review the health file for significant medical history; check auditory acuity.
- Structure the observation in authentic situations, both formal (e.g., classroom) and informal (e.g., playground, lunchroom) settings.

Implementation

✓ Observe language during verbal interactions (e.g., conversations), one-on-one interactions, and group activities, with peers and adults.

✓ Compare a sample of the student's language to that of typically developing peers to determine whether the student has age appropriate skills.

✓ Assess the student's receptive and expressive language using checklists (see Figure 3–1).

✓ Determine if student's oral skills improve when prompts, such as verbal or visual cues, are provided.

✓ Use direct observation or teacher–family interviews to assess oral language skill levels using language surveys (see Figure 3–2).

Special Considerations, Accommodations, Alternatives

- Cultural diversity, impoverished linguistic environments, or limited opportunities to use and hear language may affect communication skill.
- Oral processing or word retrieval problems may impact performance.
- If the student's response is not clear, if it is not obvious that the meaning of a word is known, or is being used appropriately, ask the student to explain further or use the word in a sentence.

FIGURE 3–1 Screening Assessment for Language Skills

	Above Average 0	*Average 1*	*Below Average 2*
Receptive Language			
1. Ability to comprehend common gestures	______	______	______
2. Enjoys listening to books	______	______	______
3. Ability to "read" picture stories	______	______	______
4. Ability to retain directions and instructions	______	______	______
5. Listening vocabulary	______	______	______
6. Response time to questions or direction	______	______	______
7. Interprets anger or teasing from others	______	______	______
Inner Language			
8. Ability to follow directions or demonstrations	______	______	______
9. Knowledge of background information	______	______	______
10. Grasp the meaning of a story/discussion	______	______	______
11. Sense of humor	______	______	______
12. Ability to stay on topic	______	______	______
13. Ability to predict what will happen next	______	______	______
14. Ability to summarize story/discussion	______	______	______
15. Ability to solve simple mental math	______	______	______
Expressive Language			
16. Pronunciation of words	______	______	______
17. Recall of people's names, places, objects	______	______	______
18. Ability to repeat a story/discussion	______	______	______
19. Regulates voice volume	______	______	______
20. Rate of speech	______	______	______
21. Use of correct words when speaking	______	______	______
22. Ability to speak in complete sentences	______	______	______
23. Uses words in correct order	______	______	______
24. Participation in class discussions	______	______	______

Score:

27 or less	Language skills seem to be developing adequately.
28–35	Skills seem to be emerging; monitor progress periodically.
36 or more	A comprehension assessment should be completed.

Source: From *Informal Assessment in Education*, by G. R. Guerin and A. S. Maier. Copyright © 1983 by Mayfield Publishing Company. Reprinted by permission of the publisher.

FIGURE 3–2 Oral Language Checklist

Oral Language Checklist	***Mastered***	***Emerging***	***Little to No Skill***
The student:			
Understands the teacher in classroom discussions	______	______	______
Understands the language of peers in social contexts	______	______	______
Understands nonverbal communication (e.g., foot tapping, nodding)	______	______	______
Understands and can follow verbal directions and instructions	______	______	______
Uses nonverbal means to communicate (e.g., gestures, facial signals)	______	______	______
Concentrates fully on speaker (e.g., attend to faces, eye contact)	______	______	______
Understands oral communication when speaker is not in full view	______	______	______
(e.g., when back is turned, when listening to taped discussion)	______	______	______
Listens attentively and follows a conversation	______	______	______
Listens attentively in a group	______	______	______
Listens attentively to a recitation or story	______	______	______
Understands simple forms of figurative language (metaphors, similes)	______	______	______
Speaks in one- or two-word sentences	______	______	______
Speaks in sentences of three or more words	______	______	______
Speaks clearly; no serious speech defects (e.g., articulation, stuttering)	______	______	______
Speaks in complete sentences	______	______	______
Articulates thoughts clearly and thoroughly	______	______	______
Speaks in a tempo appropriate to the situation	______	______	______
Responds appropriately to questions	______	______	______
Understands or "gets" jokes	______	______	______
Speaks without exerting excessive energy (e.g., head jerking, grimaces)	______	______	______
Takes time before responding	______	______	______
Uses age appropriate vocabulary	______	______	______
Gives sequenced oral directions	______	______	______
States information in a logical manner	______	______	______
Demonstrates competence using words and grammar (e.g., correct use	______	______	______
of objects, actions, events, correct tense, and word usage)	______	______	______
Expresses original thoughts rather than parrots/paraphrases	______	______	______
Communicates appropriately in different contexts (e.g., class, gym)	______	______	______
Distinguishes between relevant and irrelevant information	______	______	______
Uses appropriate distance when speaking	______	______	______
Demonstrates a variety of possibilities and perspectives	______	______	______
Assumes the point of view of the speaker	______	______	______
Uses standard English	______	______	______
Uses regional variation or dialect	______	______	______
Contributes appropriately to conversations	______	______	______
Able to retell a story	______	______	______
Takes turns when conversing	______	______	______
Holds the audience's attention	______	______	______
Stays on topic in a conversation	______	______	______

Next Step

- *Mastered*—Introduce advanced vocabulary, provide opportunities for more complex conversations, encourage leadership in group activities, promote opportunities for making oral presentations.
- *Emerging*—Increase language development experiences at home and school; continue to provide opportunities for oral interaction in dialogue, conversations, and small group discussions; stimulate receptive and expressive language by focusing on who, what, when, why, and how questions.
- *No skill yet*—Refer to speech and language therapists for comprehensive assessment.

Additional Resources

http://www.sju.edu/~cspinell/pages/source/fry_word_list.pdf

Assessment Strategy: *Phonological Awareness Assessment*

Strategy Description

This assessment examines students' knowledge of how individual sounds make words and measures their ability to hear and manipulate these sounds in words. Students' phonological awareness is measured to determine whether they understand and are able to make new words by adding, moving, or deleting phonemes (the smallest distinguishable units of sound within a word, such as /b/, /j/, /o/), recognize that speech can be segmented into phonemic units or sounds, can segment words, and identify the number of phonemes in a word. A slightly more advanced level of assessment is to determine whether students can divide sentences into words, break words into syllables, and identify common phonemes. This assessment is appropriate for students at the emergent literacy stage, ranging from kindergarten through the early primary grades. Allow approximately 5 to 15 minutes to assess each specific skill.

Questions to Ask

Is the student able to:

- Identify individual sounds (phonemes) and the number of sounds in a word?
- Blend a sequence of separate sounds into a recognizable word?
- Identify common sounds in different words?
- Break words into individual sounds?
- Identify a word when a sound is removed?
- Recognize the word with a different sound part in a series of words?
- Recognize rhyming words or identify words that do not rhyme?

Assessment Preparation

- Have a tape recorder available to record responses; this will assist in later analysis.
- Review the health file for significant medical history, including auditory or visual acuity.
- Develop a list of words and parts of words that cover all sounds and analysis categories. When assessing these skills, follow the developmental stage in the progression of phonological knowledge: rhyming, blending, counting, segmenting, deleting, and substituting.

Implementation

✓ Observe students' use of phonological skills in natural (e.g., playground) and more formal (e.g., classroom) settings.

✓ Determine students' understanding of phonemic awareness by having them count the number of phonemes in a word and also by adding, moving, or deleting a phoneme to make a new word (see Figure 3–3).

✓ Determine whether students are able to isolate sounds; blend, categorize, and segment phonemes; and rhyme words (see Figure 3–4).

✓ Determine if students' skills improve when prompts, verbal or visual cues, are provided.

Special Considerations, Accommodations, Alternatives

- Determine whether the student understands the concepts of first, last, add, delete (e.g., be sure that the child knows what *delete* means before asking him or her to delete the last sound of the word *put*).
- Consider using nonsense rather than meaningful words so the student focuses on the word and is not distracted by the word meaning.
- It is important to remember that there are only 45 phonemes in the English language but an infinite number of possible words.

FIGURE 3–3 Test of Phonological Awareness

Give the child two demonstration items to help him or her understand the task. For example, first say the word *cowboy*, then ask the child to say the word. You then tell the child to say the word again but not to say *boy*. Do the same with the word *steamboat*. Tell the child, "Say it again but don't say *steam*." If the child answers both demonstration items correctly, then give the following test.

Item	***Question***	***Correct Response***
Say *sunshine*	Now say it again, but don't say *shine*.	*sun*
Say *picnic*	Now say it again, but don't say *pic*.	*nic*
Say *cucumber*	Now say it again, but don't say *cu*.	*cumber*
Say *coat*	Now say it again, but don't say /k/.	*oat*
Say *meat*	Now say it again, but don't say /m/.	*eat*
Say *take*	Now say it again, but don't say /t/.	*ache*
Say *game*	Now say it again, but don't say /m/.	*gay*
Say *wrote*	Now say it again, but don't say /t/.	*row*
Say *please*	Now say it again, but don't say /z/.	*plea*
Say *clap*	Now say it again, but don't say /k/.	*lap*
Say *play*	Now say it again, but don't say /p/.	*lay*
Say *stale*	Now say it again, but don't say /t/.	*sale*
Say *smack*	Now say it again, but don't say /m/.	*sack*

Scoring: Give 1 point for each correct answer.

Score	***Expected Level***
1–3	Kindergarten
4–9	Grade 1
10–11	Grade 2
12–13	Grade 3

Source: From *Helping Children Overcome Learning Disabilities*, by J. Rosner. Copyright © 1993 by Jerome Rosner, Walker & Company.

Next Step

- *Mastered*—Begin instruction in phonics.
- *Emerging*—Continue instruction in phonemic skills, progressing from isolated sounds to blending, categorizing and, segmenting, to rhyming. Provide instruction in small groups; this facilitates increased teacher feedback and provides practice with peers.
- *No skill yet*—Consult with a speech and language therapist and/or remedial reading specialist. Teach sounds using word games. Provide explicit, systematic instruction progressing in skill complexity; use teacher demonstration and guided practice (Vaughn & Bos, 2009).

Additional Resources

http://www.balancedreading.com/assessment/abecedarian.pdf
http://www.k-3learningpages.net/web%20phonemic%20awareness.htm
http://teams.lacoe.edu/reading/assessments/assessments.html
http://www.nmreadingfirst.org/ANRFC/05/Lane-PhonologicalAwarenessAssessmentandInstruction.pdf

FIGURE 3–4 Phonemic Analysis Assessment Skill Activities

Phonemic Analysis	***Assessment Skill***	***Sample Assessment Activity***
	Can the student . . .	
Phonemic segmentation	break the word into its sounds and tap, clap out, or place a marker on the different syllables in words?	How many phonemes in *run?* **(3)**
Phoneme isolation	recognize individual sounds in words?	What is the first sound in *bike*? **(/b/)***
Phoneme blending	listen to a sequence of separately spoken sounds and combine them to form a recognized word?	What word is this? /f/e/t/ **(feet)**
Phoneme identity	recognize the common sound in different words?	What sound is the same in these words? *rake, rock, row* **(/r/)**
Phoneme categorization	recognize the word with the odd sound in a sequence of three or four words?	What word does not belong? *cat, cap, rat* **(rat)**
Rhyming	state whether or not two words rhyme or give a list of words that rhyme with a specific word?	What word sounds the same as *rake*? ***(cake, take, fake)***
Phoneme deletion	recognize when a word remains after a specific phoneme is removed?	What word is "pants" without the *p*? **(ants)**

Note: *Slashes (//) indicate that the sound should be pronounced.

Assessment Strategy: *Print Awareness Assessment*

Strategy Description

Print awareness assessment is a means of determining students' knowledge of print: awareness that print contains a message, recognition of the significance of letter position in words and word position in sentences, and understanding that text features (e.g., punctuation) determine meaning. This assessment also focuses on students' knowledge of print concepts, such as the order and direction of words on a page, the basic contents of a book (e.g., table of contents), and how to handle printed material (e.g., reading in a right-to-left, front-to-back order). This assessment is appropriate for students at the emergent literacy stage, ranging from kindergarten through the early primary grades. Allow approximately 10 to 15 minutes to assess this skill.

Questions to Ask

Is the student able to:

- Identify the differences between letters, words, pictures, and word sounds?
- Recognize that letters make words and words make sentences?
- Recognize the meaning of positional words (e.g., *first, last, beginning, middle, end*)?
- Identify how print is arranged on a page (e.g., where to begin reading)?
- Recognize text features, such as punctuation and boldface type (e.g., the meaning of a comma, question mark)?
- Handle a book properly (e.g., turn pages, read from left to right, front to back)?

Assessment Preparation

- Check students' visual acuity and processing skills.
- Have available a variety of letters, words, prefixes and suffixes, common logos and signs, picture cards, and print material including primer level books with basic punctuation marks and text features (e.g., boldface, paragraph indentation).

Implementation

✓ Observe the student during activities using print (e.g., reading, writing) and consult with teachers and family to determine print awareness.

✓ Provide the student with various forms of printed materials (e.g., book, list of words, common signs and logos) to complete a series of identification activities (see Figure 3–5).

Special Considerations, Accommodations, Alternatives

- Be aware of cultural/linguistic/word knowledge issues. Ensure students conceptually understand verbal directions and what they are to do on print awareness assessment tasks.
- Adjust for the students' learning style; a multisensory approach may be needed.
- Students who lack print awareness often lack an understanding of how to approach the reading act.

Next Step

- *Mastered*—Progress to alphabet knowledge skills.
- *Emerging*—Increase opportunities for interaction with print; work individually or in small groups to discuss print concepts while reading primary level books.
- *No skill yet*—Stress visual concepts using pictures or symbols. Have students use grouping and categorizing to identify the concepts of *same* and *different*. Focus on one concept at a time, and provide opportunities for physical interaction. Achieve proficiency in basic skills before introducing a new concept and continue to reinforce skills.

Additional Resources

http://www.mlpp-msl.net/assessments/conceptsofPrint/Concepts-of-Print-A.pdf

FIGURE 3–5 Survey of Print Concepts

Is the student able to:	***Yes***	***No***
• Demonstrate awareness of print (i.e., that print contains a message)?	______	______
• Recognize one-to-one correspondence between printed words and spoken words?	______	______
• Locate the title of the book?	______	______
• Hold a book correctly and turn pages appropriately?	______	______
• Distinguish between the front and back of the book?	______	______
• Identify where to begin reading on a page?	______	______
• Indicate the direction to read words (left to right)?	______	______
• Know that at the end of a line of words to continue at the beginning left of the next line of words?	______	______
• Recognize that the left page is read before the right page?	______	______
• Point to the top and bottom of a page and to an illustration?	______	______
• Identify letters by pointing to a letter on a page?	______	______
• Identify words by pointing to a word on a page?	______	______
• Recognize that there are spaces between words?	______	______
• Identify an uppercase and a lowercase letter?	______	______
• Identify why some words are printed in bold?	______	______
• Identify the meaning of punctuation marks?	______	______
• Recognize familiar signs and logos?	______	______
• Read environmental print (STOP, Exit)?	______	______
• Use picture clues as a word identification technique?	______	______
• Demonstrate awareness of inverted pages, transposed words, reversed letters?	______	______
• Recognize mismatches between pictures and text, or sentences out of sequence?	______	______
• Count the number of syllables in words (up to three syllables)?	______	______
• Identify common suffixes (*ed, es, ing, ly, s, etc.*)?	______	______
• Identify common prefixes (*un, in, re, etc.*)?	______	______
• Use context and syntax to identify unknown words?	______	______
• Recognize and/or write letters?	______	______
• Recognize and/or write his or her name?	______	______
• Demonstrate pretend writing (writing that resembles letters or numbers)?	______	______
• Recognize common sight words (e.g., *baby, cat, run*)?	______	______
• Recognize that oral language can be written down and read?	______	______

Assessment Strategy: *Knowledge of the Alphabet Assessment*

Strategy Description

Knowledge of the alphabet refers to an understanding that words are made up of individual letters and that there is a clear link between a letter and a sound. Students lacking in this skill may not be able to make letter name and sound associations. Assessment involves determining whether the student is able to easily and automatically discriminate letters, numbers, and other letterlike symbols from each other, and to quickly identify letters by name and the sound of words that begin with a particular letter. This assessment is appropriate for students at the emergent literacy stage, ranging from kindergarten through the early primary grades. Allow 5 to 15 minutes to assess this skill.

Questions to Ask

Is the student able to:

- Match upper- and lowercase letters?
- Recognize individual letter sounds (e.g., hear a letter and match it to the written form)?
- Identify letters (e.g., name letters presented randomly and in context)?

Assessment Preparation

- Gather a set of upper- and lowercase letters (at least one set for each letter of the alphabet), number (at least from 1 to 10), and symbol forms (such as +, #, :).
- Design a piece of paper with all upper- and lowercase letters clearly formed and placed in random order.

Implementation

✓ *Discriminate letters*—Have the student separate particular letters from a pile of letters, numbers, and symbols.

✓ *Assess letter-name knowledge*—Have the student match uppercase letters with their lowercase counterparts.

✓ *Assess letter recognition*—Have the student orally name a specific letter and then locate this letter from a series of letters on paper, nonverbally, by pointing.

✓ *Assess letter identification*—Show the student letters in random order, then have student verbally identify each upper- and lowercase letter (see Figure 3–6).

✓ *Assess letter-sound correspondence*—Show the student letters in random order, then have student say the letter name and letter sound (see Figure 3–7).

✓ *Assess letter-sound associations*—Have the student identify the initial letter name and beginning sound of one- and two-syllable words (see Figure 3–7).

Special Considerations, Accommodations, Alternatives

- Use a variety of color and size forms.
- Use a multisensory approach (e.g., tactile sandpaper letters).
- Make note whether identification is without hesitation or confusion.

Next Step

- *Mastered*—Begin instruction in phonics.
- *Emerging*—Once letter identification is mastered, introduce and reinforce letter-sound symbol recognition; have the student separate vowel letters from consonant letters.

- *No skill yet*—Provide large letter forms introducing one alphabet letter at a time and gradually move to matching and differentiating between upper- and lowercase letters, then group and categorize letters. Students who are not able to quickly and accurately identify all of the letters of the alphabet (both upper- and lowercase) may benefit from a letter sorting activity. Put letter tiles or letter cutouts in a pile and ask the children to sort the letters by some salient feature (e.g., put all of the letters with straight lines in one pile and all letters with curves in another), then ask children to sort them by another salient feature (e.g., diagonal lines versus lines that go up and down). Continue with additional features until students are looking at small sets of two to four letters that have similar, confusing features, but that differ in important ways (e.g., *O* and *Q*; or *b*, *d*, *p*, and *q*). When children can see confusing letters side by side, they can focus on the salient features that make those confusing letters distinct.

Additional Resources

http://www.lakeshorelearning.com/media/images/free_resources/teachers_corner/great_ideas/alphaAssessment.pdf
http://www.balancedreading.com/assessment/abecedarian.pdf

FIGURE 3–6 Alphabet Knowledge Assessment Chart

	Letter Name	*Letter Sound*		*Letter Name*	*Letter Sound*		*Letter Name*	*Letter Sound*		*Letter Name*	*Letter Sound*
A	____	____	C	____	____	a	____	____	s	____	____
Y	____	____	I	____	____	y	____	____	O	____	____
g	____	____	v	____	____	G	____	____	B	____	____
t	____	____	K	____	____	T	____	____	k	____	____
S	____	____	V	____	____	d	____	____	x	____	____
R	____	____	p	____	____	e	____	____	L	____	____
d	____	____	n	____	____	J	____	____	Z	____	____
w	____	____	l	____	____	Q	____	____	r	____	____
F	____	____	N	____	____	h	____	____	u	____	____
E	____	____	o	____	____	z	____	____	D	____	____
j	____	____	m	____	____	P	____	____	W	____	____
c	____	____	U	____	____	X	____	____	f	____	____
H	____	____	M	____	____	b	____	____	q	____	____

FIGURE 3–7 Letter-Sound Correspondence Assessment

Directions: Ask the student to give the beginning sound of each word (e.g., *cake*). The student says the initial sound of the word (i.e., /k/). Then ask the student what letter makes the sound. The student says "c." If the wrong or no response is given, repeat the directions for the student and go to the next word.

Word	*Beginning Sound*	*Beginning Letter*
cake		
boat		
yellow		
because		

READING SKILLS

Assessment Strategy: *Phonetic Analysis Assessment*

Strategy Description

Phonics assessment is used to determine students' ability to pronounce words that are not within their sight vocabulary. Students who are unable to phonetically analyze words often have difficulty with sound-symbol association and sound blending. This assessment determines whether students can quickly and easily pronounce words or struggle to sound out words. This assessment is appropriate for students during the initial reading instructional period, ranging from the primary grades to the upper elementary grades. Allow approximately 10 to 20 minutes to assess this skill.

Questions to Ask

Is the student able to identify:

- Single consonants, consonant blends, consonant digraphs?
- Short and long vowels?
- Schwa sounds?
- Vowel digraphs or diphthongs?
- Vowels with *r*, *l*, and *w*?
- Word families, homophones, and homographs?

Assessment Preparation

- Perform a health record review, especially visual and auditory acuity screenings.
- Provide a grade level list of familiar regular words that students have probably seen before and a second list of regular words with which students are not familiar.

Implementation

✓ Assess phonetic skill development by determining the ability to identify single consonants, consonant blends (consonant clusters), consonant digraphs, short and long vowels, schwa sound, vowel digraphs, vowel diphthongs, vowels with *r*, *l*, *w* word families (phonograms), homophones (homonyms), and homographs (see Figure 3–8).

✓ Assess knowledge of phonetic patterns, sound-symbol relationships, awareness of phonetic principles, generalizations, and the ability to use phonics to decode "words" that cannot be identified by sight (see Figure 3–9).

✓ Provide students with a list of grade level words to read aloud; teacher records phonetic errors made.

✓ Have the student read a grade level passage while the teacher records errors made; analyze for types of phonetic errors and error patterns.

Special Considerations, Accommodations, Alternatives

- Students who have auditory processing problems, such as discrimination, closure, and memory, often have problems that interfere with their ability to phonetically analyze word parts.

Next Step

- *Mastered*—Provide opportunities for generalization; progress with graded reading material.
- *Emerging*—Determine which phonetic skills have been mastered and while reinforcing these, introduce the next level of developmental phonetic skills. Provide opportunities to practice and develop proficiency. Provide students with memory strategies, specifically mnemonics (e.g., when two vowels go walking, the first does the talking).
- *No skill yet*—Determine whether basic auditory and visual processing skills are adequately developed and whether phonemic awareness has been mastered. Provide direct instruction in word segmentation and blending using a multisensory approach (kinesthetic, tactile, auditory, and visual activities).

FIGURE 3–8 Mastery of Phonics Skills Developmental Checklist

Directions: Check off each phonetic generalization sound and keep a tracking and monitoring system using the following skill level rating codes.

NK = no knowledge E = emerging M = mastered

Simple Consonants (Grade 1)

___b ___d ___f ___h ___j ___k ___l ___m ___n ___p ___r ___s ___t ___v ___w ___x ___y ___z

Consonant Digraphs (Grade 1)

___sh ___ ch ___ ck ___ ph ___ th ___ qu

Beginning Consonant Blends (Grade 2)

___ st ___ gr ___ cl ___ sp ___ pl ___ tr ___ br ___ dr ___ bl ___ fr ___ fl ___ pr
___ cr ___ sl ___ sw ___ gl ___ str ___ z

Ending Consonant Blends (Grade 2)

___nd ___nk ___nt ___lk ___ld ___rt ___rm ___mp ___ft ___lt ___ct ___pt ___lm

Single Long Vowels (Grades 2–3)

___ long a ___ long e ___ long i ___ long o ___ long u

Single Short Vowels (Grades 2–3)

___ short a ___ short e ___ short i ___ short o ___ short u

R-Controlled Vowels (Grade 2–3)

___ ar (car) ___ er (her) ___ ir (shirt) ___ or (for) ___ ur (fur)

Vowel Digraph Combinations (Grades 2–3)

___ ai (pail) ___ ea (each, bear) ___ oa (boat) ___ ee (bee) ___ ay (bay) ___ ea (seat, bear)

Vowel Diphthong Combinations (Grades 2–3)

___au (auto) ___aw (awful) ___oo (boot, look) ___ow (cow, low) ___ou (out) ___oi (oil) ___oy (toy)

Hard and Soft C and G (Grade 3)

___ soft c (cent) ___ hard c (cake) ___ soft g (engine) ___ hard g (gate)

Silent Letters (Grades 3–4)

___ k (knife) ___ w (write) ___ l (talk) ___ t (catch) ___ g (gnat) ___ c (lack) ___ h (hour)

FIGURE 3–9 Checklist for Assessing Phonics Generalizations Using Nonsense Words

Student Form		Teacher Scoring Form (*record student response*) Correct (+)		*Incorrect* (–)	
SIMPLE SINGLE CONSONANTS (initial and final position)					
1 bim	8 hek	1	8	1	8
2 mib	9 wot	2	9	2	9
3 pud	10 tun	3	10	3	10
4 dup	11 yat	4	11	4	11
5 gop	12 ket	5	12	5	12
6 fop	13 naw	6	13	6	13
7 cuf		7		7	
MORE DIFFICULT SINGLE CONSONANTS (initial and final position)					
1 viz	5 jev	1	5	1	5
2 liv	6 qua	2	6	2	6
3 zix	7 giz	3	7	3	7
4 cij		4		4	
CONSONANT DIGRAPHS					
1 shup	4 guan	1	4		
2 thop	5 dack	2	5		
3 chup		3			
CONSONANT BLENDS					
1 sput	6 plat	1	6		
2 crub	7 grut	2	7		
3 flig	8 pund	3	8		
4 drub	9 gert	4	9		
5 strib	10 ropt	5	10		
SINGLE VOWELS, LONG AND SHORT					
1 bam	6 nibe	1	6	1	6
2 bame	7 po	2	7	2	7
3 fot	8 pom	3	8	3	8
4 fote	9 lum	4	9	4	9
5 nib	10 lume	5	10	5	10
R-CONTROLLED VOWELS					
1 tar	3 por	1	3		
2 det	4 spir	2	4		
VOWEL COMBINATIONS					
1 foat	5 loub	1	5		
2 tay	6 jeet	2	6		
3 rew	7 sood	3	7		
4 moil		4			
HARD AND SOFT C AND G					
1 cet	3 gi	1	3	1	3
2 clep	4 gis	2	4	2	4
SILENT LETTERS					
1 knes	3 wrot	1	3		
2 gnop	4 whes	2	4		

Additional Resources

http://www.mes-english.com/phonics.php
http://teams.lacoe.edu/reading/assessments/inven.html

Assessment Strategy: *Structural Analysis Assessment*

Strategy Description

Structural analysis assessment measures students' ability to decode by subdividing words into parts or units and then blending them into meaningful words. This assessment is appropriate for students during the primary grades through the secondary grade level. Allow approximately 10 to 15 minutes to assess this skill.

Questions to Ask

Is the student able to identify:

- Base or root words?
- Prefixes, suffixes, inflections?
- Syllabication, accented syllable, compound words, and word origins?

Assessment Preparation

- Have available a list of multisyllabic nonsense words of increasing complexity.

Implementation

✓ Have student divide and write the nonsense words in syllables; then the student should pronounce each nonsense word. Record both correct and incorrect responses and note errors and error patterns (see Figure 3–10).

Special Considerations, Accommodations, Alternatives

- Be aware that students with auditory acuity or processing disorders may have difficulty with structural analysis.
- Be sensitive to cultural and linguistic diversity issues.

Next Step

- *Mastered*—Continue to challenge student with multisyllabic vocabulary.
- *Emerging*—Determine skill level and reinforce; once base words are mastered, begin to introduce prefixes and suffixes and their meaning using concrete examples. Provide visual and auditory cues and opportunities for practice by presenting more root words.
- *No skill yet*—Use concrete teaching strategies, such as clapping word parts and moving manipulatives (e.g., move blocks or paper divided into sections to write word parts).

FIGURE 3–10 Informal Test for Syllabication Skills

Student Form		Teacher Scoring Form	
Say these Nonsense Words	*Write these Words in Syllables*	*Student Pronunciation*	
		Correct (+)	Incorrect (0)
		Compound Words	
1. staybut		1.	
2. leeway		2.	
3. landom		3.	
		Structural Word Parts	
1. frogment		1.	
2. lauter		2.	
3. remanly		3.	
		Vowel Combinations	
1. lainest		1.	
2. doyter		2.	
3. spouler		3.	
		Vowel Followed by One Consonant	
1. witon		1.	
2. dowal		2.	
3. turmit		3.	
4. leton		4.	
		Vowel Followed by Two Consonants	
1. pittel		1.	
2. coddat		2.	
		Combinations	
1. kepple		1.	
2. gintle		2.	

Assessment Strategy: *Word Meaning/Vocabulary Assessment*

Strategy Description

Assessment of word meaning is a measure of students' knowledge of basic vocabulary, word classification, pronoun referents, and vocabulary relations; and the ability to use descriptive words and root words and affixes to develop new words. Word meaning competence is critical for word recognition, word attack, and reading comprehension. This assessment is appropriate for students during the initial reading instructional period, ranging from early elementary to the secondary level. Administration is generally individual. Allow approximately 15 to 20 minutes to assess this skill.

Questions to Ask

Is the student able to:

- Demonstrate knowledge of the meaning of words in isolation and in context?
- Use context clues (word knowledge) to assist in identifying unfamiliar words?
- Apply strategies to analyze word meaning and increase word knowledge and use?

Assessment Preparation

- Gather several lists of vocabulary words that are at, above, and below the student's grade level; include a list of prefixes, suffixes, and pronouns.
- Collect grade level passages with specific vocabulary highlighted.

Implementation

✓ Have student match words that have the same meaning, classify words, and identify the meaning of prefixes, suffixes, and pronouns. Record student response for later analysis (see Figure 3–11).

✓ Have student read a graded passage and define or explain specific vocabulary.

✓ Consider when evaluating the more advanced student that it is important to assess the ability to know and correctly use synonyms, antonyms, homonyms, homographs, multiple meanings, abstract and colloquial terms, neologisms ("explain the probable meaning of *edzoocate*"), euphemisms ("provide a more polite word for *sweat*"), pejoratives ("explain why a word such as *amateur* might be considered negative"), and etymology ("provide the origin of the word *sandwich*").

Special Considerations, Accommodations, Alternatives

- Word knowledge is affected by the students' family and cultural experiences, by their exposure to the vocabulary of teachers, parents, peers, and significant others, by their opportunities to converse using new vocabulary, by their previous exposure to and use of a dictionary and thesaurus, and by other language and cultural experiences.

Next Step

- *Mastered*—Advance to next grade level vocabulary words.
- *Emerging*—Provide additional practice and contextual support, create opportunities for students to make connections to prior knowledge and use the word(s) in different contexts; promote a reliance on the dictionary and the thesaurus; and develop skills using word games.
- *No skill yet*—Provide graphic examples and definitions; provide direct instruction connecting new words to known words; introduce word families; teach prefixes and suffixes to increase word knowledge; incorporate semantic mapping to promote word meaning and relationships.

Additional Resources

http://www.nifl.gov/readingprofiles/MC_Word_Meaning.htm
http://www.phschool.com/eteach/language_arts/2002_03/essay.html

FIGURE 3–11 Sample Word Meaning Assessment

Teacher's Version	Student's Version
Basic Vocabulary *Correct* / *Incorrect* 1. angry _____ _____ 2. stove _____ _____ 3. letter _____ _____ 4. wheel _____ _____	*Which word means:* 1. angry 2. stove 3. letter 4. wheel *Choose from one of the following words:* lamp mail mad running ocean oven tire tear pair
Classification *Correct* / *Incorrect* 1. body parts _____ _____ 2. places _____ _____ 3. jobs _____ _____ 4. furniture _____ _____	*Which words tell about:* 1. body parts 2. places 3. jobs 4. furniture *Choose from the following words:* table sofa church elbow park manager knee store teacher doctor lamp stomach
Affixes *Correct* / *Incorrect* 1. dis _____ _____ 2. less _____ _____ 3. re _____ _____ 4. in _____ _____	*Tell how each underlined word part changes the word meaning:* 1. disagree 2. homeless 3. rewrite 4. incorrect
Pronoun Referent *Correct* / *Incorrect* 1. Jim and Mary _____ _____ 2. you and me _____ _____ 3. a boy _____ _____ 4. a mother _____ _____	*Read the word that could mean:* 1. Jim and Mary 2. you and me 3. a boy 4. a mother *Say the word that would match:* she we they he it you
Vocabulary Relations *Correct* / *Incorrect* 1. tear _____ _____ 2. live _____ _____ 3. read _____ _____ 4. wound _____ _____	*Say the underlined word in each sentence:* 1. Don't tear your coat. 2. I live near you. 3. I read the letter yesterday. 4. The wound is bleeding.

Assessment Strategy: *Word Recognition Assessment*

Strategy Description

Word recognition assessment measures students' ability to identify a sequence of letters that form a word as a single unit. Students who read with less than 90% accuracy are unable to grasp any useful information from the text; even with 94% accuracy, comprehension is marginal (Betts, 1946). This assessment is appropriate for students from primary through the secondary level. Allow approximately 10 to 15 minutes to determine an instructional level.

Questions to Ask

Is the student able to:

- Read a list of grade level vocabulary words quickly without sounding out each word part?
- Fluently read words in context in grade level passages?

Assessment Preparation

- Prepare sight word lists based on the type of curriculum used—either developmental or functional.
- Compile developmental sight word lists that typically come from the vocabulary used in a basal reading series, graded word lists composed of words used in all subject area texts and listed by grade level, high-frequency words that make up the majority of written American English, and phonetically irregular word lists (i.e., words that do not adhere well to the phonics principles, such as *was, of, the, shoe, one, said*).
- Compile functional word lists that are based on life skill curriculum.
- Compile various forms of common print material (e.g., newspapers, signs, manuscript, and cursive). Check readability (appropriate grade level) using a readability graph (refer to Figure 2–19).

Implementation

✓ Assess students functioning at the readiness, preprimer, or primer level of skill development by having them match, point to, and/or verbally identify words in isolation and in context (see author's website: *http://www.sju.edu/~cspinell* for Fry Word Lists).

✓ Assess students functioning at the primer to secondary levels by having them pronounce grade level vocabulary words, which must be read without hesitation (about 1 second) and without sounding out individual word parts using phonetic or structural analysis.

Special Considerations, Accommodations, Alternatives

- Teachers, especially those instructing students who have special learning needs, should use more authentic assessment methods, such as real-life replications or close facsimiles (e.g., employment applications, bus schedules, rental contracts).
- Students with cognitive disabilities generally have not been exposed to or are unable to master developmental sight words. Functional vocabulary lists should be considered as they contain words critical for independence in everyday life, including words related to employment (e.g., *part time, salary, contract*), safety (e.g., *keep out, poison, beware, danger*), and building environments (e.g., *exit, bathroom*).

Example

Fry Word Lists

http://www.sju.edu/~cspinell/pages/source/fry_word_list.pdf

Next Step

- *Mastered*—Advance to words at the next grade level.
- *Emerging*—Use repeated reading and guided reading activities. Use incremental rehearsal which involves repetition and a systematic ratio of rehearsing one known followed by one unknown word (Joseph, 2006).
- *No skill yet*—Determine whether students can make sound-symbol associations and have phonemic awareness and basic phonics skills. Embed the new word(s) in a highly familiar and strongly supported print context (e.g., story); provide direct instruction by presenting words at the letter level, chunking words when necessary, and applying knowledge of letter-sound relationships. Break words apart and examine the letters and chunks within the words; use predictable books and language experience stories; provide word banks and word walls.

Additional Resources

http://www.blevinsenterprises.com/Informal_Word_Analysis_Survey_Teacher_Copy.pdf

Assessment Strategy: *Oral Reading Assessment*

Strategy Description

Assessment of oral reading competency is based on determining students' ability to accurately and fluently read aloud. Oral reading research suggests that students who read with less than 90% word recognition accuracy are unable to obtain sufficient meaning (Mercer, Mercer, & Pullen, 2010).

This assessment is appropriate for students from primary through the secondary grade level. Depending on the length of the passage and the student's reading rate, allow approximately 10 to 30 minutes to determine the instructional level.

Questions to Ask

Is the student able to read a graded passage with:

- Words read accurately?
- Adequate reading rate?
- Expression and appropriate intonation?
- Adequate phrasing (rather than read word by word)?

Assessment Preparation

- Word recognition can also be assessed using oral reading material (e.g., textbook, trade book) which has not been previously read by the student.

- Choose the next passage to be read from the classroom reading material which ensures background and context.
- Select a passage to be read that ranges from 50 words at the primary level to 400 words at the secondary level.

Implementation

✓ Observe student when reading both silently and orally (see Figure 3–12).

✓ Note whether oral reading is fluent and relaxed, with a sense of rhythm and expression.

✓ Track word identification errors, noting emergent reading skills.

✓ Determine the type of word errors and whether a pattern of errors exists (refer to miscue analysis assessment).

✓ Analyze oral reading errors to determine how the student distorts or changes the meaning of a passage (e.g., syntactic/semantic acceptability; graphic and sound similarity).

✓ Note student's ability to self-correct.

Scoring

The text is the appropriate readability (instructional) level for the student when word recognition performance scores are as follows:

- 90% to 95% accurate
- 95% accurate, when counting miscues that change the meaning of a passage
- 90% accurate, if all miscues are counted with 70% to 75% accuracy on comprehension questions (refer to the section on miscue analysis for more details)

Special Considerations, Accommodations, Alternatives

- For students with disabilities, accommodations, such as enlarging the print or reducing the number of words required to be read at one time, may be necessary.

Next Step

- *Mastered*—Advance to reading passages at the next grade level.
- *Emerging*—Provide word games to develop fluency with sight words; use peer pairing to practice accuracy and expressive oral reading.
- *No skill yet*—Introduce guided and repeated reading by having the teacher read aloud as the student follows the words by pointing to the print and patterning by reading along softly with the teacher. With each repetition, the teacher's voice slowly fades and the student's voice should become louder.

FIGURE 3–12 Silent and Oral Reading Observation Checklist

Behavioral Characteristics	***Yes***	***No***	***N/A***	***Comments***
Holds book too close	___	___	___	___
Holds book too far	___	___	___	___
Points to each word	___	___	___	___
Moves finger under each line	___	___	___	___
Runs finger down the page	___	___	___	___
Uses finger to mark place	___	___	___	___
Loses place on page	___	___	___	___
Skips words	___	___	___	___
Skips lines	___	___	___	___
Makes frequent word errors	___	___	___	___
Does not attempt unfamiliar words	___	___	___	___
Does not observe punctuation	___	___	___	___
Does not read for meaning	___	___	___	___
Does not use text structure	___	___	___	___
Does not use visual cues	___	___	___	___
Does not read clearly	___	___	___	___
Does not read in phrases	___	___	___	___
Reads too slowly	___	___	___	___
Reads too quickly	___	___	___	___
Oral reading lacks expression	___	___	___	___
Frequently requests assistance	___	___	___	___
Makes lip movements	___	___	___	___
Subvocalizes words	___	___	___	___
Moves head while reading	___	___	___	___
Tires easily when reading	___	___	___	___
Makes negative comments when reading	___	___	___	___
Refuses to continue reading a complete passage	___	___	___	___
Mispronounces words	___	___	___	___
Does not self-correct when reading	___	___	___	___
Does not use context clues	___	___	___	___
Does not read left to right	___	___	___	___
Lacks fluency; word-calls	___	___	___	___
Pauses are lengthy/frequent	___	___	___	___
Errors do not make sense	___	___	___	___
Other prominent behaviors	___	___	___	___

Assessment Strategy: *Miscue Analysis Assessment*

Strategy Description

Miscue analysis assessment determines not only the number (quantity) but the type of errors (quality) made; how oral reading errors distort or change the meaning of a passage; whether there is a pattern to the types of miscues made; and whether reading word substitutions are semantically incorrect (a meaning-related error) or syntactically incorrect (a grammatically related error). This assessment is appropriate for students from early elementary through secondary levels and is generally administered individually. Allow approximately 10 minutes per passage.

Questions to Ask

Are the miscues that the student makes:

- Affecting the meaning of the sentence?
- Contextually acceptable within the context of the passage?
- Similar to the intended word in sound and appearance?
- Indicating an error pattern?
- Self-corrected by the student?

Assessment Preparation

- Select graded reading passages, at the student's reading level, from textbooks, literature series, trade books.
- Make two copies of the passage, one for the student and one for the teacher to follow and make notations.
- Have an audio recording device available to tape the student's oral reading to replay when analyzing in order to more closely discriminate errors.

Implementation

✓ Have the student read the passage orally as the teacher records the errors for later analysis.

✓ Analyze and record the type of errors the student makes (see Figure 3–13).

✓ Determine whether there is a pattern of errors both qualitatively and quantitatively; determine how often each type of error was made and identify the most frequently made errors.

✓ Analyze errors to determine whether they are semantically unacceptable (i.e., do they distort or change the meaning?) or syntactically unacceptable (i.e., do they substitute one part of speech for another and affect the meaning of the sentence?).

✓ Analyze the student's oral reading to determine the ability to self-correct.

Scoring

- Count as a major oral reading error and deduct 1 point for a substitution error that interferes with comprehension (e.g., *house* for *horse*).
- Count as a minor oral reading error and deduct 0.5 point for any deviation from printed text that does not seem to interfere significantly with comprehension (e.g., *home* for *house*).

- Count any word the student cannot pronounce after 5 seconds as an oral reading error and deduct 1 point if the word interferes with comprehension; only deduct 0.5 point if the word does not interfere with comprehension.
- Count an inserted word as an oral reading error and deduct 0.5 point if it does not significantly change the meaning of the text.
- Count a repetition of 2 or more words as half an error, and deduct 0.5 points. Do not deduct points for repeating a single word as this suggests that the student is self-monitoring or using metacognitive skills.
- Do not count a self-correction as an error if it occurs within 5 seconds, because this indicates the student is using monitoring or metacognitive skills.
- Do not count more than one oral reading error of the same word in any one passage.
- Do not count a proper noun as an oral reading error.
- Do not count oral reading errors that seem to exemplify student's cultural/regional dialect.

How to tally results of an oral reading sample:

1. Subtract the total number of errors from the total number of words in the passage (e.g., 20.5 oral reading errors from the 280 total words in the passage) to determine how many words were correctly pronounced (e.g., 259.5 words read correctly).
2. Divide the total words in the passage into the words correctly pronounced to obtain the percentage of correct words (259.5/280 = 93%). In this example, the results indicate approximately 93% accuracy in word identification.
3. After all the oral reading errors are recorded from the material read, the teacher can determine students' reading independent, instructional and frustration levels as categorized below:
   - Independent reading level: relatively easy text level; more than 95% accuracy
   - Instructional reading level: challenging but manageable text level; 90% to 95% accuracy
   - Frustration reading level: difficult text level; less than 90% accuracy (Kuhn & Stahl, 2003)

Special Considerations, Accommodations, Alternatives

- Miscue analysis is a good method of evaluating mature readers as the focus is on passage comprehension rather than on word-for-word accuracy.

Next Step

- *Mastered*—Advance the student to the next instructional reading level.
- *Emerging*—Use repeated readings, provide good reading models and opportunities for guided practice.
- *No skill yet*—Use a language experience approach, highlight or underline words that are misread, prompt students to identify and use context clues. Provide several optional words, with only one that is clearly the correct option (e.g., cat, <u>bank</u>, dish), and gradually, make the optional words more similar and require more discrimination (e.g., bark, <u>bank</u>, bent).

FIGURE 3–13 Oral Reading Errors

Substitutions
Definition: replacing a word or series of syllables for the depicted word
Cause: may result from poor word recognition, poor word analysis, dialectic differences, or carelessness
Example (words): "the boy run" for the boy ran
Example (letters): initial: "cat" for sat; medial: "coat" for colt; final: "lap" for lab
Notation: cross out the incorrect word (or letter) and write the substituted word (or letter) above it

Omissions
Definition: leaving out a word or words
Cause: may result from poor word recognition, poor word analysis, or carelessness
Example (words): "the yellow house" for the big, yellow house
Example (letters): "tree" for three; "dog" for dogs
Notation: circle the omitted word(s) or letter(s)

Insertions
Definition: addition of a word or words
Cause: may result from poor comprehension, carelessness, or oral language that exceeds reading ability
Example (words): "the big, yellow house" for the yellow house
Example (letters): "chart" for cart; "wented" for went
Notation: place a caret (^) at the point of insertion and write inserted word (letter) above the sentence (word)

Reversals or Transpositions
Definition: confusion about the order of letters in a word or words in the sentence
Cause: may be the result of neurological or visual processing problems
Examples (words): "said Mary" for Mary said
Example (letter reversal): "bad" for dad; (letter transposition): "saw" for was
Notation: draw a line through the word (letter) and write the reversed/transposed word (letter) above it

Mispronunciations
Definition: incorrect pronunciation/may not be recognizable
Cause: may be the result of poor word recognition or word analysis or articulation problems
Example: "wabbit" for rabbit
Notation: draw a line through the mispronounced word and write the mispronunciation above it

Self-Corrections
Definition: correction of a word that was substituted, inserted, or omitted
Cause: may be the result of poor recognition/word analysis, or carelessness
Example: "she run . . . ran up the hill"
Notation: cross out the word read incorrectly, write corrected word above it

Repetitions
Definition: saying a part of a word or a complete word more than once
Cause: may be the result of attention problems, poor word recognition, or poor word analysis
Example: "What is, what is wrong?" instead of What is wrong?
Notation: underline repeated material with wavy lines

Disregards Punctuation
Definition: failure to pause for comma, periods, etc., or to change inflection for questions or exclamations
Cause: may result from not knowing the meaning of the punctuation mark or being distracted by difficulty reading
Example: "It is a dog He is a good dog." instead of It is a dog. He is a good dog.
Notation: circle the punctuation mark

Aid
Definition: assistance in pronouncing a word or waiting more than 10 seconds for the teacher to supply the word
Cause: may be the result of difficulty in word attack recognition skills
Example: "He is —" (teacher says: "wonderful")—"He is wonderful."
Notation: place a bracket ({}) around the supplied word

Assessment Strategy: *Running Records Assessment*

Strategy Description

Running records is a system used to assess the reading process, specifically for students who demonstrate developmental reading and/or fluency problems. Teachers keep a "running record" of students' oral reading by closely monitoring and recording errors made. Running records are used for instructional purposes to evaluate text difficulty, to match students with appropriate book levels for instruction and for independent reading, to make informed decisions for grouping students who make similar types of errors, to monitor and track individual progress, and to note particular strategies used by the student (Clay, 2000). This assessment is appropriate for students during the initial reading instructional period from preprimer to third grade, and is generally administered individually. Allow approximately 10 to 20 minutes per session.

Questions to Ask

Is the student reading:

- Grade level passages without making word substitutions?
- Fluently without omitting or inserting extra words or phrases?
- Without repeating or self-correcting words or phrases?
- Without needing to be told unknown words?

Assessment Preparation

- Select an appropriate level reading passage (recommended length is between 100 and 200 words).
- Prepare a form for recording results (see Figure 3–14).

Implementation

- Have the student read a grade level passage orally. Be sure the passage has not been read previously.
- Record errors on the record form.
- Note whether the student pauses while reading; if so, the teacher should wait a few seconds for the student to respond before supplying the word. The teacher should not wait too long, however, as the student may lose the meaning of the text.
- Note what the student says while reading the assigned material (e.g., word substitutions, omissions).

Scoring

- Refer to Figure 3–15 for a scoring chart.
- If a whole page is omitted, deduct the number of words omitted from the total word count.
- Pronunciation differences are not counted as errors.
- Determination of error rate: Divide the number of errors into number of total words.

- Percent of accuracy: Divide the number of words read correctly by the total number of words in the passage and multiply by 100. The percentage of accuracy data indicates the difficulty level of the material read.

Scoring is determined by the percentage correct:

- Independent reading level: 95% to 100%
- Instructional reading level: 90% to 94%
- Frustration reading level: less than 90% accuracy (Clay, 2000)

Special Considerations, Accommodations, Alternatives

- When running records are used as an ongoing instructional assessment tool, students may do a *warm read*. This is when they have already heard or have read a passage or a book. However, when running records are used directly for assessing skill levels, the reading material should not be familiar to the student, referred to as a *cold read*.
- Although running records are specifically used to assess oral reading skills, reading comprehension can be assessed by having students retell the story. If, after reading the passage or book, the child is unable to retell the story, the teacher can prompt with questions (refer to retell procedure assessment for more guidelines).

Next Step

- *Mastered*—Increase the reading instructional level.
- *Emerging*—Provide the student with guided reading instruction.
- *No skill yet*—Initiate instruction with a passage at the student's independent reading level.

Additional Resources

Running Records and Benchmark Books
http://www.readinga-z.com/assess/runrec.html#whatis

FIGURE 3–14 Running Record Recording Chart

Text	Page No.	Incorrect Response	Multiple Attempts	Self-Correction	Insertion—No Response	Word Text	Appeal for Help	Error No.

FIGURE 3–15 Scoring Running Records

Substitution (S): Error is written on top of line, correct word from text is written underneath (each incorrect response is counted as one error).	"want" (child) / went (text) — S
Multiple attempts, or repetitions (R): Student attempts to read a word several times, each attempt is recorded (counted as one error no matter how many attempts are made).	R or (ADD)
Self-correction (SC): Student corrects a word read incorrectly; the evaluator marks it SC (not counted as an error).	went / want — SC
No Response, or omission: Student provides no response or omits; the evaluator records with a dash (counted as one error).	------- / little
Insertion: Student inserts a word where one does not belong; the evaluator records with a dash (counted as one error).	many / ---------
Word told (T): Student stops because he or she realizes an error has been made or because he or she does not know the word; the evaluator provides the word, records it as T (counted as one error).	where — T
Appeal for help (A): Student requests help; evaluator marks with an A and tells the student to try it. Only the second attempt (if incorrect) is scored as an error. If student gets the word correct the second time, there is no error.	only — A
Repeated errors: Student makes an error and continues to substitute the word again and again (counts as one error each time). Exception: When a proper name is substituted, it is counted as an error only the first time it is substituted.	
Words or phrases repeated: Student accurately reads a word or phrase more than one time, no errors are counted.	

Source: From *The Literacy Center Companion*, by L. Romeo, 1999, and adapted from M. Clay, 1993.

Assessment Strategy: *Curriculum-Based Measurement: Reading Fluency Assessment*

Strategy Description

Curriculum-based measurement (CBM) uses repeated measures from the student's curriculum to evaluate the effectiveness of instruction and instructional changes to lead to more effective teaching methods and improved student achievement. Each probe contains a random sampling of the grade level curriculum material and different but equivalent subject matter, and assesses skills taught from the beginning to the end of the school year. A common type of reading probe assesses fluency, which is the student's ability to read with expression and at a steady rate. This assessment is appropriate for all grade levels and is generally administered on an individual basis. Allow approximately 5 minutes per probe for administration and scoring.

Questions to Ask

Is the student reading:

- Smoothly, without stumbling over or repeating words?
- Without pausing excessively?
- In phrases rather than word by word?
- With expression, displaying variation in rise and fall in voice rather than reading in a monotonous, expressionless tone?
- At a steady pace, not rushing through text, ignoring punctuation and sentence breaks?
- Words correctly rather than making careless mistakes on familiar words?

Assessment Preparation

- Create appropriate CBM tests, referred to as probes, based on subject content selected from the entire year's curriculum, taken from the basal series, textbooks, trade books, or a literature series. Reading probes are used to assess the student's ability to identify individual letters, identify individual words, read in context, and/or answer comprehension questions.
- Develop a page of single letters, a graded list of single words, or graded reading passages with comprehension questions, depending on the type of probe to be used.
- When the probe is a reading passage, prepare by selecting three passages, one from the beginning, middle, and end of the book. The passages should be 50 to 100 words for students in first through third grade, and 150 to 200 words for fourth grade and beyond. The selections should not contain illustrations, have minimal or no dialogue, consist of text but not play or poetry material, be free of unusual or foreign words, and make sense on their own without requiring a supporting paragraph. Reading material should not have been read previously and is generally the next page to be read in the student's text, novel, or other reading source. When counting words, consider numeral groups (e.g., 4,506) and hyphenated words (e.g., *mother-in-law*) as single-word units.
- Make a copy for the student to read and a copy for the teacher to use for marking the word recognition errors and the responses to the comprehension questions. On the teacher's copy, count and make a slash mark after the first 100 words.
- Develop a set of comprehension questions (e.g., five to eight questions) for each passage. The questions should cover the following skills: vocabulary meaning, fact and detail, inference, sequence, and main idea (see Figure 3–16).
- Prepare enough probes to administer at regular intervals (weekly, biweekly, monthly).
- Prepare a chart for graphing CBM progress (see Figure 3–17).
- Have stopwatch available.

Implementation

✓ Evaluate letter-sound fluency by giving the student a sheet of randomized letters and asking for as many sounds corresponding to the letters as possible in 1 minute.

✓ Evaluate word identification fluency by having the student read as many words as possible in 1 minute from a list of grade level words.

✓ Evaluate the ability to read words in context (a more authentic measure) by having the student read an unpracticed grade level passage. Tell the student to start at the top of the page, read the passage aloud, try to read each word, and read until told to stop. Have the student read for exactly 1 minute; stop the student at the end of 1 minute, make a notation (e.g., mark the place with "]") on the teacher's copy at the last word read at the end of the minute. Allow the student to continue reading to the end of the paragraph, however, only count the words read within 1 minute.

✓ Observe as the student reads. If the student stops or struggles with a word for 3 seconds (3-second rule), then the teacher provides the word and marks it as incorrect.

✓ Determine the word accuracy rate (number of words correctly identified) by recording word recognition errors on the teacher's copy of the reading passage. Record errors by marking a slash (/) through the incorrectly read word. Write the student's phonetic attempt at pronunciation above the printed word for later analysis of the specific types of errors made.

This is useful for designing remediation (refer to Figure 3–13 for a list of common word recognition errors).

✓ Circle unusual proper nouns read incorrectly (e.g., Zofrie), and use a caret (^) to mark insertions. Note use of expression.

Reading CBM Scoring

- For an oral reading measure, both the student's reading rate and accuracy rate can be recorded and scored. For a silent reading measure, only the reading rate score can be obtained.
- The scoring procedure is as follows:

  At the end of 1 minute, the teacher determines the student's reading fluency level by taking the total number of words read in 1 minute and subtracting the number of errors (only one error per word is counted). The final number of correct words per minute (cwpm) represents the student's fluency score. For example, if a first-grade student reads 53 words in a minute and makes seven errors, then the student has a fluency score of 46 cwpm. More accurate fluency scores can be obtained when teachers use the average of two or three fluency readings from three different passages (Vaughn & Bos, 2009).
- To determine accuracy, score as follows:

Counted as Errors	*Counted as Correct*
Substitutions	Self-corrected words within 3 seconds
Mispronunciations	Repetitions within 3 seconds
Omissions	Dialectical speech
Transpositions	Inserted words are ignored
Words read by evaluator after 3 seconds	

- A correct words per minute (cwpm) fluency standards rate for first through third grade is as follows:

  End of first grade: 60 cwpm

  End of second grade: 90 to 110 cwpm

  End of third grade: 114 cwpm (Put Reading First, 2001)
- For a letter-sounds correct (lsc) rate for kindergarten to first grade, refer to Table 3–1.
- To determine whether the student's word read correctly (wrc) fluency growth is increasing at a normal rate, the teacher compares the student's scores with published oral reading fluency norms (see Table 3–2).

Administration and scoring guidelines:

If assessing once a week, administer one CBM probe and record each score. If assessing every 3 to 5 weeks, administer three to four CBM probes and record the median (middle) score.

Special Considerations, Accommodations, Alternatives

- Informal fluency assessment can begin as early as the second semester of first grade by listening and recording rate and accuracy; more formal assessments usually begin in second grade, using fluency assessments to establish baseline data (refer to Figure 3–18).
- Administration and scoring procedures must be the same for each administration to maintain *reliability* (likelihood that a student will achieve a similar score if the test was readministered) and *validity* (likelihood that the targeted skills are the skills being tested).
- At Tier 2 and Tier 3, it is recommended that a CBM be administered one or two times each week to determine if an intervention is working for a particular student (Jenkins, Hudson, & Lee, 2007).
- Computer technology uses automated speech recognition technology to "listen" to students read aloud and monitor their fluency and accuracy. This technology allows students to engage in repeated reading with feedback by reading aloud into a microphone and the computer provides assistance by monitoring progress and tracking performance.
- Students who are slower to process and identify visual information tend to be at a disadvantage on reading fluency tasks (Lovett, Steinbach, & Frijters, 2000).

Next Step

- *Mastered*—Continue development by introducing higher level reading material.
- *Emerging*—Provide opportunities for guided practice, have students track their progress by graphing their scores which provides motivation to "beat their best score."
- *No skill yet*—Start with words that the student is most familiar with and work on increasing accuracy and reading rate. Provide individualized, guided reading instruction. Use choral reading, have the student read along with the teacher. The teacher and student read the same passage together several times with the teacher's voice fading steadily each time. Assist students with graphing their progress. Count number of correct letters or words read correctly so students are reinforced for even the smallest gain or improvement.

Additional Resources

Reading a-z.com: Fluency
http://www.readinga-z.com/fluency/index.html#assess

Calculating Correct Words per Minute
http://www.nevadareading.org/resourcecenter/literacycomponents/fluency.attachment/446/Fluency_Strategies.doc

Dibels Data System Home Page
http://dibels.uoregon.edu/

Intervention Central
http://www.interventioncentral.org/

Instructional Assessment Resources

http://www.amphi.com/departments/technology/assess/orf.html

FIGURE 3–16 Example of Elementary Level CBM Reading Comprehension Questions

Passage

The children hurried to put on their boots, coats, and mittens because they knew it was almost time to leave. Their mother called to everyone to jump into the car already crowded with suitcases and presents. Before they left, the family walked to their neighbor's house who would be taking care of their pet, Muffy, while they were away. Muffy barked loudly as they all said goodbye. Now they were off to their grandparents' house. The children knew they had a long trip ahead but they were excited and anxious to see their cousins who would also be there to celebrate grandmother's birthday. There would be cake, and ice cream, gifts, and lots of fun.

Comprehension Questions

(Fact) 1. Who were the children going to visit? (Their grandparents)
(Detail) 2. Whose birthday were they going to celebrate? (Grandmother)
(Inference) 3. During what season did the story occur? (Winter)
(Inference) 4. Would they be staying overnight? How do you know? (Yes, they took suitcases)
(Main idea) 5. Why were the children excited? (They were going to a party; they would see their cousins and grandparents)
(Detail) 6. Who was Muffy? Why do you think she did not go with them? (Their dog; because it was a long trip; maybe their grandparents didn't like dogs, there was no room in the car for the dog)
(Vocabulary) 7. What does celebration mean?
(Sequence) 8. Tell what the chidren did in this story.

FIGURE 3–17 CBM Progress Rating Recording Form

Date of administration					
Passage read/grade level					
Percent of word recognition errors					
Number of substitution errors					
Number of omission errors					
Other types of word recognition errors					
Percent of correct answers to comprehension questions					
Explicit comprehension errors					
Implicit comprehension errors					
Critical comprehension errors					
Number of seconds to read passage					
$\frac{\text{\% correct words} \times 60}{\text{time in seconds}} =$ Words read correctly (wrc) (per minute)					

FIGURE 3–18 Oral Reading Fluency Scale

Level 4	Reads primarily in larger, meaningful phrase groups. Although some regressions, repetitions, and deviations from text may be present, these do not appear to detract from the overall structure of the story. Preservation of the author's syntax is consistent. Some or most of the story is read with expressive interpretation.
Level 3	Reads primarily in three- or four-word phrase groups. Some smaller groupings may be present. However, the majority of phrasing seems appropriate and preserves the syntax of the author. Little or no expressive interpretation is present.
Level 2	Reads primarily in two-word phrases with some three- or four-word groupings. Some word-by-word reading may be present. Word groupings may seem awkward and unrelated to larger context of sentence or passage.
Level 1	Reads primarily word-by-word. Occasional two-word or three-word phrases may occur, but these are infrequent and/or they do not preserve meaningful syntax.

Source: From *Listening to Children Read Aloud*, by U.S. Department of Education, National Center for Education Statistics, 1995, p. 15.

TABLE 3–1 Oral Reading Fluency: Letter Sounds Correct

Grade	Percentile	Fall (LSC)	Winter (LSC)	Spring (LSC)
Kindergarten	90%	21	43	53
	75%	11	32	43
	50%	3	19	32
	25%	0	8	20
	10%	—	2	11
First	90%	47	59	62
	75%	37	49	52
	50%	27	38	41
	25%	16	27	30
	10%	8	16	20

TABLE 3–2 Oral Reading Fluency Norms: Words Correctly Read

Grade	Percentile	Fall (WCPM)	Winter (WCPM)	Spring (WCPM)
1	90%		81	111
	75%		47	82
	50%		23	53
	25%		12	28
	10%		6	15
2	90%	106	125	142
	75%	79	100	117
	50%	51	72	89
	25%	25	42	61
	10%	11	18	31
3	90%	145	146	162
	75%	119	120	137
	50%	94	92	107
	25%	68	62	78
	10%	45	36	48

TABLE 3–2 (*Continued*)

Grade	Percentile	Fall (WCPM)	Winter (WCPM)	Spring (WCPM)
4	90%	145	166	180
	75%	119	139	152
	50%	94	112	123
	25%	68	87	98
	10%	45	61	72
5	90%	166	182	194
	75%	139	156	168
	50%	110	127	139
	25%	85	99	109
	10%	61	74	83
6	90%	177	195	204
	75%	153	167	177
	50%	127	140	150
	25%	98	111	122
	10%	68	82	93
7	90%	180	192	202
	75%	156	165	177
	50%	128	136	150
	25%	102	109	123
	10%	79	88	98
8	90%	185	199	199
	75%	161	173	177
	50%	133	146	151
	25%	106	115	124
	10%	77	84	97

Source: Hasbrouck, J. & Tindal, G.A. (2006, April). Oral Reading Fluency Norms: A Valuable Assessment Tool for Reading Teachers. The Reading Teacher, 59(7), 636–644. doi:10.1598IRT.59.7.3.

Assessment Strategy: *Explicit, Implicit, and Critical Comprehension Assessment*

Strategy Description

Comprehension assessment determines whether students are able to comprehend, to make connections between the information in the text and the information already in their head, to draw inferences about the author's meaning, to evaluate the quality of the message, and to connect aspects of the text with other works of literature. This assessment is appropriate for students from the primary to the secondary grade levels; administration can be individual or group. Allow approximately 5 to 20 minutes per passage, depending on the passage.

Questions to Ask

Is the student able to understand, remember, and communicate what has been read and make connections to reading at the following levels?

- Explicit: Most basic: literal, factual
- Implicit: More advanced: interpretive, inferential
- Critical: Most abstract: evaluative, "reading between the lines"

Assessment Preparation

- Have graded reading passages available, with a copy for the teacher and another for the student.
- Prepare a series of comprehension questions for each passage that are explicit, implicit, and critical; use Bloom's taxonomy as a guide. Refer to text website *http://www.sju.edu/~cspinell/fnBloom'staxonomyquestionguide.*

Implementation

✓ Have the student read grade level passages and then ask specific questions starting with the explicit type. If successful answering at the explicit level, then ask the student implicit questions, followed by the higher order thinking, critical comprehension questions (see Figure 3–19).

✓ Use the comprehension strategy checklist to track students' skills. This checklist can also be used by students as a self-check (see Figure 3–20).

Scoring

Comprehension performance levels are as follows:

- Independent reading level: 90% or higher
- Instructional reading level: 75% to 89%
- Frustration reading level: 75% or lower (Mercer, Mercer, & Pullen, 2010)

Special Considerations, Accommodations, Alternatives

- It is possible for a reader to understand the explicit information contained in a passage of text but fail to grasp the implicit message contained "between the lines." Similarly, it is possible for a reader to appreciate the implicit message contained in the text, but to fail to elaborate on that message, failing to connect it to other text or background knowledge.

Next Step

- *Mastered*—Continue to increase the grade level of passages presented; challenge students to attack different genres of text and critically examine the text in a variety of ways; gather explicit information, draw inferences, and make evaluations.
- *Emerging*—Use comprehension strategies, such as K-W-L, retell, paired reading.
- *No skill yet*—Focus on explicit comprehension; initially use a passage at the student's independent reading level and provide guided instruction.

Additional Resources

http://www2.scholastic.com/content/collateral_resources/pdf/r/reading_bestpractices_comprehension_flowchartofbehavior.pdf

FIGURE 3–19 Comprehension Strategy Checklist

Comprehension Strategies	***Always***	***Occasionally***	***Rarely***	***Never***
Uses prior knowledge				
Determines purpose				
Asks self what is important about topic				
Makes predictions				
Identifies main idea				
Uses context clues				
Analyzes characters				
Adjusts reading rate				
Compares and contrasts				
Monitors understanding				
Makes generalizations				
Makes inferences				
Recognizes cause and effect				
Recalls supporting details				
Recalls sequence of ideas/facts				
Differentiates between fact and fiction				
Draws a conclusion				
Understands figurative language				
Visualizes an image				
Uses story maps				
Summarizes characters				

FIGURE 3–20 Explicit, Implicit, Critical Question Guide

Is the student able to:

_____ Identify facts directly from reading material by naming characters and settings? (explicit)

_____ Identify the main idea of a story? (explicit)

_____ Locate significant and irrelevant details? (explicit)

_____ Retell story facts in sequence? (explicit)

_____ Infer from reading material by summarizing? (implicit)

_____ Locate the implied main idea? (implicit)

_____ Predict outcomes, draw conclusions, generalize? (implicit)

_____ Compare and contrast reading material? (implicit)

_____ Identify cause-and-effect relationships? (implicit)

_____ Determine the author's mood, purpose, and intended audience? (implicit)

_____ Discriminate between fact and fiction? (critical)

_____ Evaluate the accuracy and completeness of material? (critical)

_____ Interpret figurative language? (critical)

_____ Analyze and compare material from various sources? (critical)

_____ Sense the author's biases and agenda? (critical)

_____ Respond with a more abstract response? (critical)

_____ Demonstrate higher order thinking skills? (critical)

_____ Apply prior knowledge, summarize, predict? (critical)

_____ Identify implied main idea? (critical)

_____ Distinguish between fact and fiction? (critical)

_____ Recognize propaganda techniques used in reading matter? (critical)

Assessment Strategy: *Cloze Procedure Assessment*

Strategy Description

The cloze procedure is used to assess word prediction abilities, to measure comprehension, and to determine the way students use context clues to identify words. When using the cloze method of assessment, students read a passage with selected words deleted and they supply the missing word or a semantically acceptable substitute. This requires that students use context clues to determine the missing word. This assessment is appropriate for students at the early elementary to the secondary level using grade appropriate reading passages; administration can be group or individual. Allow approximately 10 to 20 minutes per passage.

Questions to Ask

Is the student able to:

- Use word prediction abilities for comprehension?
- Use context cues to identify words?
- Demonstrate knowledge of linguistic structures?

Assessment Preparation

- Select a passage from the beginning of the story, chapter, or text of 250 to 300 words (100 to 200 words for first and second grades).
- Type the passage, using complete paragraphs. Beginning with the second sentence, delete every fifth word and replace with a blank line. Do not remove any words from the first and last sentences.
- Make blank lines of uniform length (10 to 15 spaces) to avoid spacing clues for missing words.
- Make a copy for the teacher and another for the student.

Implementation

✓ Provide a model so the procedure can be demonstrated, or provide students with a practice passage with easy sentences to ensure that they understand and can follow the directions (e.g., "Mary had a little lamb. It's fleece was white ______ snow"). The teacher directs students to do the following:

1. Read the whole passage.
2. Go back over the passage and fill in the missing words.
3. Try to use the exact words the author would have used.
4. Write one word on each line provided.
5. Skip and go to the next blank if having difficulty with one. Go back and try to fill in the remaining blanks at the end (see Figure 3–21).

✓ Provide unlimited time as this assessment focuses on comprehension rather than reading rate.

✓ Analyze answers to determine the similarity of meaning between the deleted word and the word that was written.

Scoring

- Misspellings are not counted as incorrect if the word is recognizable.
- Exact replacement words are recommended for ease of scoring, but synonyms that do not change the meaning may be accepted.

Scoring criteria:

Scoring is determined by the percentage correct, as follows:

- Independent reading level: 57% to 100%
- Instructional reading level: 44% to 56%
- Frustration reading level: less than 43% (Ekwall, 1997)

Special Considerations, Accommodations, Alternatives

- This type of procedure is best used with students who have strong language skills; it should not be used for students with word retrieval problems; instead use a maze procedure.
- Practice this procedure with students before administration. Consider using a maze procedure, then progress to a cloze procedure.
- The cloze procedure can be used to determine whether the reading content (i.e., textbook) level is appropriately matched to the student's instructional reading level.
- For students with language, learning, or physical disabilities or students who are English language learners, rather than require them to write the missing word, the teacher should allow the student to dictate the missing word to a peer, classroom aide, or another teacher.

Next Step

- *Mastered*—Increase to a higher reading level.
- *Emerging*—Have students identify context clues; provide guided reading practice.
- *No skill yet*—Start by providing a reading passage at the students' independent level focusing on identifying context clues; use a structured word bank for them to choose the missing word; use a maze procedure (limited to three word options).

FIGURE 3–21 Sample Cloze Procedure

Cloze Procedure Passage

The Miracle

I lived with my grandpa on the corner of Oak and Second Streets. We lived together in __________ large, brown cardboard box __________ we ate as many __________ of food as we __________ find. It was a __________ December and the ground __________ covered with snow. We __________ running out of food __________ were low on blankets. __________ had started coughing a __________. We needed a miracle __________ we would both die __________ starvation or frostbite. One __________ I was lying awake __________ the hard, cold cement __________ not to think of __________ very hungry I was. __________ face was flushed and __________ was frail and as __________ as a stick. I __________ I had to think __________ a way to help __________. That frigid night I __________ soundly until six in __________ morning when the bright __________ warmed my face. As __________ opened my eyes I __________ a huge table of __________ foods. It was a __________ come true. Grandpa's face __________ up as he watched __________ enjoying a hot cinnamon __________ while he drank a __________ cup of coffee and __________ a piece of freshly __________ bread. I drifted off __________ sleep dreaming happy thoughts. __________ woke suddenly to see __________ shadowy white figure in __________ distance standing beside my __________ as he slept. Grandpa __________ up and smiled at __________ figure. The white figure __________ into the sky with __________ grasping her outstretched hands. __________ is gone now but __________ has not forgotten me. He has __________ the angel back to __________ over me. Now, I have everything I need, except Grandpa.

Cloze Procedure Passage Answers

The Miracle

I lived with my grandpa on the corner of Oak and Second Streets. We lived together in a large, brown cardboard box and we ate as many scraps of food as we could find. It was a cold December and the ground was covered with snow. We were running out of food and were low on blankets. Grandpa had started coughing a lot. We needed a miracle or we would both die of starvation or frostbite. One night I was lying awake on the hard, cold cement trying not to think of how very hungry I was. Grandpa's face was flushed and he was frail and as thin as a stick. I knew I had to think of a way to help him. That frigid night I slept soundly until six in the morning when the bright sunshine warmed my face. As I opened my eyes I saw a huge table of delicious foods. It was a dream come true. Grandpa's face lit up as he watched me enjoying a hot cinnamon bun while he drank a steaming cup of coffee and ate a piece of freshly baked bread. I drifted off to sleep dreaming happy thoughts. I woke suddenly to see a shadowy white figure in the distance standing beside my Grandpa as he slept. Grandpa sat up and smiled at the figure. The white figure flew into the sky with Grandpa grasping her outstretched hands. Grandpa is gone now but he has not forgotten me. He has sent the angel back to watch over me. Now, I have everything I need, except Grandpa.

Assessment Strategy: *Maze Procedure Assessment*

Strategy Description

The maze procedure assesses reading comprehension and knowledge of linguistic structures. It is similar to the cloze procedure except that word choices are provided rather than blank spaces. This assessment can identify students who have poor comprehension, and those who do not use context clues and are unable to choose the correct missing word after reading a graded passage. This assessment is appropriate for students at the early elementary to the secondary level using grade level reading passages; administration can be group or individual. Allow approximately 10 to 15 minutes per passage.

Questions to Ask

Is the student able to:

- Use context cues to identify the appropriate word?
- Demonstrate knowledge of linguistic structures?
- Use word prediction abilities for comprehension?

Assessment Preparation

- Select a passage from the beginning of the story/chapter/text of 250 to 300 words (100 to 200 words for first and second grades).
- Type the passage, using complete paragraphs. Delete every fifth word and replace with a blank, beginning with the second sentence. Do not delete any words in the first or last sentence.
- Make blanks of uniform length (10 to 15 spaces) to avoid providing clues for word length.
- Rather than leave blank spaces for students' responses as in the cloze method, the maze method provides students with choices, presented in vertical or horizontal format. This gives students a choice of three words, only one of which is correct.
- Make a copy for the teacher and another student.

Implementation

✓ Provide a model so the procedure can be demonstrated, or provide students with a practice passage with easy sentences to ensure that they understand and can follow the directions (e.g., "Mary had a little lamb. It's fleece was white ______________ snow"). The teacher directs students to do the following: *(at, as, all)*

1. Read over the whole passage.
2. Go back over the passage, and choose one word that fits best from the three choices provided.
3. Write the word on the line provided (or allow student to circle the correct word).
4. Skip and go to the next blank if you have difficulty with one; go back and try to fill in the remaining blanks at the end (refer to Figure 3–22).

✓ Do not impose a time limit since the focus is on comprehension rather than reading rate.

Scoring

- Misspellings are not counted as incorrect if the word is recognizable.
- A percentage score is determined by: number of correct responses divided by the number of possible correct responses times 100.
- The criteria for determining reading levels when using the maze procedure are based on percentage of correct responses (words correctly read = wcr), as follows:

  Independent reading level: over 85%

  Instructional reading level: 50% to 84%

  Frustration reading level: 49% or less (Ekwall, 1997)
- To graph progress, refer to Tables 3–3 and 3–4 for maze norms and expected weekly growth rate.

Special Considerations, Accommodations, Alternatives

- This procedure is a more valid indicator of reading comprehension for children who have word retrieval problems than the cloze procedure, because it provides optional choices other than requiring them to produce their own words.
- Students whose primary language is other than English also profit from language cues (word options) provided in the maze procedure.
- For students with language, learning, or physical disabilities, rather than require them to write the missing word, have them dictate the word to a peer, classroom aide, or teacher.

Next Step

- *Mastered*—Increase to a higher readability level use a cloze procedure.
- *Emerging*—Have students identify context clues; provide guided reading practice.
- *No skill yet*—Start the process by providing a reading passage at the student's independent reading level while the student focuses on identifying context clues; provide student with three very different word choices (configuration/meaning) and gradually use increasingly similar word choices as the student becomes more proficient.

FIGURE 3–22 Example of the Maze Procedure

The following sentences are examples of the maze procedure.

foot it buy
Jim did not have foam so he went shopping in the grocery store to bake food.
food on bite

or:

Jane went back to ____________________ because she was tired.
(school, work, sleep)

TABLE 3–3 Norms for Maze CBM: Words Correctly Restored

Grade	Percentile	Fall (WCR)	Winter (WCR)	Spring (WCR)
1	90%	8	13	18
	75%	3	7	12
	50%	1	3	7
	25%	0	1	3
	10%	0	0	1
2	90%	13	21	25
	75%	8	16	19
	50%	4	10	14
	25%	2	6	9
	10%	0	3	5
3	90%	21	25	27
	75%	16	19	21
	50%	11	14	15
	25%	7	9	10
	10%	3	6	7
4	90%	22	31	33
	75%	17	25	26
	50%	12	18	19
	25%	8	13	13
	10%	5	8	9
5	90%	27	32	36
	75%	21	26	30
	50%	16	20	24
	25%	10	14	17
	10%	7	10	12
6	90%	31	38	41
	75%	25	31	32
	50%	19	24	25
	25%	13	17	18
	10%	8	11	12

(*Continued*)

TABLE 3–3 (*Continued*)

Grade	Percentile	Fall (WCR)	Winter (WCR)	Spring (WCR)
7	90%	33	36	42
	75%	27	29	34
	50%	20	22	26
	25%	14	16	18
	10%	10	12	13
8	90%	34	33	40
	75%	27	26	32
	50%	20	20	25
	25%	15	15	19
	10%	11	11	14

Source:

TABLE 3–4 Weekly Growth Rate for Maze: Words Correctly Restored

Grade	Ambitious Growth Rates Per Week (WCR)
1	0.4
2	0.4
3	0.4
4	0.4
5	0.4
6	0.4

Source: Fuchs & Fuchs, 2004.

Assessment Strategy: *Think-Aloud Procedure*

Strategy Description

The think-aloud procedure is a method of gaining insight into the reader's approach to text processing. Verbalizations made before, during, and after reading a selection are used to assess thinking processes and the application of metacognitive strategies. Students who do not have a strategic approach when processing reading material often have poor comprehension. This assessment is appropriate particularly for students from third grade and above; is administered individually, and is focused more on process than content. Allow 10 to 20 minutes per passage, based on grade level and length of passage read.

Questions to Ask

Is the student able to:

- Demonstrate how to construct meaning from reading material?
- Determine what is important in a particular passage?
- Relate information across sentences and paragraphs?
- Use strategies to deal with unfamiliar words and concepts?

Assessment Preparation

- Choose a graded reading passage.
- Consider audio recording students as they read and respond, for later analysis.

Implementation

✓ Provide the student with a graded reading passage.

✓ Tell the student the title of the selected passage; ask student to reflect on the topic and share feelings about it.

✓ Ask the student to read the passage but to stop after each sentence and think aloud about what was read and about what processes and strategies were used during this reflection.

✓ Note when the student has finished reading the passage; ask about its content, structure, and difficulty level (see Figure 3–23 for sample questions).

Special Considerations, Accommodations, Alternatives

- Student may be uncomfortable or be inexperienced with this procedure and need a model, coaching, and/or practice before actual results are useful.
- A student who is an English language learner (ELL) or has a disability may need extra accomodations for this assessment. Consider pairing the student with a peer; provide a visual guide, such as a structured organizer or outline, and provide verbal prompts, as needed.

Next Step

- *Mastered*—Encourage critical, higher order thinking; challenge students to connect reading to real-life experiences and to analyze text for more complex details.
- *Emerging*—Reinforce by modeling and sharing predictions; encourage interaction with the text by rereading, revisiting, rethinking, and reflecting.
- *No skill yet*—Select reading material content that is familiar to the reader, activate prior knowledge and interest, preteach vocabulary, and focus attention on key concepts.

Additional Resources

http://www2.scholastic.com/browse/article.jsp?id=4464
http://literacy.kent.edu/eureka/strategies/think_aloud.pdf

FIGURE 3–23 Sample Think-Aloud Questions

How does the student use existing information?
Can the student relate existing information with new information?
Can the student integrate new information with prior knowledge?
How does the student deal with new words and concepts?
Is the student using any metacognitive strategies to facilitate comprehension?
Can the student predict or anticipate upcoming events in a story?

Assessment Strategy: *Retell Procedure Assessment*

Strategy Description

The retell procedure is used to demonstrate understanding of reading material by the retelling or paraphrasing of a passage. Students can be rated on how they describe the events in the story (story structure) or their response to the content read based on the quantity, quality, and organization of the material. This assessment is appropriate for all grade levels. Administration can be either individual or in groups for written retells, but needs to be individual for oral retells. Allow 10 to 20 minutes per passage, based on grade level and length of passage read.

Questions to Ask

Is the student able to:

- Retell reading material in his/her own words rather than repeat the reading content verbatim?
- Demonstrate comprehension of the reading material by providing some personal reflection rather than just recall specific facts?
- Retell the passage as if relating it to someone who has never heard it before?

Assessment Preparation

- Select a grade level reading passage; determine whether responses will be recorded orally or in written form.
- Prepare checklist to record the important components of the passage (refer to Figure 3–24).

Implementation

✓ Explain to students that they need to tell everything they remember from the story or passage in as much detail as possible.

✓ Have the student read a grade level narrative reading passage; then direct the student to retell the story in a structured, sequential manner and identify the following:

Setting and characters

Goal, problem, and main events

Story resolution

✓ Have the student read a grade level expositive reading passage; then direct the student to retell the passage in an organized, sequential manner, and to recall the main idea and identify supporting details.

✓ Use retell before asking comprehension questions.

✓ Use prompts, such as "What comes next?" or "Then what happened?" only when necessary.

Scoring

Use rating scale as a guide (see Figure 3–25).

Independent Level Will Generally Reflect the Following

- Text structure
- Organization of how the material was presented
- Main ideas and details contained in the text

Instructional Level Will Generally Reflect the Following

- Less content than at the independent level
- Some minor misrepresentations and inaccuracies
- Organization that differs from the actual text

Frustration Level Will Generally Be Described as Follows

- Haphazard
- Incomplete
- Containing bits of information not related logically or sequentially (Johns & Lenski, 1997)

Special Considerations, Accommodations, Alternatives

- This type of assessment may not be a reliable indicator for students who are English language learners or who have an expressive language disorder.
- An accommodation for students with language-based learning or communication disorders or those with limited English language proficiency is to provide oral and/or visual prompts with the teacher asking structured questions. Provide a model so the student has an example of what is expected.
- Retelling can be enhanced by using role-playing, blackboards/felt boards, or puppets.
- Ensure students know that they have to retell in detail and in logical (sequential) order, not just summarize what they have read, as this may skew the results.

Next Step

- *Mastered*—Encourage student to retell story in an increasingly sequential, detailed manner.
- *Emerging*—Allow students to revisit the text material after initial reading; provide structure and physical and/or visual prompts; provide practice opportunities through cooperative storytelling; use prompts that have a symbolic link to help trigger the story.
- *No skill yet*—Provide pictures that the student can sequence and then retell; provide simulated activities, such as "show and tell."

Additional Resources

http://www.liketoread.com/read_strats_retell.php
http://www.readinga-z.com/assess/rubrics.html

FIGURE 3–24 Retell Skill Checklist

Can the student:

_____ Explain the central theme?
_____ Identify the main points?
_____ Tell story events in sequential order?
_____ Include supporting details?
_____ Refer to story characters by name?
_____ Define personal traits of the characters?
_____ Describe story problems and solutions?
_____ Respond with literal interpretation?
_____ Include only important and exclude unimportant information?
_____ Respond with interpretation reflecting higher level thinking?
_____ Provide adequate responses to teacher's questions and prompts?
_____ Retell the entire story needing no more than two or three questions or prompts?

S = satisfactory   I = improving   NI = needs improvement

FIGURE 3–25 Retell Rating Scale

Rating	*Interpretation*
5	Generalizations are made beyond the text; includes central thesis and major points, supporting details, and relevant supplemental information; exhibits coherence, completeness, and comprehensibility
4	Includes central thesis, major points, supporting details, and relevant supplemental information; exhibits coherence, completeness, and comprehensibility
3	Relates major ideas, includes supporting details and relevant supplemental information; exhibits adequate coherence, completeness, and comprehensibility
2	Relates a few major ideas, supporting details, and relevant supplemental information; exhibits some coherence, completeness, and comprehensibility
1	Relates no major ideas, and details only irrelevant supplemental information; low degree of coherence, completeness, and comprehensibility

Pass: rating of 4 or 5
No pass: rating of 3, 2, 1

Assessment Strategy: *Metacognition Assessment*

Strategy Description

Metacognition assessment evaluates students' awareness of their own thinking processes. It combines thinking and reflection, the understanding of when, where, and how to apply, regulate, and assess these processes or strategies to ensure successful learning. This assessment is appropriate for students in the middle to upper grades; it can be individual or group administered. Allow generally 15 to 20 minutes to assess this skill.

Questions to Ask

Is the student:

- Aware of own thinking process?
- Aware of own reading strategies?
- Able to regulate his/her reading processes or strategies to ensure successful learning?

Assessment Preparation

- Develop or use a metacognition checklist or inventory sheet.

Implementation

✓ Have the student reflect on and share the processes used before, during, and after reading.
✓ Consider the terms the student used in the self-analysis/self-assessment.
✓ Have the student complete a self-report regarding the ability to do the following:
Prepare and plan for learning
Select and use metacognitive strategies
Monitor strategy use
Use a range of strategies
Evaluate each strategy used and its personal benefits (see Figure 3–26)

Special Considerations, Accommodations, Alternatives

- Students who have difficulty reading and comprehending frequently do not understand or adequately use metacognitive strategies, including reflection or comprehension monitoring (Mercer & Pullen, 2009).

Next Step

- *Mastered*—Encourage students to read various genres and higher levels of material and self-analyze their comprehension.
- *Emerging*—Assist students in identifying their metacognitive strengths; discuss various ways of applying metacognition and identify several for students to use.
- *No skill yet*—Provide examples and assist students in guided practice using metacognitive strategies.

FIGURE 3–26 Student Metacognitive Skill Self-Analysis

Before beginning to read, have I . . .	***Regularly***	***Sometimes***	***Not Yet***
Identified the purpose for reading?	______	______	______
Thought about what I already know about the topic?	______	______	______
Asked myself what I need to know about the topic?	______	______	______
Thought about or discussed experiences related to the topic?	______	______	______
Asked myself what I expect to learn from this reading?	______	______	______
Thought about strategies to help me understand the material?	______	______	______
Looked over and thought about the title and illustrations?	______	______	______
Used headings/topic sentences to predict what I will be reading?	______	______	______
Predicted what will happen in the story?	______	______	______
Thought about the characters and setting of the story?	______	______	______
While reading, have I . . .			
Stopped and checked my understanding of what I just read?	______	______	______
Adjusted my reading rate if material gets confusing or difficult?	______	______	______
Paid attention to signal words (e.g., *therefore, such as, finally*)?	______	______	______
Highlighted and/or underlined parts that are important or unclear?	______	______	______
Written questions or comments in the margin to reread or check later?	______	______	______
Made predictions about what might happen next?	______	______	______
Made an outline to organize and remember characters, plot, etc.?	______	______	______
After reading, have I . . .			
Asked myself if I learned what I wanted to know?	______	______	______
Gone back to reread specific sections that were confusing or unclear?	______	______	______
Thought about what the author was trying to convey?	______	______	______
Determined if my predictions were correct or incorrect?	______	______	______
Summarized what I have read?	______	______	______
Asked myself if I agree or disagree with what I read, and why?	______	______	______
Thought about how I might use this information in the future?	______	______	______
Decided whether I need to read more about this topic?	______	______	______

Assessment Strategy: *Informal Reading Inventory Assessment*

Strategy Description

An informal reading inventory (IRI) assesses reading levels and specific strengths and weaknesses in reading strategies, knowledge, and skills. It may be prepared commercially or by the teacher. An IRI typically consists of graded word lists and graded reading passages. Inventory results provide students' independent, instructional, and frustration levels for word recognition and oral, silent, and listening comprehension. IRIs are appropriate for students from early elementary through 12th grade (this grade range varies according to the specific commercial IRI used). Time allotment varies, depending on the length of the passage and the student's reading fluency; however, generally allow at least 30 minutes for the student to read and respond to several graded passages.

Questions to Ask

Is the student able to:

- Identify sight vocabulary—isolated words, words in context?
- Decode unknown words?
- Understand grade level vocabulary word meaning?
- Answer comprehension questions after reading a passage orally and/or silently?
- Answer comprehension questions after listening to a passage read orally?

Assessment Preparation

- Develop a graded word list by randomly selecting 20 to 25 words from the glossary list for each grade level of the basal reading series.
- Select five passages from reading material used in class (two below the student's grade level, one at grade level, and two above grade level).
- Passage should range from about 50-words at the preprimer level to from 150 to 250 words for the secondary level.
- Construct five questions for each passage based on recalling facts, making inferences, and defining vocabulary to assess comprehension. Make two copies of each passage, one for the teacher to record errors and one for the student to use for reading orally.

Implementation

✓ Begin by asking the student to read a list of vocabulary words in isolation start with a list that is at least one grade below his or her estimated reading level. Continue until the words become too difficult to read (frustration level).

✓ Mark errors as the student reads from the word list and determine the word recognition independent instructional and frustration levels.

✓ Have the student read passages at the highest independent level and continue reading passages at each subsequent grade level until the material becomes too difficult to decode and/or comprehend (frustration level).

✓ Record the percentage of words read accurately for each passage (divide the number of words read accurately by the number of words in the passage) to determine the student's word recognition score and whether it is within the independent, instructional, or frustration level.

✓ Ask five questions for each passage based on recalling facts, making inferences, and defining vocabulary to determine whether the student's comprehension is within the independent, instructional, or frustration level. Additional questions may need to be asked to probe for the student's level of understanding. Be alert for signs of frustration.

✓ Have student read passages at the next highest level when the independent or instructional level is determined, or the next lowest level passage if the student has scored at the frustration level. Once the independent, instructional, and frustration level has been established, stop testing.

✓ Determine student's listening comprehension level by following directions above; however, read the passage aloud to the student, rather than having the student read the passage orally or silently.

Scoring

Performance levels—independent, instructional, frustration—and listening are determined according to the number of words read accurately and the percent of comprehension questions answered correctly.

Independent level:

- Level at which reading is fluent, understandable, and requires no assistance
- Level chosen for pleasure reading
- Comprehension question accuracy rate of 90% or higher for oral reading; higher rate for silent reading
- Correct word recognition (in context) rate of 98%
- Reads fluently without tension

Instructional level:

- Level at which the material is challenging but neither too difficult nor too easy
- Critical score—the level where instruction should begin
- Comprehension question accuracy rate for oral reading of 70% to 89%; substantially higher rate for silent reading
- Correct word recognition range of 90% to 97%
- Ability to anticipate meaning with freedom from tension

Frustration level:

- Level at which reading material is too difficult to read or understand
- Comprehension question accuracy rate below 70%
- Correct word recognition of less than 90%
- Slow, halting reading and signs of tension

Listening comprehension level:

- Level at which material read to student is understood
- Typically exceeds frustration level

Scoring Criteria for Determining Independent, Instructional, and Frustration Levels Are as Follows

- Word identification in isolation (word lists): number of words correctly identified (divided by) the total number of words
- Word identification in context (oral reading of passages): number of words in a passage (minus) number of miscues/word recognition errors (divided by) number of words in the passage
- Comprehension (questions): number of questions correctly answered (divided by) total number of questions
- Reading rate (words per minute, or wpm): number of words in passage times 60 (divided by) number of seconds to read passage. Correct words per minute = wpm-miscues. (Leslie & Caldwell, 2005)

Special Considerations, Accommodations, Alternatives

- When using selections from textbooks for teacher-generated IRI samples, teachers need to realize that the readability of texts may vary from subject to subject.
- To select instructional materials and texts that appropriately match the student's reading level, a readability measure, such as a readability graph, can be used.
- Computer software is also available to determine the readability of printed material.
- There are numerous commercially prepared informal reading inventories. However, if administering a commercially published IRI, it is important to carefully read the directions, scoring, and interpretation prior to administration because each inventory has specific criteria and procedures that need to be followed for valid and reliable results.

Next Step

- *Mastered*—Proceed to the next grade level reading material.
- *Emerging*—Have the student read along while listening to a taped version of the passage; begin with explicit comprehension questions and move into higher order thinking questions.
- *No skill yet*—Start at the student's independent level and use a paired reading partnership or a guided reading approach to build competence and confidence.

Assessment Strategy: *Performance-Based Assessment*

Strategy Description

Performance assessment of reading entails having students read a passage or story for a purpose, then demonstrate their comprehension and construct meaning from the text by performing an authentic task about what they read. This type of assessment puts students in realistic situations in which they can demonstrate their ability to integrate knowledge and skills to perform a target activity. This assessment is appropriate for all grades and administration can be either group or individual. Time allotment varies according to the task.

Questions to Ask

Is the student able to:

- Plan and problem solve?
- Create a product, collaborate, use resources and higher order thinking skills as opposed to regurgitating answers on a test form?
- Demonstrate the ability to cognitively process and use reasoning skills?

Assessment Preparation

- Determine the outcome(s) to be measured.
- Devise clear instructions to be provided to students.
- Determine conditions for assessment (e.g., setting, time needed).
- Gather all the equipment or resource materials that may be used.
- Establish whether the student will have a choice in how to respond (e.g., oral response).
- Determine whether the student will require accommodations or modifications.
- Develop the scoring criteria to be used.

Implementation

- ✓ Share the performance criteria (the expected outcome) with students when assigning the task.
- ✓ Engage students in the development of the performance task (see Figures 3–27 and 3–28).
- ✓ Involve students in comparing and contrasting examples of performance.
- ✓ Involve students in the development of the evaluation process, including rating scales, checklists, and progress monitoring charts; have students help rate and track progress by converting progress points to graphs.
- ✓ Assess generalization and application skills using meaningful, relevant learning activities.
- ✓ Store samples of students' performance products over time (e.g., in a portfolio, videotape); have students note areas of strength and areas still needing improvement.
- ✓ Evaluate students' ability to create an authentic product that demonstrates knowledge and skill.

Scoring

90–100	exceptional performance = competency
80–89	mastery level = competency
70–79	minor types and/or number of errors = adequate
60–69	many types and/or number of errors = adequate
40–59	fails to complete = inadequate
20–39	inability to begin task = inadequate
0–19	no attempt

Special Considerations, Accommodations, Alternatives

- Performance assessment provides a means for students with disabilities to demonstrate skills that are not evident on pencil-paper tests; however, these students may need various accommodations (e.g., special equipment, extra time) to carry out these activities.
- Students may require prompts or varying degrees of direction to carry out performance tasks.

Next Step

- *Mastered*—Challenge students to use higher order, creative thinking during performance tasks.
- *Emerging*—Provide guided instruction and supportive feedback; provide a skilled, supportive partner to assist in planning and follow through.
- *No skill yet*—Provide clear, specific, sequential directions, monitor closely, and provide feedback at each step. Pair with a peer partner.

Additional Resources

http://teacher.scholastic.com/professional/assessment/readingassess.htm

FIGURE 3–27 Suggested Reading Performance Activities

Write and act out plays	Write dialogue for narrative story
Present original writing	Compare a film to a novel
Perform a production through mime	Follow directions to program a VCR
Write an editorial after reading articles	Read and critique children's stories
Read and act out a puppet show	Dramatize characters in a story
Perform a role-play	Illustrate a story

FIGURE 3–28 Nonverbal Performance Assessments

Physical Demonstrations

Students can point to objects; use gestures or hands-on tasks; or act out vocabulary, concepts, or events. The students can respond with a thumbs up or a thumbs down or other affirming gesture when the teacher has grouped a category of items correctly (e.g., food groups, animal habitats). The teacher can use a checklist to record individual responses. Audiotaping or videotaping of work in process, presentations, or demonstrations is a good way to capture skill mastery or areas needing attention; program a DVR to record a show.

Pictorial Products

Students can produce and manipulate drawings, models, dioramas, graphs, and charts, for example, students can label the names of the states and their products on a map. Labeling can be used across the curriculum with diagrams, webs, and illustrations.

Illustrations

Students can draw rather than explain. Pictorial journals can be kept during units to record and illustrate comprehension (e.g., the life cycle of a plant, a butterfly).

Written Products

Students can be assessed using reading response logs, dialogue journals, narrative story writing, and so forth.

K-W-L Charts

Students can use K-W-L charts (what I know, what I want to know, what I've learned) to begin and conclude a unit of study. This strategy helps teachers to gain an awareness of background knowledge and interests and to assess the content material learned. For students with limited English proficiency, the chart can be completed in the child's first language or with illustrations.

REFERENCES

AIMSweb. (2008). Oral reading fluency norms [data file]. Retrieved May 12, 2009, from *http://www.aimsweb.com*

Betts, E. A. (1946). *Foundation of reading instruction*. New York: American Book.

Clay, M. (2000). *Running records for classroom teachers*. Westport, CT: Heinemann.

Ekwall, E. (1997). *Locating and correcting reading difficulties* (7th ed.). Upper Saddle River, NJ: Merrill/Prentice Hall.

Fuchs, L. S., & Fuchs, D. (2004). *Using CBM for progress monitoring*. Retrieved from *http://www.studentprogress.org*

Gersten, R., Fuchs, D., Williams, J., & Baker, S. (2001). Teaching reading comprehension strategies to students with learning disabilities. *Review of Educational Research, 71*, 279–320.

Guerin, G. R., & Maier, A. S. (1983). *Informal assessment in education*. Palo Alto, CA: Mayfield Publishing Company.

Hasbrouck, J., & Tindal, G. A. (2006, April). Oral reading fluency norms: A valuable assessment tool for reading teachers. *The Reading Teacher, 59*(7), 636–644.

Jenkins, J. R., Hudson, R. F., & Lee, S. H. (2007). Using CBM-reading assessment to monitor progress. *Perspectives on Language and Literacy, 33*(2). International Dyslexia Association.

Johns, J. L., & Lenski, S. D. (1997). *Improving reading: A handbook of strategies* (2nd ed.). Dubuque, IA: Kendall/Hunt.

Joseph, L. M. (2006). Incremental rehearsal: A flash card drill technique for increasing retention of reading words. *The Reading Teacher, 59*, 803–807.

Kuhn, M. R., & Stahl, S. A. (2003). Fluency: A review of developmental and remedial practices. *Journal of Educational Psychology, 95*, 3–21.

Leslie, L., & Caldwell, J. (2005). *Qualitative reading inventory—4*. Boston: Allyn & Bacon.

Lovett, M. W., Steinbach, K. A., & Frijters, J. C. (2000). Remediating the core deficits of developmental reading disability: A double-deficit perspective. *Journal of Learning Disabilities, 33*(4), 334–358.

Lyon, G. R. (1997). *Report on learning disabilities research*. Adapted from testimony of Dr. Reid Lyon before the Committee on Education and the Workforce, U. S. House of Representatives, July 10.

Lyon, G. R. (2001). Measuring success: Using assessments and accountability to raise student achievement. Statement from the U.S. House Committee on Education and the Workforce Hearing. The National Right to Read Foundation, *http://www.nrrf.org/lyon_statement3-01.htm*

Lyon, G. R. (2003). Reading disabilities: Why do some children have difficulty learning to read? What can be done about it? *Perspectives, 29*(2), 4.

Mercer, C. D., Mercer, A. R., & Pullen, P. C. (2010). *Teaching students with learning problems* (8th ed.). Upper Saddle River, NJ: Merrill/Prentice Hall.

Mercer, C. D., & Pullen, P. C. (2009). *Students with learning disabilities* (7th ed.). Upper Saddle River, NJ: Merrill/Prentice Hall.

National Assessment of Educational Progress. (2005). *The nation's report card*. Washington, DC: National Center for Education Statistics.

National Center for Educational Statistics. (1995). *Listening to children read aloud*. Washington, DC: U.S. Department of Education.

National Center for Educational Statistics. (2005). *The nation's report card*. Retrieved August 20, 2004, from *http://nces.ed.gov/nationsreportcard/reading/*

National Reading Panel. (2005). *Teaching children to read: An evidence-based assessment of the scientific research literature on reading and its implications for Put Reading First: The research building blocks for teaching children to read*. Jessup, MD: National Institute for Literacy.

Put reading first: The research building blocks for teaching children to read, (2001). Jessup, MD: National Institute for Literacy.

Riddle-Buly, M., & Valencia, S. W. (2002). Below the bar: Profiles of students who fail state reading assessments. *Educational Evaluation and Policy Analysis, 24*, 219–239.

Rosner, J. (1993). *Helping children overcome learning disabilities*. New York: Walker & Company.

Torgesen, J. K., Wagner, R. K., Rashotte, C. A., Rose, E., Lindamood, P., Conway, T., & Garvan, C. (1999). Preventing reading failure in young children with phonological processing disabilities: Group and individual responses to instruction. *Journal of Educational Psychology, 91*(4), 579–594.

Vaughn, S., & Bos, C. S. (2009). *Strategies for teaching students with learning and behavior problems* (7th ed.). Upper Saddle River, NJ: Pearson.

Chapter 4

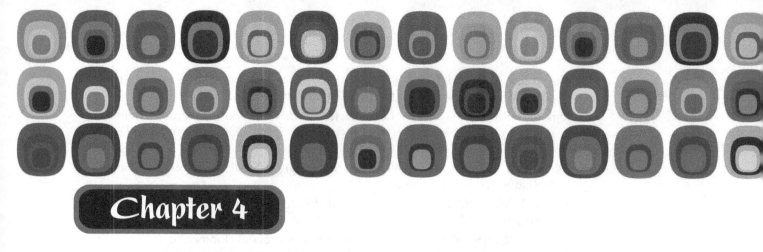

Written Language and Related Skills Assessment

INTRODUCTION

Written language, the ability to communicate effectively in writing, is one of the highest forms of communication, yet is the most complex language task. It requires complex thought processes based on multiple skills, including talking, listening, reading, penmanship, and spelling, and requires the linking of language, thought, and motor skills. The three components of written language are interwoven; therefore, when students have difficulty in one aspect of writing, such as spelling or handwriting, the other aspect, written expression, the ability to express ideas in a readable manner, is affected, thus limiting their ability to communicate effectively (Lerner & Johns, 2009).

Inability to write legibly or encode can also affect the way individuals are perceived by others, their level of confidence, and their willingness to attempt writing tasks. Writing requires the coordination of several modalities simultaneously and more synchronization than any other school task. Poor written expression skills can have a negative impact on individuals' ability to cope and succeed, not only in school but also in employment situations (Adelman & Vogel, 2003). Therefore, as teachers, we need to be knowledgeable about the various components that affect students' written language competencies and develop the assessment skills necessary to diagnose specific problems, initiate interventions, and monitor progress.

WRITTEN LANGUAGE ASSESSMENT

Assessment Strategy: *Written Language: Assessment of the Writing Process*

Strategy Description

Teachers need to determine whether students know and can apply the developmental writing process. This assessment measures students' ability to preplan before beginning to write, write drafts, revise and edit written work, proofread, and share the final product. In order to construct instructional programs that increase writing competence and to determine appropriate interventions, it is critical to identify and prioritize the areas of need and of strength, and to determine students' present performance levels. This assessment is appropriate for primary through secondary level students. Allow 15 to 30 minutes, depending on the length and complexity of students' writing samples.

Questions to Ask

Does the student:

- Take time to think before beginning to write?
- Produce a writing sample of sufficient quality and quantity?
- Edit the writing sample and make appropriate revisions?
- Ask others to read the final product and use feedback for improvement?

Assessment Preparation

- It is always useful to administer an interest inventory so that motivating prompts can be presented to get the student started in the writing process.
- Provide plenty of paper and pencils and access to a computer or word processor, as needed.

Implementation

✓ Have the student produce a writing sample (e.g., narrative story, expository essay).

✓ Provide a writing prompt, if necessary.

✓ Read the written product and, before each skill statement, mark the skill as either M for mastered, E for emerging, or B for beginning if the student is either just being introduced to the skill or has not been successful at the early stages (see Figure 4–1).

✓ After having assessed the writing piece, return the paper and the checklist to the student. Once the student has found and corrected the errors, recheck the piece with the student.

Special Considerations, Accommodations, Alternatives

- Keeping a notebook or journal allows students to record their work as well as their attitudes and feelings about their writing and the writing of other authors.
- Journals are useful for monitoring progress on a daily basis, for providing rehearsal opportunities to practice new skills, for providing regular supportive and corrective feedback, for program planning, and for program evaluation.
- Provide necessary supports to facilitate writing, such as a computer, a pencil guard, dictionary, thesaurus, extra time, a peer partner.

Next Step

- *Mastered*—Encourage students to write in a range of genres and increase their production rate.
- *Emerging*—Provide outlines, structured organizers, story starters, word banks; provide peer support.
- *No skill yet*—Have students talk through a story; the teacher guides students to complete a partially constructed outline; partner students with more proficient writers.

Additional Resources

Ideas for Teaching the Writing Process
http://www.kimskorner4teachertalk.com/writing/writingprocess/menu.html

FIGURE 4–1 Assessing the Steps in the Writing Process

Writing Process Analysis

Step 1: Prewriting or Planning Stage

Did the writer:

_____ Generate or select a suitable topic?
_____ Determine the purpose and audience before writing?
_____ Use various strategies to explore ideas and plan for writing (e.g., brainstorming, semantic webbing, charting, graphing, using graphic organizers)?
_____ Discuss ideas before beginning to write?

Step 2: Writing or Drafting Stage

Did the writer:

_____ Complete the first draft without focusing on mechanics or spelling?
_____ Transform prewriting, planning, and organization into complete sentences/paragraphs?
_____ Construct a written piece appropriate for the purpose and audience?
_____ Develop a title and topic sentence that is interesting and suits the topic?
_____ Write a piece that has a clear beginning, middle, and end?
_____ Develop ideas that are detailed and provide vivid descriptions?
_____ Write a piece that incorporates personal experiences and observations?
_____ Use a range of sentence types (declarative, interrogatory, exclamatory)?
_____ Write a piece that is clear, organized, and written in sequential order?
_____ Use age- and grade-appropriate vocabulary levels when writing?
_____ Incorporate smooth transitions between sentences and paragraphs?
_____ Use figurative language, interesting words, realistic dialogue, and/or descriptions?
_____ End the written piece with a good concluding paragraph?
_____ Use technical supports (e.g., encyclopedia, dictionary, thesaurus)?

Step 3: Revising or Editing Stage

Does the writer:

_____ Review the work for possible changes and revisions?
_____ Focus content, clarifying that the purpose and intended meaning is conveyed?
_____ Participate in peer sharing and conferencing as part of this step?
_____ Take and give suggestions for improvement?
_____ Begin sentences and proper nouns with a capital letter?
_____ End sentences with a period, a question mark, or an exclamation mark?
_____ Write sentences that are complete thoughts and include subjects and predicates?
_____ Separate independent clauses with a semicolon or a comma and conjunction?
_____ Use singular subjects with singular verbs; do plural subjects agree with plural verbs?
_____ Use pronouns correctly for subjects and objects?
_____ Use singular and plural pronouns correctly?
_____ Spell all words correctly; use prefixes and suffixes accurately?
_____ Correctly use verbs that are frequently confused (e.g., *rise/raise, lie/lay*)?
_____ Avoid using double negatives?
_____ Check that words are not omitted?
_____ Indent paragraphs; space letters and words adequately?
_____ Use apostrophes correctly with contractions and possessive nouns?
_____ Punctuate and capitalize dialogue correctly?

Step 4: Proofreading Stage

Does the writer:

_____ Reread the draft, inspect for mechanical errors, revise and edit based on suggestions for change?
_____ Make careful revisions to the writing piece?
_____ Produce a legible final product with minimal errors?

Step 5: Publishing or Sharing Stage

Does the writer:

_____ Share the work via oral presentation or reading to peers or a younger class?
_____ Publish and distribute the final draft?

Assessment Strategy: *Written Language: Writing Sample Analysis*

Strategy Description

Analyzing a writing sample can provide the teacher with important information about a student's overall written language skills, including the ability to organize thoughts, vocabulary usage, creativity, spelling, and handwriting skills. This assessment is appropriate for students from the primary level through secondary grade levels, and can be administered individually or in a group setting. Allow approximately 15 to 20 minutes, depending on the length of the sample.

Questions to Ask

Is the student:

- Having difficulty expressing thoughts clearly in writing?
- Unable to write comprehendible passages?
- Producing limited written output, in quality or quantity?

Assessment Preparation

- Provide plenty of paper and pencils and access to a computer or word processor, if needed.
- Be prepared with a writing prompt, such as a few sentences to begin the writing, a picture, or an object that is of interest to the student.

Implementation

✓ Ask the student to produce a writing sample. This may include writing a story, responding to a prompt, or composing an expository essay.

✓ Require several writing samples from different subject areas (e.g., science and math as well as language arts) and various types of written assignments (e.g., in-class writing, homework, note-taking).

✓ Focus of the writing sample assessment should be on several criteria, including content, organization, structure, word choice, usage, and mechanics (see Figure 4–2).

✓ Determine competency by analyzing both quality and quantity.

Special Considerations, Accommodations, Alternatives

- Comparisons should be made from earlier in the school year (or last year, if possible) to the student's current functioning to note progress.
- Depending on the type of problem, the student may require prompts, organizational supports, or extended time for planning and writing.
- When the goal is to determine how the student writes independently, the teacher should not help with spelling, mechanics, and so forth.

Next Step

- *Mastered*—Encourage the use of expanded vocabulary and different genres of writing (e.g., letter, journal entry, newspaper report, essay, research paper).
- *Emerging*—Expand on aspects of writing that have developed well; focus instruction on one component at a time for remediation.
- *No skill yet*—Encourage more writing without stressing conventions (e.g., spelling, grammar); focus on communicating ideas (let students know they can edit later). Give students regular opportunities for writing a topic of their choice.

Additional Resources

General Ideas for Teaching Writing

http://www.kimskorner4teachertalk.com/writing/general/menu.htm
http://teacher.scholastic.com/professional/teachwriting/
http://www.adlit.org/article/22323

FIGURE 4–2 Writing Sample Analysis

- Does the student write in manuscript or cursive form consistently? ____________
- Is the handwriting legible? ____________
- Is there evidence of handwriting problems with letter and number formation or spacing? ____________
- Is the print properly signed within line boundaries? ____________
- Are the letters and numbers proportionate to each other? ____________
- Is the letter or number slant appropriate? ____________
- Is line quality precise, consistent? ____________
- Is there evidence of excessive erasures? ____________
- Does student write in left-to-right progression? ____________
- Are any letters or numbers reversed, transposed, or inverted? ____________
- Can the student spell phonetically regular words? ____________
- Can the student spell phonetically irregular words? ____________
- Does the student substitute, omit, or add sounds in words? ____________
- Does the student confuse common synonyms (*house* for *home*) ____________
- Does the student confuse common homonyms (*blue* for *blew*)? ____________
- Does the student confuse vowel sounds (*sit* for *sat*)? ____________

Assessment Strategy: *Written Language: Beginning Writer's Continuum*

Strategy Description

The Beginning Writer's Continuum (BWC) is an assessment for determining developmental early writing skills. The BWC is used to assess skills for letter formation and early drawing and storytelling skills to the beginning stages of written expression when the student is starting to write a complete sentence. This assessment is appropriate for preschool through approximately the latter third-grade level. A group of students may be working at the same time; however, each student's final product is assessed individually. Time allotment will vary depending on the individual writing project.

Questions to Ask

When trying to determine whether to use the BWC or the 6+1 Trait® Assessment (Figure 4–3), consider the following:

- Which will give the student and teacher the best information to improve performance next time?
- How complex is the writing piece? Is the writing sample only a few sentences? If so, regardless of the quality, use the BWC assessment.
- Has the writing matured to the point where the student can produce a complete paragraph or two? If so, then begin transitioning to the 6+1 Trait® Assessment.

Assessment Preparation

- Have available crayons, markers, sharpies, pens, colored pencils, all kinds of paper, including lined sheets. Use a computer to make your own lined sheets to adjust spacing and thickness.
- Be prepared with a writing prompt, such as pictures, special hobby items, any objects of interest to the student, and provide as needed.

Implementation

✓ Have the student produce a writing sample based on developmental age (e.g., pictures with primitive labeling for beginning primary level to a paragraph for a third grader).

Use the BWC as a guide to analytically assess these attempts at early writing. The rubric is used to measure appropriate stages of development using various writing-related work samples (see Figure 4–3).

✓ Note that the BWC criteria for level 3 is similar to the criteria for 6+1 Trait® Assessment, which is the criterion for more advanced writing.

Special Considerations, Accommodations, Alternatives

- This is a particularly useful method for assessing students with cultural and linguistic differences.
- This is a flexible technique, and can be used to facilitate communication for students with special learning needs.

Next Step

- *Mastered*—If students have developed the ability to write in paragraphs, begin to use the 6+1 Trait® Assessment.
- *Emerging*—Encourage students to expand their writing (e.g., adding details), provide writing prompts, develop a structured outline, a word bank, brainstorm pre-writing ideas, partner with a peer, and provide many opportunities for writing.
- *No skill yet*—Focus on creating sentences, have students tell what happened "next" if they are able to write one or two sentences; encourage students to verbally tell their story and then attempt to write it down or draw it, depending on their developmental stage.

Additional Resources

Beginner's Writing Continuum
http://educationnorthwest.org/webfm_send/145

Six-Trait Assessment for Beginning Writers
http://apps.educationnorthwest.org/toolkit98/six.html

FIGURE 4–3 Beginning Writer's Continuum Assessment Scale

6-Trait Assessment for Beginning Writers

1 **Experimenting**	2 **Emerging**	3 **Developing**	4 **Capable**	5 **Experienced**
IDEAS — Uses scribbles for writing — Dictates labels or a story — Shapes that look like letters — Line forms that imitate best — Writes letters randomly	IDEAS — Some recognizable words present — Labels pictures — Uses drawings that show detail — Pictures are supported by some words	IDEAS — Attempts a story or to make a point — Illustration supports the writing — Meaning of the general idea is recognizable/ understandable — Some ideas clear but some are still fuzzy	IDEAS — Writing tells a story or makes a point — Illustration (if present) enhances the writing — Idea is generally on topic — Details are present but not developed (lists)	IDEAS — Presents a fresh/original idea — Topic is narrowed and focused — Develops one clear, main idea — Uses interesting, important details for support — Writer understands topic well
ORGANIZATION — Ability to order or group not yet present — No sense of beginning or end — Connections between ideas are confusing	ORGANIZATION — No title (if requested) — Experiments with beginnings — Begins to group like-words/pictures — Transitions or evidence of sequencing are haphazard	ORGANIZATION — A title is present (if requested) — Limited transitions present — Beginning but no ending except "The End" — Attempts at sequencing and transitions	ORGANIZATION — An appropriate title is present (if requested) — Attempts transitions from sentence to sentence — Beginning works well and attempts an ending — Logical sequencing — Key ideas begin to surface	ORGANIZATION — An original title is present (if requested) — Transitions connect main idea — The opening attracts — An effective ending is tried — Easy to follow — Important ideas stand out
VOICE — Communicates feeling with size, color, shape, line in drawing or letter imitation — Work is similar to everyone else's — Unclear response to task — Awareness of audience not present	VOICE — Hints of voice present in words and phrases — Looks different from most others — Energy/mood is present — Treatment of topic predictable — Audience is fuzzy could be anybody, anywhere	VOICE — Expresses some predictable feelings — Moments of individual sparkle, but then hides — Repetition of familiar ideas reduces energy — Awareness that the writing will be read by someone else — Reader had limited connection to writer	VOICE — Writing is individual and expressive — Individual perspective becomes evident — Personal treatment of a standard topic — Writes to convey a story or idea to the reader — Attempts non-standard point of view	VOICE — Uses text to elicit a variety of emotions — Takes some risks to say more than what is expected — Point of view is evident — Writes with a clear sense of audience — Cares deeply about the topic

WORD CHOICE — Writes letters in strings — Imitates word patterns — Pictures stand for words and phrases — Copies environmental print	WORD CHOICE — Recognizable words — Environmental words used correctly — Attempts at phrases — Functional language	WORD CHOICE — General or ordinary words — Attempts new words but they don't always fit — Settles for the word or phrase that "will do" — Big words used only to impress reader — Relies on slang clichés, or repetition	WORD CHOICE — Uses favorite words correctly — Experiments with new and different words with some success — Tries to choose words for specificity — Attempts to use descriptive words to create images	WORD CHOICE — Everyday words used well — Presice, accurate, fresh original words — Creates vivid images in a natural way — Avoids repetition, cliches, or vague language — Attempts at figurative language
SENTENCE FLUENCY — Mimics letters and words across the page — Words stand alone — Patterns for sentences not in evidence — Sentence sense not yet present	SENTENCE FLUENCY — Strings words together into phrases — Attempts simple sentences — Short, repetitive sentence patterns — Dialogue present but not understandable	SENTENCE FLUENCY — Uses simple sentences — Sentences tend to begin the same — Experiments with other sentence patterns — Reader may have to reread to follow the meaning — Dialogue present but needs interpretation	SENTENCE FLUENCY — Simple and compound sentences present and effective — Attempts complex sentences — Not all sentences begin the same — Sections of writing have rhythm and flow	SENTENCE FLUENCY — Consistently uses sentence variety — Sentence structure is correct and creative — Variety of sentence beginnings — Natural rhythm, cadence, and flow — Sentences have features which clarify the important idea
CONVENTIONS — Writes letter strings (pre-phonetic: dmRxzz) — Attempts to create standard letters — Attempts spacing of words, letters, symbols, or pictures — Attempts to write left to right — Attempts to write top/down — Punctuation, capitalization, etc. not making sense, yet — Student interpretation needed to understand text/pictures	CONVENTIONS — Attempts semi-phonetic spelling (MTR, UM, KO, etc.) — Uses mixed upper and lowercase letters — Uses spaces between letters and words — Consistently writes left to right — Consistently makes effective use of top to bottom spacing — Random punctuation — Nonstandard grammar is common	CONVENTIONS — Uses phonetic spelling (MOSTR, HUMN, KLOSD, etc.) on personal words — Spelling of high frequency words still spotty — Uses capitals at the beginning of sentences — Usually uses end punctuation correctly (.!?) — Experiments with other punctuation — Long paper may be written as one paragraph — Attempts standard grammar	CONVENTIONS — Transitional spelling on less frequent words (MONSTUR, HUMUN, CLOSSED, etc.) — Spelling of high frequency words usually correct — Capitals at the beginning of sentences and variable use on proper nouns — End punctuation is correct (.!?) and other punctuation is attempted (such as commas) — Paragraphing variable but present — Noun/pronoun agreement, verb senses, subject/verb agreement	CONVENTIONS — High frequency words are spelled correctly and very close on other words — Capitals used for obvious proper nouns as well as sentence beginnings — Basic punctuation is used correctly and/or creatively — Indents consistently to show paragraphs — Shows control over standard grammar

Source: Northwest Regional Educational Laboratory. Copyright 2010. Printed with permission.

Assessment Strategy: *Written Language: 6+1 Trait® Assessment*

Strategy Description

The 6+1 Trait® Assessment is designed to pinpoint areas of strength and weakness as students focus on improving their writing. This assessment, basically a rubric analytic framework, is a guide for learning and using a common language to refer to the characteristics of writing. It provides a common vision of what "good" writing looks like. It is used for students who are actually beginning to write, and assesses a range of performances across the traits (beginning to strong)(see Figure 4–4). This assessment is appropriate for latter third grade through the secondary level grades. While a large group can be writing at the same time, each student's final product is assessed individually. Allow generally 20 minutes, but time will vary depending on the individual writing project.

Questions to Ask

Is the student able to focus on:

- Ideas: write informative, interesting pieces with a main theme, and sufficient supporting detail?
- Organization: write in an organized manner with a clear theme, supporting sentences, and a strong conclusion with sentences that are sequential and logical?
- Voice: write in a manner that engages the reader with the topic and contains a personal tone and flavor?
- Word choice: write using rich, colorful, precise language that communicates clearly, and clarifies and expands ideas?
- Sentence fluency: write sentences that vary in length and style so that the words and phrases flow together as they are read?
- Conventions: produce a written piece with accuracy in spelling, grammar, usage, paragraphing, capitalization, and/or punctuation?
- Presentation: produce a final written product that is neat, clear, and well organized, with illustrations, graphs, or charts as needed?

Assessment Preparation

- Provide plenty of paper and pencils and access to a computer or word processor, as needed.
- Be prepared with a writing prompt, such as a few sentences to begin the writing, a picture, or an object that is of interest to the student.

Special Considerations, Accommodations, Alternatives

- Students with learning difficulties may need to work in groups or with writing partners.
- Students who are English language learners (ELL) may benefit from orally discussing and then dictating ideas before attempting to write.

Next Step

- *Mastered*—Encourage more creativity; promote varied genres of writing with more details.
- *Emerging*—Start with small writing samples to revise and provide guided practice to enable the student to move to more complex revision, such as adding, deleting, moving, and substituting words; expand sentence length by combining short sentences; add specific detail and sensory images; vary kinds of sentences, and paragraph lengths by moving, removing, or adding sentences and including transitions.

FIGURE 4–4 6+1 Trait® Assessment Writing Analysis Scoring Guide

6+1 Trait® Condensed Scoring Guide		
Ideas: The heart of the message, the content of the piece, the main theme, with details that enrich and develop that theme.	**Organization:** The internal structure, the thread of central meaning, the logical and sometimes intriguing pattern of the ideas.	**Voice:** The unique perspective of the writer evident in the piece through the use of compelling ideas, engaging language, and revealing details.
⑤ *This paper is clear and focused. It holds the reader's attention. Relevant anecdotes and details enrich the central theme.* A. The topic is narrow and manageable. B. Relevant, telling, quality details go beyond the obvious. C. Reasonably accurate details. D. Writing from knowledge or experience; ideas are fresh and original. E. Reader's questions are anticipated and answered. F. Insight	⑤ *The organizational structure of this paper enhances and showcases the central idea or theme of the paper; includes a satisfying introduction and conclusion.* A. An inviting introduction draws the reader in; a satisfying conclusion leaves the reader with a sense of closure and resolution. B. Thoughtful transitions. C. Sequencing is logical and effective. D. Pacing is well controlled. E. The title, if desired, is original. F. Flows so smoothly, the reader hardly thinks about it.	⑤ *The writer of this paper speaks directly to the reader in a manner that is individual, compelling, engaging, and shows respect for the audience.* A. Uses topic details, and language to strongly connect with the audience. B. Purpose is reflected by content and arrangement of ideas. C. The writer takes a risk with revealing details. D. Expository or persuasive reflects understanding and commitment to topic. E. Narrative writing is honest, personal, and engaging.
③ *The writer is beginning to define the topic, even though development is still basic or general.* A. The topic is fairly broad. B. Support is attempted. C. Ideas are reasonably clear. D. Writer has difficulty going from general observations to specifics. E. The reader is left with questions. F. The writer generally stays on topic.	③ *The organizational structure is strong enough to move the reader through the text without too much confusion.* A. The paper has a recognizable introduction and conclusion. B. Transitions often work well. C. Sequencing shows some logic, yet structure takes attention away from the content. D. Pacing is fairly well controlled. E. A title (if desired) is present. F. Organization sometimes supports the main point or story line.	③ *The writer seems sincere, but not fully engaged or involved. The result is pleasant or even personable, but not compelling.* A. Attempt to connect with audience is earnest but impersonal. B. Attempts to include content and structure to reflect purpose. C. Occasionally reveals personal details, but avoids risk. D. Expository or persuasive writing lacks consistent engagement with the topic. E. Narrative writing reflects limited individual perspective.
① *The paper has no clear sense of purpose or central theme. The reader must make inferences based on sketchy or missing details.* A. The writer is still in search of a topic. B. Information is limited or unclear or the length is not adequate for development. C. The idea is a simple restatement or a simple answer to the question. D. The writer has not begun to define the topic. E. Everything seems as important as everything else. F. The text may be repetitious, disconnected, and contains too many random thoughts.	① *The writing lacks a clear sense of direction.* A. No real lead. B. Connections between ideas are confusing. C. Sequencing needs work. D. Pacing feels awkward. E. No title is present (if requested). F. Problems with organization make it hard for the reader to get a grip on the main point or story line.	① *The writer seems uninvolved with the topic and the audience.* A. Fails to connect with the audience. B. Purpose is unclear. C. Writing is risk free, with no sense of the writer. D. Expository or persuasive writing is mechanical, showing no engagement with the topic. E. Narrative writing lacks development of a point of view.
Key Question: *Did the writer stay focused and share original and fresh information or perspective about the topic?*	**Key Question:** *Does the organizational structure enhance the ideas and make it easier to understand?*	**Key Question:** *Would you keep reading this piece if it were longer?*

(*Continued*)

FIGURE 4–4 (*Continued*)

6+1 Trait® Condensed Scoring Guide		
Word Choice: The use of rich, colorful, precise language that moves and enlightens the reader.	**Sentence Fluency:** The rhythm and flow of the language, the sound of word patterns, the way in which the writing plays to the ear, not just to the eye.	**Conventions:** The mechanical correctness of the piece; spelling, grammar and usage, paragraphing, use of capitals, and punctuation.
⑤ *Words convey the intended message in a precise, interesting, and natural way.* A. Words are specific and accurate. B. Striking words and phrases. C. Natural, effective and appropriate language. D. Lively verbs, specific nouns, and modifiers. E. Language enhances and clarifies meaning. F. Precision is obvious. ③ *The language is functional, even if it lacks much energy.* A. Words are adequate and correct in a general sense. B. Familiar words and phrases communicate. C. Attempts at colorful language. D. Passive verbs, everyday nouns, mundane modifiers. E. Functional, with one or two fine moments. F. Occasionally, the words show refinement and precision. ① *The writer struggles with a limited vocabulary* A. Words are nonspecific or distracting. B. Many of the words don't work. C. Language is used incorrectly. D. Limited vocabulary, misuse of parts of speech. E. Words and phrases are unimaginative and lifeless. F. Jargon or clichés, persistent redundancy.	⑤ *The writing has an easy flow, rhythm, and cadence. Sentences are well built.* A. Sentences enhance the meaning. B. Sentences vary in length as well as structure. C. Purposeful and varied sentence beginnings. D. Creative and appropriate connectives. E. The writing has cadence. ③ *The text hums along with a steady beat, but tends to be more pleasant or businesslike than musical.* A. Sentences get the job done in a routine fashion. B. Sentences are usually constructed correctly. C. Sentence beginnings are not ALL alike; some variety is attempted. D. The reader sometimes has to hunt for clues. E. Parts of the text invite expressive oral reading; others may be stiff, awkward, choppy, or gangly. ① *The reader has to practice quite a bit in order to give this paper a fair interpretive reading.* A. Sentences are choppy, incomplete, rambling, or awkward. Phrasing does not sound natural. B. No "sentence sense" present. C. Sentences begin the same way. D. Endless connectives. E. Does not invite expressive oral reading.	⑤ *The writer demonstrates a good grasp of standard writing conventions (e.g., spelling, punctuation, capitalization, grammar, usage, paragraphing)* A. Spelling is generally correct. B. Punctuation is accurate. C. Capitalization skills are present. D. Grammar and usage are correct. E. Paragraphing tends to be sound. F. The writer may manipulate conventions for stylistic effect; and it works! ③ *The writer shows reasonable control over a limited range of standard writing conventions* A. Spelling is usually correct or reasonably phonetic on common words. B. End punctuation is usually correct. C. Most words are capitalized correctly. D. Problems with grammar and usage are not serious. E. Paragraphing is attempted. F. Moderate (a little of this, a little of that) editing. ① *Errors in spelling, punctuation, capitalization, usage and grammar and/or paragraphing repeatedly distract the reader and make text difficult to read.* A. Spelling errors are frequent. B. Punctuation missing or incorrect. C. Capitalization is random. D. Errors in grammar or usage are very noticeable. E. Paragraphing is missing. F. The reader must read once to decode, then again for meaning.
Key Question: *Do the words and phrases create vivid pictures and linger in your mind?*	**Key Question:** *Can you FEEL the words and phrases flow together as you read it aloud?*	**Key Question:** *How much editing would have to be done to be ready to share with an outside source?* • A whole lot? Score in the 1–2 range. • A moderate amount? Score in the 3 range. • Very little? Score in the 4–5 range.
		**Grades 7 and Up Only: The writing is sufficiently complex to allow the writer to show skill in using a wide range of conventions.*

Source: Northwest Regional Educational Laboratory. Copyright 2010. Printed with Permission

- *No skill yet*—Provide picture books as models. Start simply and teach revisions as student progresses. Use idea prompts and structure frames or guides so the student can focus on the important content. Slowly take away scaffolding (student supports), let student create the whole piece.

Additional Resources

6+1 Trait® Writing: *http://educationnorthwest.org/webfm_send/140*

Assessment Strategy: *Written Language: Portfolio Assessment*

Strategy Description

Portfolio assessment involves the continuous and purposeful collection of authentic work products, which provide evidence of the student's efforts, progress, and achievements in one or more areas, completed over time, often spanning over years as artifacts are collected from grade to grade. Portfolios focus on the process as well as the product of learning rather than solely on the outcome, and may be final writing drafts, completed products, or works in progress. This assessment is appropriate for all grade levels from preschool through secondary grades. Time allotment will vary depending on the individual project.

Questions to Ask

Is the student able to:

- Display his/her range of skills?
- Show the processes used?
- Demonstrate the effort put into each work project?
- Clearly express his/her range of abilities?
- Demonstrate long- and short-term progress?

Assessment Preparation

It is important to determine the following before starting the portfolio process.

- Contents of the portfolio
- Who will select the portfolio items
- Intended audience
- Whether the portfolio should contain the student's best work, a progressive record of growth, or both
- Whether the portfolio should include only finished pieces or items in progress, such as sketches and revisions
- How and when entries will be selected
- How selected items will be related to learning goals and content standards
- What the portfolio will look like (e.g., the organization of the contents)
- How the portfolio entries will be evaluated
- To whom the portfolio will be passed (e.g., home to parents, from grade to grade)

Implementation

✓ Select and date the work sample items to be included in the portfolio.

✓ Collect and store several samples of each student's performance over time, either as papers kept in a folder or on audio or videotape, as appropriate.

✓ Have students compare old performance to new and discuss in terms of specific ratings (see Figure 4–5).

✓ Provide students with criteria for evaluating, monitoring individual student progress, and grading so they can be involved in monitoring and improving their performance (see Figure 7–17 later in the text).

✓ Align portfolio criteria to letter grades or points (see Figure 7–18 later in the text).

Special Considerations, Accommodations, Alternatives

- This is a useful method for assessing students with cultural and linguistic differences. It is particularly useful for students from immigrant families as the portfolio can be taken from one school to another, to provide evidence of students' progress.
- It is important to keep in mind that this is a flexible technique, and can be used to facilitate communication for students with special learning needs.

Next Step

- *Mastered*—The portfolio is an ongoing process; as each skill/concept is mastered, the next level should be introduced.
- *Emerging*—Use the portfolio as a means for students to evaluate their progress, to identify strengths and weaknesses, and learn to plan how to improve performance.
- *No skill yet*—The most basic work product can be submitted to the portfolio since the intent is to collect students' work to monitor ongoing progress.

FIGURE 4–5 Teacher, Peer, and Self-Assessment Checklist

	Self-Evaluation			Peer Evaluation		
Content	***Yes***	***No***		***Yes***	***No***	***Teacher's Comments***
1. Is each word group a sentence?						
2. Is each sentence worded clearly?						
3. Are descriptive words used?						
4. Is the main idea clear?						
5. Are more sentences needed to tell about the main idea?						
Organization						
1. Does the composition have a clear beginning, middle, and end?						
2. Are the ideas grouped into paragraphs?						
3. Are the sentences in a paragraph put in logical order?						
Mechanics						
1. Are capital letters used correctly?						
2. Are punctuation marks used correctly?						
3. Are words spelled correctly?						
4. Are tenses (present, past, or future) used appropriately throughout the composition?						
5. Is the handwriting neat and readable?						
6. Can this composition be improved? If so, how?						

Teacher: ______________________

Student: ______________________

Peer: ______________________

Additional Resources

Portfolio Final Evaluation: Teacher Rating (Grades 6–12)
http://www.teachervision.fen.com/tv/printables/07AAAM51.pdf

Assessment Strategy: *Written Language: Curriculum-Based Measurement*

Strategy Description

Written language ability can be assessed through repeated 3-minute writing samples using stimulus story starters or topic sentences. The number of words written correctly can be used as the criterion for monitoring progress. These timed writing samples (probes) are general assessments of writing skill rather than diagnostic assessments of specific writing deficits. This type of evaluation allows the teacher to base instructional decisions on direct, repeated measurement. This assessment is appropriate for all grade levels and can be administered individually or in a group. Allow approximately 5 minutes for administration and scoring.

Questions to Ask

Is the student able to write:

- A short piece with a sufficient number of words according to grade norms?
- A passage using correct spelling and grammar, at an adequate pace?

Assessment Preparation

- Obtain lined paper, pencils or pens, and a watch or timer that records seconds.
- For a writing CBM, prepare a writing prompt (story starter) based on the student's individual interests (refer to Figure 2–9).

Implementation

- ✓ Provide students with a lined sheet of paper and a story starter or topic sentence.
- ✓ Read the story starter to the students (see Figure 4–6).
- ✓ Have the students brainstorm ideas for writing for 1 minute.
- ✓ Next, tell the students to write for 3 minutes. If students stop before the 3 minutes are up, strongly encourage continued writing.
- ✓ At the end of the 3-minute period, tell students to stop writing and immediately collect their papers.
- ✓ To establish a baseline (students' present level of performance), administer three writing CBMs over a period of 1 week (e.g., administer one every other day). The administration of 3 CBM probes can provide a more reliable index of students' performance. Provide students with a new story starter or topic sentence for each CBM probe administration.
- ✓ Option: Provide students with a prewritten short story that focuses on written language skills, such as grammar or spelling (see Figure 4–7).

Scoring

- *Step 1*—For each administration, count the number of words written. Do not deduct credit for spelling errors. Include the story starter in the count, if it is repeated.
- *Step 2*—Divide total number of words written by 3 to determine words written per minute. If the student stops writing before the 3 minutes, count the number of words

written divided by the number of seconds used for writing these words times 60 = correct words per minute.

- Refer to Chapter 7 for how to score/chart, establish a baseline, and goal to monitor progress.

Scoring norms for writing CBM:

The following is the expected number of words written per minute (wpm) on a writing sample according to grade norms at the end of the school year at the 50th to the 75th percentile.

Grade 1 = 9–15 wpm
Grade 2 = 20–29 wpm
Grade 3 = 29–40 wpm
Grade 4 = 39–52 wpm
Grade 5 = 45–59 wpm
Grade 6 = 50–63 wpm
Grade 7 = 52–67 wpm
Grade 8 = 56–70 wpm (AIMSweb, 2008; Alper & Mills, 2001)

Special Considerations, Accommodations, Alternatives

- Although CBM/fluency measures based on national norms are used to monitor and plot individual student progress, comparisons can be made between students to determine how a particular student is functioning in relation to his or her age group or grade level peers, to establish a local norm; however, compare the test results of average students, not those above or below the average range.
- CBM computer software programs are available to collect, graph, and analyze student performance data and to evaluate progress toward annual IEP goals and objectives.
- Writing probes can also be a useful screening method to identify serious language problems with a more in-depth evaluation to follow, as needed.
- A writing CBM probe can be modified for beginning writers to track more discrete progress; providing credit for each correct letter or word sequence.

Next Step

- *Mastered*—Increase the level of skill of the probes administered.
- *Emerging*—Focus on increasing performance accuracy and/or rate.
- *No skill yet*—Extend instructional time, change a teaching technique or way of presenting the material, or change the grouping arrangement. Monitor the scores on the graph to determine whether the change is helping the student.

FIGURE 4–6 Sample CBM Writing Prompt

Today, a playful kangaroo hopped into our classroom and . . .

____

____

____

FIGURE 4–7 Sample Written Expression: Capitalization Probe

Directions: Circle the words that should *not* be capitalized, and draw a line under the words that *should be* capitalized.

It was drew's birthday - august 12, 2001. it was sunday, and there was no School, drew and his sister julie went to the Store to buy items for the party. they bought candy, ice cream chocolate layer cake with fluffy vanilla icing, soda, chips, and pretzels. On the way back home, they decided to walk to fifty-second street and stopped at mrs. smith's craft Store to buy balloons and ribbons to decorate the playroom, kitchen and porch.

Directions: Put in all of the commas, periods, and apostrophes that should be in the story.

It was Drew's birthday August 12 2001 it was Sunday and there was no school Drew and his sister. Julie, went to the store to buy items for the party They bought candy ice cream chocolate layer cake with fluffy vanilla icing soda chips and pretzels On the way back home they decided to walk to Fifty second Street and stopped at Mrs Smiths craft store to buy balloons and ribbons to decorate the playroom kitchen and porch

Assessment Strategy: *Written Language: Performance Assessment*

Strategy Description

Performance assessment of writing abilities measures students' competence on specific tasks that are meaningful to their life experiences and identifies developmental levels. This type of assessment also helps the teacher to develop meaningful instructional tasks and remedial interventions, to assess students' skill proficiency, and to monitor progress on an ongoing basis. This assessment is appropriate for all grade levels and can be administered individually or in a small group. Time allotment varies with the task.

Questions to Ask

Is the student able to:

- Follow directions and work with others on a project?
- Analyze a project and properly sequence the steps involved?
- Sufficiently demonstrate skill proficiency?
- Maintain attention and focus, and follow through to completion?

Assessment Preparation

- When developing performance assessment tasks, the teacher needs to consider what the specific performance to be evaluated will be, prepare the performance task, and devise a system for scoring and recording assessment results.
- Refer to Figure 4–8 for writing activity suggestions that incorporate many basic writing skills that are appropriate for assessment and for devising practical instruction-remedial procedures.
- Do a task analysis to break down the skills involved in the performance task; develop a checklist of these skills.

Implementation

✓ Provide students with a practical, meaningful task assignment and be sure that the instructions are specific and materials are easily accessible.

✓ Monitor how the student attacks the task and problem solves, and note the aspects of the task that are easily completed and those that are not mastered.

Special Considerations, Accommodations, Alternatives

- Performance tasks tend to be meaningful, to help the student see a direct connection between what, how, why, and how much learning takes place.
- For students who have language or learning differences, tasks should be individualized, geared to specific instructional levels, and modified to accommodate students' individual strengths and weaknesses. Be sure directions are clear, with color coding or picture cues provided, if needed.
- For students with special learning needs, activity-based performance tasks can help ease test anxiety; use a teach-test-(re)teach cycle.
- For students who are English language learners, communicate step-by-step procedures or project descriptions supported by diagrams.

Next Step

- *Mastered*—Challenge student with higher order thinking tasks and projects.
- *Emerging*—Provide guided instruction and supportive feedback; provide a skilled, supportive partner to assist.
- *No skill yet*—Provide clear, specific, sequential directions, monitor closely and provide feedback at each step.

FIGURE 4–8 Examples of Performance Assessment Tasks

Writing friendly letters, business letters, thank-you letters, inquiry letters, letters to the editor	Requires using salutations and closings; addressing an envelope with the correct postal abbreviations; capitalizing titles and places; punctuating, indenting, writing legibility, spelling, and so forth
Writing a story of a field trip, a family party, a special school event, a news happening, an article for the school paper	Requires using the writing process: preplanning, writing, revising, rewriting, editing, publishing; using indentation, topic and closing sentences, main idea, sequencing, summarizing, and so forth
Writing poems, a school play, a speech, a puppet show	Requires using direct quotes and punctuation: underlining titles, using exclamation points and colons, and capitalizing titles, the first line of verses, first word in a direct quote, and so forth
Writing descriptions, lists of items, recipes, directions, party invitation	Requires writing numbers, using tense and plurals, sequential organization, punctuation (e.g., using semicolons and commas for lists) and capitalizing proper nouns (e.g., holidays and street names)
Writing a resume, completing a job application, writing an advertisement	Requires knowing how to read and fill in a form, make an outline, write abbreviations, when to use hyphens and contractions, and so forth

SPELLING ASSESSMENT

Assessment Strategy: *Spelling: Informal Spelling Inventory*

Strategy Description

An informal spelling inventory (ISI) can be used to determine the approximate grade level proficiency for spelling words in isolation and to determine specific skills needing further evaluation. Teachers can construct their own ISI based on their spelling curriculum, using words taken from the basal spelling series, from spelling texts, from graded textbooks in basal and content area subjects, literature series, and trade books. This assessment is appropriate for students from kindergarten through the secondary grades and can be administered individually or in a group. Allow approximately 10 to 15 minutes.

Questions to Ask

Based on graded spelling curriculum, is the student able to spell words correctly:

- In isolation?
- In sentences?

Assessment Preparation

- Each ISI graded word list generally consists of 20 words for grades 2 through 8, with fewer words, generally about 15, for grade 1.
- To ensure random selection of these words, divide the total number of words at each random selection level by 20. For example, from a grade level word list of 300 spelling words based on the year's curriculum, dividing by 20 equals 15; therefore, include every 15th word in the ISI.
- For students in fourth grade and below, testing should begin with first-grade level words.
- For students in fifth grade and above, assessments should start with third-grade level words.

Implementation

✓ Dictate the list of words to the student; say the word, use it in a sentence, repeat the word.

✓ Provide a 7- to 10-second interval between words.

✓ Conclude the test when the student reaches a ceiling level, with six consecutive words spelled incorrectly.

✓ Use an error analysis technique with the ISI to provide additional diagnostic information. Use the inventory (see Figure 4–9) designed for a typical second- and third-grade spelling curriculum as a model for developing an inventory based on the student's grade level curriculum.

Scoring

- Independent level: 90% to 100% mastery
- Instructional level: 75% to 89%
- Frustration level: below 75%

Special Considerations, Accommodations, Alternatives

- Some students do better when the word is dictated only and not used in a sentence.

Next Step

- *Mastered*—Challenge students with the next level spelling list; practice skills by generalizing to writing complex sentences.
- *Emerging*—Teach strategies for learning and remembering words: patterns, families, mnemonic tricks, word walls, personal lists, and spelling on a computer.
- *No skill yet*—Focus on monosyllabic words and instruction on specific patterns or groups of words to help students understand a rule or generalization.

FIGURE 4–9 Dictated Spelling Test and Objectives

Spelling Word	*Spelling Objectives*	*Spelling Words Used in Sentences*
1. man	short vowels and	The *man* is big.
2. pit	selected consonants	The *pit* in the fruit was hard.
3. dug		We *dug* a hole.
4. web		She saw the spider's *web*.
5. dot		Don't forget to *dot* the i.
6. mask	words beginning and/or	On Halloween the child wore a *mask*.
7. drum	ending with consonant blends	He beat the *drum* in the parade.
8. line	consonant-vowel-	Get in *line* for lunch.
9. cake	consonant—silent *e*	We had a birthday *cake*.
10. coat	two vowels together	Put on your winter *coat*.
11. rain		Take an umbrella in the *rain*.
12. ice	variant consonant sounds	*Ice* is frozen water.
13. large	for *c* and *g*	This is a *large* room.
14. mouth	words containing vowel	Open your *mouth* to brush your teeth.
15. town	diphthongs	We went to *town* to shop.
16. boy		The *boy* and girl went to school.
17. bikes	plurals	The children got new *bikes* for their birthday.
18. glasses		Get some *glasses* for the drinks.
19. happy	short *i* sounds of *y*	John is very *happy* now.
20. monkey		We saw a *monkey* at the zoo.
21. war	words with *r*-controlled	Bombs were used in the *war*.
22. dirt	vowels	The pigs were in the *dirt*.
23. foot	two sounds of *oo*	Put the shoe on your *foot*.
24. moon		Three men walked on the *moon*.
25. light	words with silent	Turn on the *light* so we can see.
26. knife	letters	Get a fork and *knife*.
27. pill	final consonant doubled	The doctor gave me a *pill*.
28. bat	consonant-vowel-consonant	The baseball player got a new *bat*.
29. batter	pattern in which final consonant is doubled before adding ending	The *batter* hit a home run.
30. didn't	contractions	They *didn't* want to come.
31. isn't		It *isn't* raining today.
32. take	final *e* is dropped before	Please *take* off your coat.
33. taking	adding suffix	He is *taking* me to the show.
34. any	nonphonetic spellings	I did not have *any* lunch.
35. could		Maybe you *could* go on a trip.
36. ate	homonyms	Mary *ate* breakfast at home.
37. eight		There are *eight* children in the family.
38. blue		The sky is *blue*.
39. blew		The wind *blew* away the hat.
40. baseball	compound words	They played *baseball* outside.

Source: From *Teaching Students with Learning Problems* (8th ed.), by C. D. Mercer, A. R. Mercer, and P.C. Pullen, p. 345. Copyright © 2010. Reprinted by permission of Pearson Education Inc., Upper Saddle River, NJ 07458.

Additional Resources

Sylvia Greene's Informal Word Analysis Inventory
http://www.nifl.gov/readingprofiles/PF_SG_All_Docs.htm

Primary and Elementary Spelling Inventories
http://teams.lacoe.edu/documentation/classrooms/patti/k-1/teacher/assessment/spelling.html

Assessment Strategy: *Spelling: Phonemic Awareness Spelling Assessment*

Strategy Description

To determine whether young students have phonemic awareness, the teacher asks them to spell words that they do not already know, thus they must rely on invented spelling, the inner capacity to forge connections between letters and sounds. Analyzing students' invented productions can be an effective strategy for determining their word knowledge. This assessment is appropriate for students from the early primary to middle elementary grades, and can be administered individually or to a large group. Allow approximately 5 to 15 minutes.

Questions to Ask

Does the student have:

- An understanding of phonemic awareness?
- The ability to apply phonemic awareness to spell unfamiliar words?

Assessment Preparation

- Using Figure 4–10 as a model, develop a word list that is based on grade level vocabulary and spelling curriculum.
- Break words into phonemes and assign credit points.

Implementation

✓ Call out each word on the list at least twice, or as many times as the student requests.
✓ Tell students to spell each word, writing each sound they hear in the word.
✓ Tell students to write a dash (—) if they are unable to spell a particular sound in a word.

Scoring

- After all 10 words are dictated (or fewer if modifications are needed), count the number of reasonable letters written for each word.
- Compare the number of letters written to the phonemes in the word.
- Each word is scored according to the points designated at the right of each word. Points are assigned one point for each phoneme. Then the total number of points received is compared with the total number of possible points.

Scoring criteria/interpretation:

- Students who consistently write three or four letters have some ability to segment phonemes.
- Students who write nothing or string together letters indiscriminately have not learned to segment phonemes.
- Students who write only one or two reasonable letters per word are beginning to segment phonemes (Gillet, Temple, & Crawford, 2008).

Special Considerations, Accommodations, Alternatives

- Students with specific language learning disabilities may have particular difficulty breaking words into phonemes.
- Provide students with practice using manipulatives, such as block and hand clapping, to isolate and count individual sounds.

Next Step

- *Mastered*—Provide students with more advanced words and word patterns.
- *Emerging*—Review by using flashcards or word rings to reinforce the letter(s) that comprise each phoneme; have students tap out the phonemes before attempting to write the word (e.g., *cat*—/c/ /a/ /t/, tapping one finger as each phoneme is said).
- *No skill yet*—Practice identifying the first phoneme (onset) in a number of words (e.g., *pat, pan, pot, pin, pen, pun*) and ask what sound each word begins with (/p/), then do the same for the final phoneme; continue to practice finger tapping individual phonemes in small groups. Students who continue to have difficulty may need their auditory acuity and/or speech and language development assessed.

FIGURE 4–10 Procedure for Assessing Phonemic Awareness

Phonemic Awareness Word List

bite	(three phonemes: BIT = 3 points; BT = 2 points; B = 1 point)
seat	(three phonemes: SET or CET = 3 points; ST, CT = 2 points)
dear	(three phonemes: DER = 3 points; DIR or DR = 2 points)
bones	(four phonemes: BONS or BONZ = 4 points; BOS or BOZ = 3 points)
mint	(four phonemes: MENT or MINT = 4 points; MET or MIT = 3 points; MT = 2 points)
rolled	(four phonemes: ROLD = 4 points; ROL or ROD = 3 points)
race	(three phonemes: RAS, RAC, or RAEC = 3 points; RC or RS = 2 points)
roar	(three phonemes: ROR or ROER = 3 points; RR = 2 points)
beast	(four phonemes: BEST = 4 points; BES or BST = 3 points; BS or BT = 2 points)
groan	(four phonemes: GRON = 4 points; GRN = 3 points; GN = 2 points)
Total:	35 points

Source: From *Understanding Reading Problems: Assessment and Instruction* (7th ed.), by J. W. Gillet, C. Temple, and A. Crawford. Copyright © 2008 by Allyn & Bacon. Reprinted by permission.

Assessment Strategy: *Spelling: Curriculum-Based Assessment*

Strategy Description

A spelling curriculum-based measurement (CBM) is a procedure for determining students' accuracy and fluency in spelling. There are several options for determining spelling proficiency using a CBM. One method is to assess the number of vocabulary words from grade level curricular material that the student can spell within a specific period of time. Another type involves counting the number of words written in correct sequence. This extends beyond considering the word in isolation but considers units in writing and their relation to one another (words spelled correctly in a sequence). An additional type consists of measuring smaller units (spelling words broken into letters) which provides credit for partial competencies, credit for each letter in a word that is placed in the proper order. These spelling CBMs are most appropriate for students from kindergarten through the upper elementary grades and can be administered individually or in a group. Allow about 5 minutes for administration and scoring.

Questions to Ask

Is the student able to:

- Correctly spell words from the curriculum within a set period of time?
- Correctly write and sequence words or letters in words from the curriculum within a set period of time?

Assessment Preparation

- For the CBM spelling word list, the teacher randomly selects 15 to 20 words from the grade level spelling curriculum which can consist of spelling word lists, vocabulary from literature, or other subjects such as math, science, and social studies.
- Prepare for an alternative by constructing a spelling word probe which would consist of a list of words with a line for the student to fill in the coordinating missing word (e.g., homonyms, as noted in Figure 4–11).
- For the CBM correct word sequence, the teacher provides a writing prompt based on the student's interest (see Figure 4–12).
- For the CBM correct letter sequence, the teacher randomly selects three sets of six words from the grade level curriculum (see Figure 4–13).

Implementation

CBM Spelling Word List

- Present each student with lined, numbered paper.
- Provide directions and administer the spelling test by pronouncing each word on the list first in isolation, then in a dictated sentence, and again in isolation.
- Dictate the words at a pace of one every 7 to 10 seconds, or sooner if all students are finished. Stop the test at 2 minutes.
- Provide an alternative to the typical spelling dictation test using a spelling word probe in which the student will spell the missing word. Allow 1 minute for the spelling word probe.
- Note any error patterns. Chart and graph students' scores to determine the efficacy of instructional procedures and to plot progress.

CBM Writing Sample or Correct Writing (Word) Sequence

- Give each student a lined sheet of paper.
- Provide a writing prompt for each student.
- Have students brainstorm ideas for 1 minute before starting to write.
- Ask students to write for 3 minutes. If they stop before the 3 minutes are up, strongly encourage continued writing.
- Tell students to stop writing, and immediately collect their papers at the end of the 3-minute period. Score and graph results.

CBM Correct Letter Sequence per Minute (CLS)

- Provide each student with a lined sheet of paper.
- Dictate three sets of six words from the spelling curriculum.

- Dictate one word every 10 seconds, for the 3-minute probe.
- Score and graph results.

Scoring for CBM Spelling Word List

- Count the words written and subtract the number of words spelled incorrectly to determine the total number of words correctly spelled. Divide the total number of words spelled correctly by 2, to determine the correct words spelled per minute.

Scoring for Correct Word Sequence

- Count the number of words written correctly in sequence. A correct word sequence (cws) is two adjacent, correctly spelled words that are grammatically correct within the context of the phrase.
- Words at the beginning of the sentence must be spelled correctly and capitalized to be credited with one correct word sequence. Words at the end of the sentence must be spelled correctly and followed by the correct punctuation to be credited with one correct word sequence. Insert a caret (^) for a correct word sequence and an inverted caret (v) for an incorrect word sequence (insert the inverted caret before and after misspelled words).
- Divide the number of correct word sequences by the total number of sequences (possible number of cws) to get the proportion of correct word sequences.

Scoring for Correct Letter Sequence

- Credit 1 point and mark with a caret (^) the space before the first letter in the word, if the first letter is correct. Place a caret in the space after the last letter of the word, if the last letter of the word is correct.

  For each correct letter-pair, or sequence, written in the correct order, give 1 point (marked with a caret).
- Count the carets to determine the number of earned cls. The number of letter sequences within a word, plus the first and last letters, equals the total possible number of correct letter sequences (cls) in a word (King-Sears, 1998).

  For example, the word *truck* has six correct letter sequences:

  1. ^ t = the first letter sequence (space-letter)
  2. t^r = the second letter sequence
  3. r^u = the third letter sequence
  4. u ^c = the fourth letter sequence
  5. c ^k = the fifth letter sequence
  6. k ^ = the sixth letter sequence (letter-space)
- The total number of correct letters is divided by 3 to get the letter sequence per minute (lspm) (Alper & Mills, 2001; King-Sears, 1998).

Scoring

- Guidelines for letter sequence per minute (lspm) instructional ranges and projected goal ranges are as follows (Alper & Mills, 2001):

	Grades 1–2	*Grades 3–6*
Mastery	more than 60 lspm	more than 80 lspm
Upper instructional	40–59 lspm	60–79 lspm
Instructional	20–39 lspm	40–59 lspm
Frustration	less than 20 lspm	less than 40 lspm

- The following is the expected weekly growth rate for correct letter sequences (cls) (Fuchs, Fuchs, Hamlett, Walz, & Germann, 1993).

  Grade 2 = 1 to 1.5 cls

  Grade 3 = 0.65 to 1 cls

  Grade 4 = 0.45 to 0.85 cls

  Grade 5 = 0.3 to 0.65 cls

  Grade 6 = 0.3 to 0.65 cls

Special Considerations, Accommodations, Alternatives

- Each probe can be administered several times to provide a more reliable index of student performance.
- For students with specific learning disabilities, the correct letter sequence is a good way to recognize and track more discrete indications of progress as this form of the CBM is particularly sensitive to small, short-term student gains.

Next Step

- *Mastered*—Provide students with more challenging words, include those from basic skills and content area subjects; generalize from single words to spelling words in sentences.
- *Emerging*—Reinforce vocabulary words learned in writing activities; each time a word list probe is administered, include review words from previously mastered lists.
- *No skill yet*—Focus on phoneme segmentation; correspondence of sounds to letters; use repeated practice of these skills.

FIGURE 4–11
Sample CBM Spelling Word Probe

Directions: Write homonyms for the spelling words listed below.

here	____________	read	____________
see	____________	eye	____________
bye	____________	sun	____________
there	____________	way	____________
blew	____________	knot	____________
too	____________	hare	____________
knight	____________	break	____________
weak	____________	board	____________

Time: 1 minute
Number of correct words written: ____________
Number of incorrect words written: ____________

FIGURE 4–12
Example of CBM Correct Word Sequence

Model: ^The^playful,^ fluffy^ pup^ is^ happy^ to^ see^ his^ master.^ = 11
Example of errors: the plaful, flufie pup^ is hapy to^ see^ his master = 3
v v v v v v v v

FIGURE 4–13
Example of CBM Correct Letter Sequence

Word	**Student Spelling**	**Scoring**
cat	^c^a^t^	cls = 4
cat	kc^a^t^	cls = 3
cat	ka^t^	cls = 2

HANDWRITING ASSESSMENT

Assessment Strategy: *Handwriting: Error Analysis Assessment*

Strategy Description

Teachers can assess handwriting legibility (the clarity and readability of handwriting) and fluency (the rate of written production) by observing students as they write and by analyzing their writing samples. This assessment is appropriate for students from first through eighth grades and can be administered individually or in a group. Allow generally 10 to 15 minutes to assess this skill.

Questions to Ask

Is the student able to:

- Write legibly by correctly forming upper- and lowercase letters and numbers?
- Correctly align and space letters and words with accurate size and slant?
- Complete handwritten assignments within a reasonable period of time?

Assessment Preparation

- Choose a writing sample for the student to copy, generally one sentence is sufficient.
- An example of an ideal sentence to use that contains all the alphabet letters is: *The quick brown fox jumps over the lazy brown dog.*

Implementation

✓ Have students write three sample sentences. For each sample, they should copy the same sentence three times. Ask students to produce a sample of their usual writing, best writing, and fastest writing. For the usual sample, the writing should be done under typical, nonfatiguing conditions. When getting the best sample, students should be told to take their time and put forth their best effort. For the fastest sample, have students write the sentence as many times as possible within a specified period of time (e.g., 2 to 3 minutes).

✓ Analyze the writing samples for errors and patterns of errors (see Figure 4–14).

✓ Evaluate the three samples; focus on legibility and fluency (see Figure 4–15).

Scoring

Handwriting Skill	*Fluency Goal*
Freewriting	60% to 100% correct characteristics (letters/digits) per minute
Dictation	70% of freewriting goal
Near-point copying	75% to 80% of freewriting goal
Far-point copying	75% to 80% of freewriting goal (Hallahan, Lloyd, Kauffman, Weiss, & Martinez, 2005)

Special Considerations, Accommodations, Alternatives

Copying from the chalkboard or a text can be frustrating and difficult due to:

- Inattention or difficulty forming letters individually rather than as a connected series.
- Poor visual memory, which results in students copying letters in words one by one, rather than as whole words or even whole sentences.

- Lack of automatized skill in letter formation, requiring students to look several times at a single letter being copied to see how it is formed (Graham, Harris, & Fink, 2000).

Next Step

- *Mastered*—Once mastery has been reached, encourage practice for maintenance.
- *Emerging*—Have students practice writing strokes for forming each letter; use a "pencil space" between words to encourage proper spacing.
- *No skill yet*—Provide models to trace, provide trays of sand for students to trace letters with their fingers; create flashcards with letters traced in glue and have students touch the raised glue modeling as if they were writing would write the letter.

FIGURE 4–14 Checklist of Handwriting Skills

Readiness Skills	***Yes***	***No***	***N/A***	***Comments***
Moves hand up and down	____	____	____	__________
Moves hand left to right	____	____	____	__________
Moves hand backward and forward	____	____	____	__________
Connects dots on paper	____	____	____	__________
Traces dotted lines	____	____	____	__________
Traces geometric shapes	____	____	____	__________
Draws horizontal line from left to right	____	____	____	__________
Draws vertical line from top to bottom	____	____	____	__________
Draws vertical line from bottom to top	____	____	____	__________
Draws a forward circle	____	____	____	__________
Draws a backward circle	____	____	____	__________
Draws a curved line	____	____	____	__________
Draws slanted lines vertically	____	____	____	__________
Copies simple designs and shapes	____	____	____	__________
Names letters	____	____	____	__________
Identifies likenesses and differences in letters	____	____	____	__________
General Observations				
Adequate grasp of writing instrument	____	____	____	__________
Proper slant of paper	____	____	____	__________
Appropriate posture when writing	____	____	____	__________
Even pencil pressure	____	____	____	__________
Handwriting size adjusted for a given paper	____	____	____	__________
Neat writing in final copy	____	____	____	__________
Handwriting evaluated by student according to established criteria	____	____	____	__________
Letter Formation, Alignment, Line Quality				
Closed letters are closed	____	____	____	__________
Looped letters are looped	____	____	____	__________
Straight letters are not looped	____	____	____	__________
Dotted letters (*j*/*i*) are dotted directly above	____	____	____	__________
Crossed letters (*x*/*t*) are crossed accurately	____	____	____	__________
*M*s and *N*s have the correct number of humps	____	____	____	__________
*Y*s and *U*s are clearly differentiated	____	____	____	__________
Connecting strokes of *v* and *y* are clearly not *rv* and *ry*	____	____	____	__________
Uppercase letters are accurately formed	____	____	____	__________
Numbers are correctly formed	____	____	____	__________
Letters are not reversed	____	____	____	__________
Lowercase letters begin on line (unless they follow *b*, *o*, *v*, or *w*)	____	____	____	__________
Lowercase letters (except *b*, *o*, *v*, and *w*) end on the line	____	____	____	__________
Letters are aligned correctly (not formed within line boundaries)	____	____	____	__________
Letter line quality is not too heavy or too light	____	____	____	__________

FIGURE 4–15 Analysis of Handwriting Errors

Directions: Score 2 for developed skill, score 1 for emerging skill, 0 for no attempt.

I. Letter formation

A. Capitals (score each letter 1 or 2)

A _____	G _____	M _____	S _____	Y _____
B _____	H _____	N _____	T _____	Z _____
C _____	I _____	O _____	U _____	
D _____	J _____	P _____	V _____	
E _____	K _____	Q _____	W _____	
F _____	L _____	R _____	X _____	Total _____

B. Lowercase (score by groups) Score (1 or 2)

1. Round letters
   a. Counterclockwise: *a, c, d, g, o, q* _____
   b. Clockwise: *k, p* _____
2. Looped letters
   a. Above line: *b, d, e, f, h, k, l* _____
   b. Below line: *f, g, j, p, q, y* _____
3. Retraced letters: *u, t, i, w, y* _____
4. Humped letters: *h, m, n, v, x, z* _____
5. Others: *r, s* _____ Total _____

C. Numerals (score each number 1 or 2)

1. _____	4. _____	7. _____	10–20. _____	
2. _____	5. _____	8. _____	21–99. _____	
3. _____	6. _____	9. _____	100–1,000. _____	Total _____

II. Spatial relationships Score (1 or 2)

A. Alignment (letters on line) _____
B. Uniform slant _____
C. Size of letters
   1. To each other _____
   2. To available space _____
D. Space between letters _____
E. Space between words _____
F. Anticipation of end of the line [hyphenates, moves to next line] _____ Total _____

III. Rate of writing [letters per minute] Score (1 or 2)

Grade			
	1:20	4:45	7 and above:75
	2:30	5:55	
	3:35	6:65	

Total _____

Scoring	*Underdeveloped Skill*	*Developing Skill*	*Developed Skill*
I. Letter formation			
A. Capitals	36	39	40+
B. Lowercase	7	10	11+
C. Numerals	12	18	19+
II. Spatial relationships	7	10	11+
III. Rate of writing	1	2	6+

Source: From *Informal Assessment in Education,* by G. R. Guerin and A. S. Maier. Copyright © 1983 by Mayfield Publishing Company. Reprinted by permission of the publisher.

Assessment Strategy: *Handwriting: Zaner-Bloser Evaluation Scale*

Strategy Description

The Zaner-Bloser Evaluation Scale is a holistic method of assessing manuscript and cursive writing to determine whether students' handwriting is significantly below average, average, or above average when compared with grade norms. This untimed evaluation measures students' penmanship compared to graded samples provided for comparison (see Figure 4–16). This assessment is appropriate for evaluating manuscript writing for first and second grades, and cursive writing for second through sixth grades. Allow about 15 to 20 minutes to assess this skill.

Questions to Ask

Based on handwriting samples, does the student have grade level skill in:

- Letter formation, slant, alignment?
- Proportion, spacing, line quality?

Assessment Preparation

- Obtain lined paper, writing utensils, and the Zaner-Bloser sentence samples.

Implementation

✓ Write a sentence from the evaluation guide on the chalkboard.
✓ Have the student practice writing the sentence written on the chalkboard on a lined paper.
✓ Give the student lined paper to copy the Zaner-Bloser sample sentence. Ask the student to use best handwriting to write the sentence again.
✓ Allow the student 2 minutes to complete the task.
✓ Compare the student's writing with the five examples on the evaluation guide, using the keys to legibility. The keys are the characteristics of handwriting: shape, size, spacing, and slant (see Figure 4–16).
✓ Repeat this evaluation procedure at least once each grading period.

Scoring

- Evaluation Guide

  Excellent: all keys acceptable

  Good: at least three keys acceptable

  Average: only two keys acceptable

  Poor: only one or no key acceptable

- Handwriting fluency rates are as follows:

Grade	*Lines per Minute*
1	2
2	3
3	38
4	45
5	60
6	67 (Zaner Bloser, 2008)

Special Considerations, Accommodations, Alternatives

- To get the most information benefit from using this scale, carefully analyze students' errors (using examples of common errors noted earlier) to formulate a remedial program.

Next Step

- *Mastered*—Provide opportunities for skilled handwriting practice.
- *Emerging*—Provide handwriting models and opportunities for guided practice.
- *No skill yet*—Provide good models of single letters and numbers for students to trace, supports such as guidelines on paper, dotted patterns of letters to copy, pencil grips, and markers to guide spacing between words.

FIGURE 4–16 Zaner-Bloser Evaluation Scale

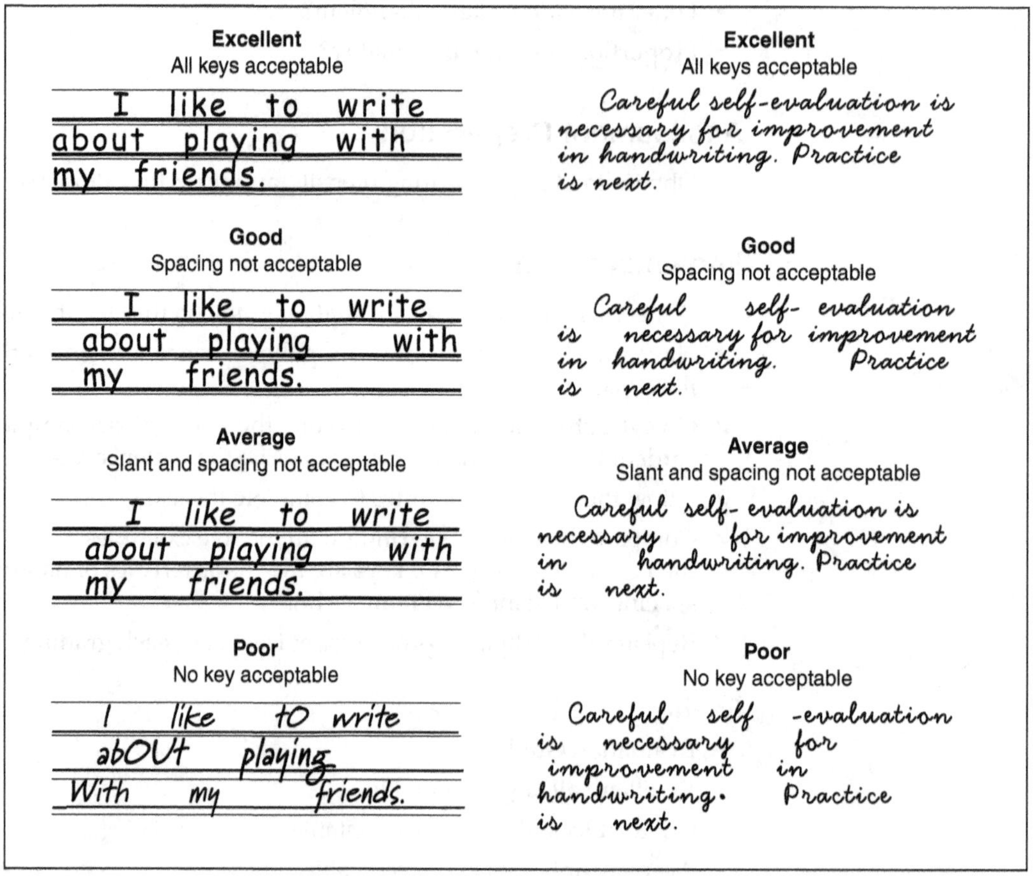

Source: From Zaner-Bloser Evaluation Scale. (2008). Columbus, OH: Zaner-Bloser Educational Publishers. Used with permission from Zaner-Bloser, Inc.

REFERENCES

Adelman, O., & Vogel, S. (2003). Lifestyle issues of adults with learning disabilities, 8–15 years after college. In S. Vogel, F. Sharoni, & D. Dagan (Eds.), *Learning disabilities in higher education and beyond: An international perspective.* Toronto: York Press.

Alper, S., & Mills, K. (2001). Nonstandardized assessment in inclusive school settings. In A. S. Alper, D. L. Ryndak, & C. N. Schloss (Eds.), *Alternate assessment of students with disabilities in inclusive settings* (pp. 54–74). Needham Heights, MA: Allyn & Bacon.

Fuchs, L. S., Fuchs, D., Hamlett, C., Walz, L., & Germann, G. (1993). Formative evaluation of academic progress: How much growth can we expect? *School Psychology Review, 22,* 27–49.

Gillet, J. W., Temple, C., & Crawford, A. (2008). *Understanding reading problems: Assessment and instruction* (7th ed). Boston: Pearson.

Graham, S., Harris, K. R., & Fink, B. (2000). Is hand-writing causally related to learning to write? Treatment of handwriting problems in beginning writers. *Journal of Educational Psychology, 92,* 620–633.

Guerin, G. R., & Maier, A. S. (1983). *Informal assessment in education.* Palo Alto, CA: Mayfield.

Hallahan, D. P., Lloyd, J. W., Kauffman, J. M., Weiss, M. P., & Martinez, E. A. (2005). *Learning disabilities: Foundations, characteristics, and effective teaching* (3rd ed.). Boston: Allyn & Bacon.

King-Sears, M. E. (1998). *Curriculum-based assessment in special education.* San Diego, CA: Singular Publishing Group.

Lerner, J., & Johns, B. (2009). *Learning disabilities and related mild disabilities: Characteristics, teaching strategies, and new directions* (11th ed.). Boston: Houghton Mifflin.

Mercer, C. D., Mercer, A. R., & Pullen, P. C. (2010). *Teaching students with learning problems* (8th ed.). Upper Saddle River, NJ: Merrill/Prentice Hall.

Mirkin, P. K., Deno, S. L., Fuchs, L., Wesson, C., Tindal, G., Marston, D., & Kuehnle, K. (1981). *Procedures to develop and monitor progress on IEP goals.* Minneapolis, MN: University of Minnesota, Institute for Research on Learning Disabilities.

Zaner-Bloser Evaluation Scale. (2008). Columbus, OH: Zaner-Bloser Educational Publishers.

Chapter 5

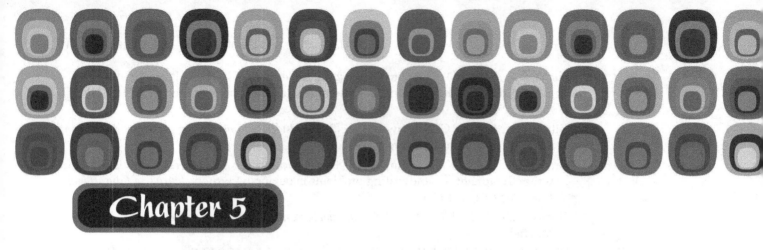

Mathematics and the Content Areas Assessment

INTRODUCTION

A major purpose of educational assessment is to direct teaching practice. Assessment in math and the content area subjects needs to be developmentally appropriate, systematic, and language and culturally sensitive. Mathematics is a multidimensional, cumulative process in which skills and concepts become increasingly complex and abstract. Skills learned during the earliest school years provide the foundation for mathematical conceptual development as well as the structure for subsequent higher level skill mastery. For example, the concept of fractional parts that is introduced at the readiness level when the teacher cuts an apple in half is continued throughout elementary and secondary grades as students learn to compute all basic operational functions with fractions and apply these concepts in advanced algebraic and geometric formats. This chapter provides assessments that focus on your classroom curriculum and emphasize a performance-based approach.

Content area assessment should be a fluid, ongoing process that is instructionally embedded; contextual and realistic rather than contribed or staged; developmentally and linguistically appropriate; and intrinsically linked to program goals. The assessments covered in this chapter help us, as classroom teachers, meet the instructional needs of our students by determining students' background knowledge, by identifying what students need to know, by monitoring how well they are acquiring new skills and concepts, by ascertaining how fluent and proficient they are in applying what they have learned, and by noting whether they can generalize mastered skills to new situations.

MATHEMATICAL ASSESSMENT

Assessment Strategy: *Mathematics Language Assessment*

Strategy Description

An important step in the assessment process is to determine students' understanding of mathematical terms, both in written and oral form. The ability to correctly use and understand the language of mathematics is a critical developmental skill. This assessment is appropriate for the elementary and secondary grades and is generally administered on a one-to-one basis. Allow approximately 15 to 20 minutes to assess this skill.

Questions to Ask

Does the student:

- Comprehend the meaning of commonly used math terms (e.g., *equivalent, place value, minus*)?
- Recognize the multiple meanings of math terms, such as the same word used as a noun ("color the *circle* red") and as a verb ("*circle* the group of four")?
- Grasp the meaning of synonyms that describe the same operation (e.g., *subtract, minus, take away*)?
- Understand and distinguish between operational signs and symbols (e.g., +, −, *x*, < or >)?
- Have the ability to use math language appropriately to ask clear questions and, if needed, to say he/she is confused while solving math tasks?

Assessment Preparation

- Develop a list of math terms and concepts specific to the student's grade level.
- Design a set of instructions using key terms and concepts for the student to follow.
- Develop a series of word problems that incorporate key terms and concepts.
- Have manipulatives available for identification of key math terms, such as a calendar, clock, cards with math terms, numbers, items to count, measuring tape, shapes, colors.

Implementation

✓ Have students demonstrate their understanding of and ability to use math terms correctly (see Figure 5–1 for checklist).

✓ Have students demonstrate their ability to communicate using math terms (e.g., explain how they solved the problem, what difficulties they experienced while solving the problem, and what they learned during the process) by writing in a journal (see Figure 5–2).

Special Considerations, Accommodations, Alternatives

- Manipulatives can be used for this assessment; however, be sure that students describe what they are doing with these items as they use them for problem solving.
- Using words to describe math is a difficult skill especially for students who are English language learners or who have language-based learning disabilities; provide verbal prompts, as needed.

Next Step

- *Mastered*—Promote language as a problem-solving tool; have students read and restate the math word problem, and discuss the problem with peers.
- *Emerging*—Reinforce new vocabulary through visual aids and manipulatives; build on prior knowledge.
- *No skill yet*—Restate math language questions in different ways, paraphrase, use visual aids and draw schematic diagrams to introduce and reinforce new vocabulary. Use terms clearly and consistently, and introduce only two or three words per lesson. Use symbols and manipulatives to teach confusing terms such as GCF and LCM.

FIGURE 5–1 Math Language Checklist

The student can identify:	**Mastered**	**Emerging**	**Unmastered**
Relationship words			
• Temporal: before, after, first, last, early, late	______	______	______
• Positional: top, bottom, under, over, on, in, off, over, under	______	______	______
• Comparative: greater than, less than, bigger, shorter, longer	______	______	______
• Spatial: long, narrow, near, far, tall, short, thin, fat, wide, narrow	______	______	______
• Sequential: next, between, after, in front of, behind, before	______	______	______
Number words			
• Counting: numbers starting with 1, 2, 3, 4, 5, . . .	______	______	______
• Whole: numbers including zero—0, 1, 2, 3, 4, 5, . . .	______	______	______
• Cardinal: the total of a set (e.g., //// = 4)	______	______	______
• Ordinal: identify a position—first, second, third, . . .	______	______	______
Time words			
• General time: morning, early, night, noon, tomorrow, day, yesterday	______	______	______
• Clock words: watch, hour hand, seconds, long hand, minutes, alarm clock	______	______	______
• Calendar words: date, birthday, vacation, holiday, days of the week, month, annual, yesterday, names of the seasons	______	______	______
Shape words			
• Round, corners, flat, triangle, cylinder, sides, square, rectangle	______	______	______
Symbols of math			
• Ideas: numbers (1, 2, 3), elements (X, Y)	______	______	______
• Relations: $=$, $\neq$, $<$, $>$	______	______	______
• Operations: $+$, $-$, $\times$, $\div$	______	______	______
• Punctuation	______	______	______
decimal point: \$4.50	______	______	______
comma: 4,500	______	______	______
parentheses: $7 + (9 - 4) = 12$	______	______	______
brackets: $5 \times [2 + (3 + 2)] = 35$	______	______	______
braces $(C = \{2, 4, 6\})$	______	______	______

FIGURE 5–2 Math Journal Writing

Your math journal is for you to think about and write about your experience with math.

- Ideas for math topics include: ______

Select a math problem that you solved successfully.

- What processes did you use to solve the problem? ______
- What part(s) were easy for you? ______
- What part(s) were difficult for you? ______
- What did you learn? ______

Select a math problem that you could not solve successfully.

- What part of the problem was difficult for you? ______
- What area(s) were you able to solve successfully? ______
- What would you need to solve this problem? ______

Describe what you learned today.

- What did you learn to do during today's lesson? ______
- What was difficult about today's lesson? ______
- What do you like about working by yourself when solving problems? ______
- What do you like about working in a group to solve problems? ______

Write about how you learn.

- Do you like working on math problems? ______
- What could be done to help you during math class? ______
- How are you doing with math homework? ______
- How could you use the math skills you learned outside of school? ______

Assessment Strategy: *Mathematics Attitude and Disposition Assessment*

Strategy Description

This assessment, involving an oral interview, is a means of assessing students' social-emotional reaction to math by determining whether they have a negative attitude toward math tasks or feel anxious when working with math equations or word problems. This assessment is appropriate for the elementary and secondary grades and can be administered individually or in a group. Allow generally 15 to 20 minutes to assess this skill.

Questions to Ask

Does the student:

- Seem to be anxious, depressed, or respond negatively when working on math-related tasks?
- Have difficulty concentrating when solving math problems or during instruction, or have difficulty remembering number facts, rules, or directions?
- Become overly dependent on the teacher, seeking an excessive amount of help with math tasks?
- Actively avoid working on math, yet not avoid other subjects?

Assessment Preparation

- Determine appropriate times and math-related activities to observe.
- Develop interview questions to ask the students based on the observation.

Implementation

✓ Observe the student during math period and while working on math assignments, both individually and in groups (see Figure 5–3).

✓ Interview the student about his or her feelings toward math. Have student complete the self-report on attitude toward math (see Figures 5–4 and 5–5).

FIGURE 5–3 Math Attitude and Disposition: Teacher Observation Checklist

Does the student:

_____ Perform poorly on math tests?
_____ Display a serious dislike and avoidance of math activities?
_____ Appear apathetic?
_____ Have low self-confidence?
_____ Lack motivation; give up easily or make excuses?
_____ Demonstrate classroom behavior problems?
_____ Erase excessively?
_____ Become inattentive or fidgety during math class?
_____ Try to avoid doing any math tasks?
_____ Fail to do math assignments?
_____ Submit assignments that are incomplete or done carelessly?
_____ Complete work at an extremely slow pace or in a compulsive manner?
_____ Tend to make self-deprecating comments about his or her poor ability?
_____ Make excuses to avoid doing the math assignments; show reluctance to even attempt math task?
_____ Demonstrate symptoms of anxiety or phobia (e.g., rapid heart rate, increased breathing pace, stomach upset, onset of tension headaches, dizziness)?

FIGURE 5–4 Math Affective Self-Report Inventory

Do you enjoy mathematics? _____
How do you feel in math class? _____
What was the best thing you learned today or this week in math class? _____
What type of math activities do you like most? _____
What math activities do you do particularly well? _____
What types of math activities do you like least? _____
What math activities are the hardest for you? _____
What would you like more help with in math? _____
Describe one particular problem that you found difficult. _____
What do you do when you can't solve a math problem? _____
What errors do you make most often in math? _____
Why do you think you make math errors? _____
Tell about one new problem that you can now solve. _____
How do you use math outside of school? _____
Do you feel you learn best in math when:
You discover the answer by trial and error? _____
Tasks are demonstrated? _____
You have a model? _____
You use manipulatives (e.g., sticks, a number line)? _____
Do you learn best when you work:
With a whole class? _____
In small groups? _____
By yourself? _____
How could math class be improved? _____

Special Considerations, Accommodations, Alternatives

- Students who are English language learners may have difficulty describing problems they are experiencing; this difficulty may also be mistaken for general math anxiety rather than generalized difficulty and anxiety related to language.
- Students with language-based learning disabilities often have difficulty with math terms, symbols, and processes, specifically with identification, retention, and application.
- Math anxiety can block initial learning and hinder working memory needed for application, generalization, and the ability to transfer learning (Cavanagh, 2007).

Next Step

- *Mastered*—Encourage students to make personal goals and track their progress; check for understanding; when errors are evident, teach corrective strategies.
- *Emerging*—Provide interesting, authentic, and challenging opportunities for success, as easy successes are not necessarily helpful; performance feedback or verbal prompting used appropriately can foster positive dispositions.
- *No skill yet*—Provide math tasks related to student interest; personalize math tasks with student's name, interests, real events, and so forth. Provide scaffolding and sufficient support so that the student experiences success so they feel good about the math process.

FIGURE 5–5 Math Performance Inventory

Student seems to exhibit:	**Consistently**	**Inconsistently**	**Not Evident**
• Confidence in working with math equations and word problems			
• Flexibility in arriving at strategies and solutions			
• Perseverance by making several attempts at problem solving			
• Curiosity in investigating various ways to tackle a problem			
• Reflection in thinking of all possible methods and aspects of a problem			
• Skill in applying math strategies to real-life situations			
• Appreciation of the importance of mathematics in everyday activities			

Assessment Strategy: *Mathematics: Oral Interview and Task Analysis*

Strategy Description

An oral math interview is an effective method for gaining insight into how students approach a task, process information, and use mathematical strategies. The student explains the steps necessary to reach the final product. This method of assessment helps to uncover misunderstandings and faulty procedures, and allows the teacher to hear and identify specific problems—to better understand students' thought processes, to identify whether steps were omitted or whether the sequence was incorrect—while students "think aloud" the solution to math problems. The interview is also useful for planning instruction. This assessment is appropriate for the elementary and secondary grades and is generally administered on a one-to-one basis. Allow generally 15 to 20 minutes to assess this skill.

Questions to Ask

Based on graded math curriculum, is the student able to:

- Conceptualize the steps required to solve word problems and math equations without omitting or reordering steps?
- Explain the thought process as he/she analyzes, plans, calculates, and carries out the steps to solve equations and/or word problems?

Assessment Preparation

- Identify the area of difficulty so that the oral interview assessment can be focused. This can be done by observing the student in class and identifying errors made on math worksheets, math homework assignments, and standardized and informal classroom tests.
- Have all materials ready, such as paper or a chalkboard where math equations or word problems are prewritten, so the teacher can closely observe and listen to the student rather than fumble for items during the interview.
- Plan to begin the process slowly and on a small scale. The first interview session should be short, and subsequant sessions should increase in length and complexity as the student becomes more experienced in this process. Have an audio tape recorder available to record the interview, so it can be analyzed later.
- Since the interview is one on one, keep in mind both length of time and the environment so the process runs smoothly and is free of distractions.

Implementation

✓ Explain the purpose of the interview, make sure the student is comfortable, and establish rapport. If a tape recorder is used, be sure the student is aware that the session is taped.

✓ Analyze the types of problems (refer to upcoming section on error analysis, see page 126); choose one of the simplest or easiest types of errors to begin. Use a task analysis approach (see Figure 5–6) making sure to choose the first type of problem according to its hierarchy in a task analysis. For example, if the student is making errors on addition, multiplication, and division equations, choose the addition equation first and then move to multiplication before division and then more difficult equations.

✓ Provide student with a problem to solve on paper or on a chalkboard while the teacher orally explains the process. (Note: This is a diagnostic exercise, not an instructional lesson.)

✓ Stop if the student begins to write the problem without orally explaining the process or steps involved. Ask the student, "Why did you do that?"

✓ Allow the student to solve the problem without making comments, providing clues, asking leading questions, or answering questions. If the student asks a question or seeks guidance, stress the importance of trying to solve the problem without help.

✓ Reinforce student's responses by nodding, smiling, and providing affirming feedback (e.g. "good work"). If the student's response is unclear, repeat the last statement and pause as if waiting for the student to continue, or ask the student to think of another way to describe the process.

✓ Guide students through the process as they solve an equation or word problem by asking leading questions (e.g., "Can you tell me why you put the number 3 there?") and giving prompts, particularly if this is a new procedure or the student's response lacks sufficient detail.

✓ Have the student self-evaluate own skills (see Figure 5–7).

✓ Continue until all problems are presented and orally explained by the student. Stop and reschedule for another time if the student becomes tired, distracted, or discouraged.

✓ Formulate a summary of the student's strengths and weaknesses in each skill area (see Figure 5–8).

Special Considerations, Accommodations, Alternatives

- Manipulatives can be used for this assessment; however, be sure students describe what they are doing with these items as they use them for problem solving.
- Using words to describe math is a difficult skill especially for students who are English language learners or who have language-based learning disabilities.

FIGURE 5–6 Sample Task Analysis Checklist

Task: Solve this addition equation: 571 +299

	Mastered	Emerging	Not Mastered
Prerequisite Skills			
Follows written and oral directions	______	______	______
Matches numerals	______	______	______
Visually discriminates numbers	______	______	______
Identifies numerals	______	______	______
Writes numerals	______	______	______
Identifies the addition sign	______	______	______
States the concept of adding numbers	______	______	______
States the concept of place value	______	______	______
Demonstrates the ability to regroup numbers	______	______	______
Computation Skills			
Identifies the equation as addition	______	______	______
Adds in right-to-left direction	______	______	______
Recognizes the starting point	______	______	______
Adds 1 and 9	______	______	______
Writes a 0 under the 9, in the ones column	______	______	______
Writes the 1 above the tens column	______	______	______
Moves to the tens place	______	______	______
Adds 7 and 9 and 1 carried into the tens column	______	______	______
Writes the 7 under the 9, in the tens column	______	______	______
Moves to the hundreds place	______	______	______
Adds the 5 and 2 and the carried 1	______	______	______
Writes the 8 under the 2 in the hundreds column	______	______	______

FIGURE 5–7 Math Self-Evaluation Questions

Have I:

_____ Carefully read/analyzed the problem or equation?

_____ Restated the problem?

_____ Determined what mathematical process is needed?

_____ Remembered from previous performances what I should do to be successful?

_____ Developed a plan?

_____ Underlined the relevant and crossed out irrelevant information?

_____ Visualized and drawn the problem?

_____ Organized multiple steps into a correct sequence?

_____ Selected the correct operation?

_____ Estimated the answer?

_____ Solved the problem?

_____ Carefully checked the answer?

Next Step

- *Mastered*—Provide opportunities for more challenging math tasks.
- *Emerging*—Provide corrective feedback and opportunities for guided practice; provide reinforcement activities working with a peer partner.
- *No skill yet*—Provide explicit examples; model the oral interview process on a one-to-one basis by providing visuals, manipulatives, and verbal prompts.

FIGURE 5–8 Math Skills Assessment Scale

Nov	Mar	June		
☐	☐	☐	**Beginning**	Solves problems and completes assignments with support; shows some understanding of math concepts; requires support to produce accurate work in learning to use math facts
☐	☐	☐	**Developing**	Completes required assignments; solves problems with assistance; needs assistance learning math concepts; needs support to produce accurate assignments; beginning to use math facts with manipulatives
☐	☐	☐	**Capable**	Completes required assignments; solves problems with occasional assistance; understands math concepts; mostly accurate on assignments; recalls and uses math facts
☐	☐	☐	**Strong**	Does some enrichment/extra credit math work; solves problems independently; applies previously learned math concepts; accurately completes assignments; confidently recalls and uses math facts
☐	☐	☐	**Exceptional**	Uses higher order thinking strategies extensively to solve problems independently; independently applies previously learned math concepts; demonstrates high level of accuracy on assignments; confidently recalls and uses all math facts

Assessment Strategy: *Math Error Analysis*

Strategy Description

A common way to grade math papers is to look at the answer and mark it correct or incorrect, calculate the percentage or rate of correct responses, and place the score or letter grade at the top of the paper. When a teacher uses this method of evaluation, important diagnostic information can be omitted. Math error analysis enables the teacher to (a) identify the types of errors being made; (b) figure out why the student is making these errors, and (c) determine if there is a pattern to the errors. It can also determine whether the error is the result of poor attention and carelessness or lack of knowledge. This assessment is appropriate for all grade levels. This math assessment can be administered in groups, but the error analysis needs to be individual. Allow approximately 15 to 20 minutes to assess this skill, depending on the number and complexity of the tasks to analyze.

Questions to Ask

Based on graded math curriculum:

- What type of errors is the student making?
- Is there a pattern of specific type of errors made?

Assessment Preparation

- Develop a worksheet of math equations and math problems from the student's math curriculum; include at least three to four items of each type. These math equations and problems can be obtained from recent class work, math workbook pages, homework; and worksheets can also be used to initially analyze the skills that have been mastered, those that are emerging, and those that have not yet been acquired.

Implementation

✓ Grade the math inventory or work sample. Identify types of errors that were made, focusing on the particular pattern of mistakes.

✓ Use a task analysis to break down the particular equation or problem into small steps or components if the reason for the errors is not obvious. (refer to task analysis, see Figure 5–6). This will help isolate the point in the mathematical process where the problem is occurring.

✓ Do an oral math interview with the student (refer to oral math interview on page 123). This allows the student to verbally describe the thought process used while working to solve the equation or word problem. This is an excellent way to determine how students tackle a problem, if they are using the correct mathematical operation, if they are correctly sequencing the steps, at which step in the process they become confused, if they are using good reasoning skills, and so forth.

✓ Analyze word problems, check to determine the magnitude of the discrepancy between correct and incorrect responses. Often, small discrepancies for large numbers indicate carelessness in the computational aspect of the task. Also, the magnitude of the response may indicate the selection of the wrong operation (e.g., the teacher expects the answer to be a small number because the requested operation is division but the student gives a large answer, which suggests he or she may have incorrectly used the multiplication process). Check whether the response could have resulted from calculating the wrong numerical data in the problem (e.g., when extraneous information is present).

✓ Conduct a reading miscue analysis to identify whether the student is using correct strategies for solving story problems. This analysis is used to identify reading behaviors that can interfere with problem solving, such as substituting incorrect words or omitting key words. Students first read the passage silently, and then orally. Errors due to decoding or comprehension breakdowns are noted. Miscue errors often affect the semantic or syntactic integrity of the passage (e.g., vocabulary or grammar errors). Thus, word problem inaccuracies may result from reading problems rather than inability to compute accurately or inability to accurately use computation in applied situations.

✓ Determine whether errors are systemic or sporadic. This is an important step in analyzing both written equation calculations and word problems. Systemic errors result from the consistent use of an incorrect number fact, operation, or algorithm. This type of error generally means that the student does not understand a rule or fact and consistently misapplies it. Sporadic errors are inconsistent and random with no particular pattern. This type of error usually indicates that the student is guessing because he or she has not learned or cannot remember the facts or rules to apply.

✓ Determine whether the error is procedural when the procedure or steps to solve the problem were not followed; factual when facts (e.g., multiplication) needed to solve the problem cannot be recalled; or conceptual when the error is due to a lack of understanding of the concept involved, which is not always as clearly evident or may be combined with procedural or factual errors.

✓ Analyze and categorize the errors by type. This step is needed to determine the pattern of errors that occurs consistently over several problems and frequently over time. Common types of mistakes include random errors (especially for students with achievement problems), incorrect algorithms (the most common for all other students), inaccurate number facts, and incorrect operations. More than one type of error may be noted for many math problems (see Figures 5–9 and 5–10).

FIGURE 5–9 Types of Math Errors

Basic fact error. Was the operation performed correctly but a simple calculation error made due to inaccurate recall of number facts? For example, the student doesn't know the multiplication facts:

$$6 \times 7 = 49$$

Regrouping. Was there confusion about place value, either carrying or borrowing numerals incorrectly or failing to regroup when appropriate? For example, the student writes the entire sum of each column without regrouping:

$$\begin{array}{r} 28 \\ +\ 8 \\ \hline 216 \end{array}$$

Incorrect operation. Was the wrong operation or process used during one or more of the computation steps, creating a different algorithm that resulted in an incorrect answer? For example, the student used the addition process to solve a multiplication equation:

$$\begin{array}{r} 34 \\ \times\ 2 \\ \hline 36 \end{array}$$

Incorrect algorithm. Were the procedures used to solve the problem inappropriate? Was a step skipped, were steps out of sequence, or was the operation performed inappropriately? For example, the student subtracted the smaller number from the larger number:

$$\begin{array}{r} 43 \\ -\ 29 \\ \hline 26 \end{array}$$

Directional. Although the computation is accurate, were the steps performed in the wrong direction or order? For example, the student used a left-to-right progression when calculating:

$$\begin{array}{r} [3] \\ 57 \\ +\ 85 \\ \hline 115 \end{array}$$

Omission. Is a step in the process missing or has part of the answer been left out? For example, the student failed to multiply in the tens place.

$$\begin{array}{r} 423 \\ \times\ 241 \\ \hline 423 \\ 846 \\ \hline 85023 \end{array}$$

Placement. Is the computation correct but the answer inaccurate because numbers were written in the wrong column? For example, the student misaligned numbers in the multiplication process:

$$\begin{array}{r} 72 \\ \times\ 31 \\ \hline 72 \\ 216 \\ \hline 288 \end{array}$$

Attention to sign. Was the operational sign ignored, causing the wrong mathematical operation to be performed? Did the student fail to attend to, understand, or perceive the correct shape of the computation sign, such as failing to note the difference between the addition sign (+), the subtraction sign (−), and the multiplication sign (×)? For example, the student confused the process, using the subtraction process on an addition equation:

$$\begin{array}{r} 765 \\ +\ 24 \\ \hline 741 \end{array}$$

Random error. Is the response incorrect and apparently a guess? Do the errors demonstrate a lack of basic understanding of the processes or skills being assessed? For example, the student made careless errors:

$$\begin{array}{r} 25 \\ +\ 43 \\ \hline 100 \end{array}$$

✓ Rate the developmental level of performance.

✓ Summarize and graph the types of errors. This is helpful for instructional planning purposes and for monitoring progress (refer to Chapter 6).

Special Considerations, Accommodations, Alternatives

- For students with specific learning disabilities, provide extra time, allow the use of a calculator, read directions and/or word problems aloud.

Next Step

- *Mastered*—Move to the next instructional level or increase the complexity of the problems.
- *Emerging*—Provide corrective feedback by identifying the type of errors, prompt or model the correct response, and follow up by providing practice activities.
- *No skill yet*—Ensure that instruction is aligned with ability and task variables; provide scaffolding with explicit directions, clear examples, and manipulatives.

FIGURE 5–10 Basic Math Computation and Problem-Solving Checklist

Does the student:	**Yes**	**Inconsistent**	**No**
Correctly carry ones and tens when adding?	______	______	______
Remember to carry tens and hundreds when adding?	______	______	______
Remember to regroup when subtracting tens and hundreds?	______	______	______
Regroup accurately when adding?	______	______	______
Regroup accurately when subtracting?	______	______	______
Perform the correct operation (e.g., adds, subtracts)?	______	______	______
Know basic addition number facts?	______	______	______
Know basic subtraction number facts?	______	______	______
Carry correctly when multiplying?	______	______	______
Regroup accurately when dividing?	______	______	______
Use place value correctly when dividing?	______	______	______
Calculate and record answers in right-to-left order?	______	______	______
Align numbers in correct columns?	______	______	______
Know multiplication number facts?	______	______	______
Cancel fractions correctly?	______	______	______
Reduce fractions to lowest common denominators?	______	______	______
Remember to identify the remainder?	______	______	______
Convert mixed numbers to fractions?	______	______	______
Read and comprehend word problems?	______	______	______
Comprehend and focus on the context of word problems?	______	______	______
Comprehend the question to be answered?	______	______	______
Comprehend the language and vocabulary of the problem?	______	______	______
Differentiate between relevant and irrelevant information?	______	______	______
Develop a plan before proceeding with a word problem?	______	______	______
Use the correct mathematical operation?	______	______	______
Identify the number and sequence of steps in word problems?	______	______	______
Perform all mathematical operations (e.g., $+$, $-$, $\times$, $\div$)?	______	______	______
Check calculations and whether question was answered?	______	______	______

Assessment Strategy: *Math Curriculum-Based Measurement*

Strategy Description

A math curriculum-based measurement (CBM) is a system of measuring student progress, specifically, an increase in the number of correct items on probes, which are timed samples that assess skill accuracy and fluency. When administered on a regular basis, CBM probes are an excellent means of progress monitoring. Graphing results can provide current, week-by-week data to track students' rate of learning and mastery of the content being taught. This assessment is appropriate from early elementary through the secondary grades and can be administered individually or to a group. Allow approximately 1 to 5 minutes per administration.

Questions to Ask

Is the student able to increase:

- The number of correct responses (accuracy) to regularly administered prompts (e.g., math equations, word problems)?
- The rate of response (fluency) to regularly administered prompts within a set period of time?

Assessment Preparation

- Prepare worksheets with computation problems randomly chosen from the entire year's curriculum (refer to Figure 5–11).
- When constructing math probes, at least three to four items per target skill should be included in order to provide an adequate sampling of the skills covered in the curriculum and for error analysis. This helps to determine whether the mistake was a random error or if a pattern of errors exists.
- Develop a checklist to track and monitor math skill progress (refer to Figure 5–12).
- Have a stopwatch available.

Implementation

✓ Give students a sheet of math equations. For a single-skill probe, only one type of equation (e.g., single-digit addition or subtraction) is on the probe sheet. For a multiple-skill probe, several types of equations (e.g., a mixture of several addition and subtraction equations not requiring regrouping, several requiring regrouping, several single-digit multiplication equations, and several single-digit division equations) are on the probe sheet.

✓ Tell students to start with the first equation on the top left row (show where to begin), to work across and then to go to the next row, and to continue without skipping any equations or rows.

✓ Tell students to complete the page as quickly and carefully as possible.

✓ Tell students who have difficulty with an equation to write their best answer, then move on.

✓ Monitor students to make sure that they are following directions and working in sequential order rather than randomly skipping around to solve the easier problems.

✓ Stop students at 1 minute or a few minutes longer (depending on the grade level).

✓ Score by counting the number of correctly placed digits.

Scoring

- Count the number of correctly written digits, even if the equation is not completed.
- Place value is important; the number must be in the correct column to be marked correct.
- Do not give points to numbers marked at the top of a number column used as reminders to regroup or carry (e.g., in the multiplication equation example below, the 2 carried in the tens place is not counted).
- Do not mark reversed or rotated numbers as incorrect.
- Do not give points for remainders of zero.
- Give full credit (the total number of correct digits) for the correct answer even if the calculation work is not shown.

- If the calculation work is shown but the answer is incorrect, give 1 point for each correct digit in the answer.
- Each correct digit is counted (rather than scoring 1 point for total correct answer) because digit count scores are more sensitive to changes in student performance (Tindal & Marston, 1990). On complicated equations, point values need to be assigned, with points assigned to each correctly performed step in the equation. For example, a correct digit (CD) is a digit in the equation that is in the proper place-value location, as follows:

			12r35 (4 CD)
		(2)	42 ⟌ 539
4	56	47	42x
+ 5	− 23	× 3	119 (3 CD)
9 (1 CD)	33 (2 CD)	141 (3 CD)	84 (2 CD)
			35 (2 CD) = (11 CD)

- To determine correct digits per minute (cdpm), divide the number of correct digits on a 2-minute probe by 2. If the student completes the probe in less than 2 minutes, calculate the correct digits per minute by dividing the number of correct digits by the number of seconds and multiplying by 60.

  Number of correct digits/Number of seconds × 60 = correct digits per minute (cdpm)

- The following cutoff levels can be used to determine whether the student is functioning at an independent, instructional, or frustration level (Alper & Mills, 2001):

	Grades 1–3	*Grades 4+*
Mastery	20+ cdpm	40+ cdpm
Instructional	10–19 cdpm	20–39 cdpm
Frustration	0–9 cdpm	0–19 cdpm

Students should master a minimum of one operation each year (Crawford, 2000). Researched math calculation scoring guides for basic addition, subtraction, multiplication, and division equations for math CBMs are provided below. Refer to Tables 5–1 and 5–2 for CBM math norms and expected growth scales; and refer to Chapter 7 for methods of graphing scores.

Grade Level Computation Scoring Guide

Objective	*Grade Level*	*Time*	*Number Completed*	*Number of Errors*
Addition facts (0–9)	2–3	1 minute	20–30 digits	2 or fewer
Subtraction facts (difference to 5)	2–3	1 minute	20–30 digits	2 or fewer
Addition and subtraction facts	3–4	1 minute	40–60 digits	2 or fewer
Addition: two columns w/regrouping	4–5	1 minute	40–60 digits	2 or fewer
Subtraction: two columns w/regrouping	4–6	1 minute	40–60 digits	2 or fewer
Multiplication facts	5–6	1 minute	40–60 digits	2 or fewer
Division facts	6	1 minute	40–60 digits	2 or fewer

Special Considerations, Accommodations, Alternatives

- Rate can vary depending on the student's age and motor skill competence (ability to form numbers), as well as the difficulty level of the task. Some students may have difficulty writing 100 digits in 1 minute. When writing numbers is difficult, the response mode should be changed. For example, the student can respond orally as the teacher records the response.

Next Step

- *Mastered*—Once a specific skill is mastered, move to the next skill level while maintaining focus on increasing accuracy and pace. Continue periodic review of mastered skills.
- *Emerging*—Provide opportunities for guided practice, have students track their progress by graphing their scores which provides motivation to "beat their best score." Once they become more proficient, begin to mix types of calculation skills (e.g., addition, subtraction, multiplication, or addition with and without regrouping).
- *No skill yet*—Start with one type of calculation equation or problem and reinforce until the student begins to progress. Allow the use of manipulatives and provide feedback. Assist students with graphing their progress, count the number of correct digits so students are reinforced for more discrete improvement (one digit at a time).

FIGURE 5–11 CBM Mixed Calculations Probe

Primary Level Math CBM

Directions: Fill in the missing number.

1 ___ 3	2 ___ 4	1 2 ___	2 3 ___	___ / 4 of 4
5 6 ___ 7	7 ___ 9	___ 6 7	4 ___ 5	___ / 4 of 8
___ 8 9	___ 4 5	___ 9 10	6 7 ___	___ / 4 of 12

Elementary Math CBM

Directions: Perform the calculations required for each of the following problems and write your answer in the space provided.

Addition:

1. 4 + 3
2. 3 + 5
3. 6 + 2

Subtraction:

4. 5 − 4
5. 9 − 7
6. 7 − 3

Missing addend:

7. 6 + _____ = 8
8. 3 + _____ = 9
9. 9 + _____ = 19

Two-digit addition:

10. 76 + 12
11. 54 + 45
12. 32 + 67

Two-digit subtraction:

13. 47 − 23
14. 56 − 42
15. 74 − 63

Write the numbers:

16. 4 tens, 3 ones _____
17. 5 hundreds, 7 tens, 3 ones _____
18. 8 thousands, 7 ones _____

Tell what place 5 holds:

19. 256 _____
20. 583 _____
21. 495 _____

Compare the numbers using > or <:

22. 64 _____ 46
23. 12 _____ 2 × 4
24. 26 _____ 24

Fill in the missing number:

25. 12, 13, _____ 15
26. _____ 29 30
27. 36 _____ 38

Secondary Math CBM

Directions: Fill in the missing number in the space provided:

1. 7 + 2 − ____ = 3
2. 6 × 47 × _____ = 282
3. 98 − 49 + ____ = 77
4. 81 − _____ + 37 = 46
5. 64 / _____ × 33 = 528
6. 45 / _____ + 26 = 31
7. _____ × 26 + 47 = 255
8. _____ / 9 × 25 = 125
9. 76 × 43 − _____ = 3,265

TABLE 5–1 Norms for Math CBM: Correct Digits

Grade	Percentile	Fall (CD)	Winter (CD)	Spring (CD)
1	90%	11	22	28
	75%	8	16	20
	50%	5	11	15
	25%	2	7	10
	10%	0	4	6
2	90%	19	35	41
	75%	14	29	31
	50%	10	22	22
	25%	7	15	16
	10%	5	10	11
3	90%	27	39	46
	75%	21	31	37
	50%	15	24	28
	25%	11	18	21
	10%	9	12	15
4	90%	60	76	87
	75%	45	60	70
	50%	33	44	52
	25%	24	33	38
	10%	16	23	27
5	90%	48	60	71
	75%	39	49	60
	50%	30	38	47
	25%	23	28	35
	10%	16	19	25
6	90%	51	65	66
	75%	38	49	50
	50%	28	36	34
	25%	21	26	26
	10%	16	20	20

FIGURE 5–12 Mathematics CBM Mastery Checklist

Concepts	Problem Numbers	Day 1	Day 2	Day 3	Total Score	Mastery 8/9
Addition facts (0–9)	1, 2, 3	_ /3	_ /3	_ /3	_ /9	_
Addition facts (10–19)	4, 5, 6	_ /3	_ /3	_ /3	_ /9	_
Subtraction facts (0–9)	7, 8, 9	_ /3	_ /3	_ /3	_ /9	_
Subtraction facts (10–19)	10, 11, 12	_ /3	_ /3	_ /3	_ /9	_
Missing addends (0–9)	13, 14, 15	_ /3	_ /3	_ /3	_ /9	_
Missing addends (10–19)	16, 17, 18	_ /3	_ /3	_ /3	_ /9	_
Add 2 digits (no regrouping)	19, 20, 21	_ /3	_ /3	_ /3	_ /9	_
Add 2 digits (regrouping)	22, 23, 24	_ /3	_ /3	_ /3	_ /9	_
Add 3 digits (1 regrouping)	25, 26, 27	_ /3	_ /3	_ /3	_ /9	_
Add 3 digits (2 regroupings)	28, 29, 30	_ /3	_ /3	_ /3	_ /9	_
Subtraction facts (2 digit − 1 digit)	31, 32, 33	_ /3	_ /3	_ /3	_ /9	_
Subtract 2 digits (no regrouping)	34, 35, 36	_ /3	_ /3	_ /3	_ /9	_
Write digits	37, 38, 39	_ /3	_ /3	_ /3	_ /9	_
Place value	40, 41, 42	_ /3	_ /3	_ /3	_ /9	_
Compare numbers	43, 44, 45	_ /3	_ /3	_ /3	_ /9	_

Time: 1 minute
Materials: Student—response sheet, pencils
Teacher—timer

TABLE 5–2 Weekly Growth Rates for Math CBM: Correct Digits

Grade	Realistic Growth Rates per Week (CD)	Ambitious Growth Rates per Week (CD)
1	0.30	0.50
2	0.30	0.50
3	0.30	0.50
4	0.70	1.15
5	0.70	1.20
6	0.45	1.00

Source: From "Formative Evaluation of Academic Progress: How Much Growth Can We Expect," by L. S. Fuchs, D. Fuchs, C. L. Hamlett, L. Walz, & G. Germann, 1993, *School Psychologist Review, 22,* 27–49. Reprinted with permission.

Assessment Strategy: *Math Portfolio*

Strategy Description

Math portfolios are used to document and assess mathematical ability by collecting a representative sampling of students' work over a period of time. Portfolios provide information about students' conceptual understanding of the math process; their problem solving, reasoning, creativity, work habits, and communication skills; as well as their attitude toward mathematics. An important aspect of portfolio assessment is that students participate in selecting portfolio content, have input in the criteria selected for judging merit, and have an opportunity for self-reflection and analysis. This assessment is appropriate for all grade levels. Time allotment varies according to the projects selected for inclusion in the portfolio.

Questions to Ask

When developing a math portfolio, the following must be determined.

- What should go into the portfolio (see Figure 5–13)?
- What is the criteria used to select the entries?
- Who will select the entries?
- When will the entries be selected?
- What should the portfolio look like, how should the entries be arranged?
- How will the portfolio entries be evaluated (see Figure 5–14)?
- Will the portfolio be passed from grade to grade?

Assessment Preparation

- Determine content guidelines for submission to the portfolio.
- Develop a rubric with evaluative criteria.

Implementation

Have student select, with teacher guidance, the items to be entered into the portfolio. Monitor for steady improvement in mathematical knowledge and skills. Considerations for improvement may include whether:

✓ Answers to the math problems are correct
✓ The process involved in solving the equations and problems is accurate
✓ There is evidence of organizational, sequencing, or placement errors
✓ Reading problems contributed to incorrect solutions
✓ Math strategies were used appropriately for solving problems
✓ Visual aids, such as pictures, graphs, tallies, were used
✓ A rubric should be used to determine progress

Special Considerations, Accommodations, Alternatives

- Portfolios are particularly good for communicating student progress to parents who do not speak English well because they contain actual work samples.
- Portfolios are also beneficial for children of migrant workers, military families, and other families who are transient because, as permanent records, they can be taken from place to place.

Next Step

- *Mastered*—Move on to the next topic following the same process, continue to monitor progress, reinforce student participation in portfolio piece selection.
- *Emerging*—Identify patterns of errors, use teacher modeling and guided practice for areas in need of improvement; provide student with further opportunities to demonstrate increased skill level proficiency.
- *No skill yet*—Based on the projects submitted to the portfolio, determine areas in need of remediation; break down steps that need to be mastered and, using task analysis, provide step-by-step directions and modeling. Once the particular skill has been acquired, provide opportunities for guided practice and reinforcement.

FIGURE 5–13 Math Portfolio Options

- Written math reports
- Learning log entries regarding problem-solving strategies
- Checklists of student progress in math
- Art illustrations related to math
- Photographs of student involved in math activities
- Printout of computer math work
- Write-up of structured observation during math period
- Math quizzes and assignments
- Group and individual math projects
- Student interest survey
- Journal entry, including self-assessments
- Photographs of students' math projects
- Artifacts from projects, such as designing new shapes
- Performance task using their concept of geometry
- Experiments that involve calculating probability
- Audiotape of students discussing how to finance a car or a home
- Videotapes of students collaborating on math projects
- Reports on math investigations
- Homework assignment samples
- Teacher conference notes
- Descriptions, diagrams, and graphs of math grades

FIGURE 5–14 Math Portfolio Assessment Checklist

Portfolio Scoring:

3 – consistently demonstrated
2 – usually demonstrated
1 – inconsistently demonstrated
0 – not demonstrated

Evidence that the student:

_____ Selects portfolio artifacts with a clear rationale
_____ Chooses artifacts that are relevant and appropriate
_____ Keeps materials well organized
_____ Includes artifacts demonstrating a variety of concepts and skills
_____ Can articulate why specific items are selected for inclusion
_____ Is able to state learning goals for each artifact
_____ Can note areas of strength and those in need of improvement
_____ Works cooperatively on portfolio projects
_____ Is able to summarize progress in reaching standards
_____ Demonstrates pride and an interest in making progress

Maximum points = 30

Assessment Strategy: *Performance-Based Assessment*

Strategy Description

Performance-based assessment is used to evaluate students' ability to develop a product or demonstrate a skill indicating proficiency. This method of assessment is effective for monitoring authentic skill mastery and for evaluating whether students can apply and generalize what they have learned in real-life situations. These assessment results are also used for program planning and evaluation. This assessment is appropriate for all students and administration can be individual or group. Time allotment varies according to the task.

Questions to Ask

When using a performance assessment, does the student:

- Have a workable plan for data collection?
- Work well individually; work cooperatively with a group of students?
- Access outside resources, such as the library, computers, the Internet?
- Use appropriate mathematical procedures and strategies?
- Organize information in a reasonable manner?
- Communicate ideas and results?
- Go beyond the immediate problem and ask new questions?

Assessment Preparation

- Construct the task—a problem to solve (see Figure 5–15)
- Develop a task description
- Determine whether the task can be completed during one or more time periods
- Determine whether the task will be an individual or a group project
- Gather materials required
- Assign specific performance criteria to tasks using a scoring rubric to rate performance

Implementation

✓ Ask the student to write a task question.

✓ Have student complete a performance-based assessment checklist (see Figure 5–16).

✓ Observe and note student performance, focusing on the following:

Did the student tackle the task in a logical, consistent manner?

How did the student deal with difficulties; was he or she able to problem solve?

Did the student ask further questions or make generalizations based on the task?

Does the final product demonstrate evidence of learning?

✓ The evaluation includes noting the progress students made through their choice of appropriate mathematical procedures and strategies, as well as in decision making, problem solving, observing, making connections, evaluating alternatives, drawing conclusions, applying, generalizing, and extending math skills and concepts to real-life situations.

Special Considerations, Accommodations, Alternatives

- For students with learning or language problems, provide explicit directions, pair with an able partner, assign tasks that are likely to result in success, allow extended time.

Next Step

- *Mastered*—Challenge the student with higher level questions, provide extra opportunities for the child to review, use, and expand on mastered skills.
- *Emerging*—Use teacher modeling to demonstrate how to address the task in relation to the project checklist, encourage students to work in groups and share their thought process with peers.
- *No skill yet*—Break task into smaller steps, scaffold support, use real-life situations from the students' own life to model or test performance skills.

FIGURE 5–15 Sample Performance Assessments

Role Play

Role play can be used to express skills across grade levels, across curriculum and content, individually, or in groups. An example is a teacher who assumes the role of a character who knows less than the students about the subject area. Students are motivated to convey facts or information.

Role play can be used to assess specific subject matter skills, such as math concepts by having students assume the role of a denominator, a numerator, a proper or an improper fraction, a number line, or an equivalent fraction; science concepts by having students assume the role of the life cycle; history by assuming the role of the explorers; reading or writing by assuming the role of characters in a literature story, and so forth.

FIGURE 5–16 Performance-Based Project Checklist

Student Response:

State the project goal: ______________________________

Describe the problem that needed to be solved: ______________________________

____

Identify how you used the following skills to solve the problem: classifying, observing, measuring, inferring/predicting, communicating, and experimenting: ______________________________

____

What did you find from your investigation? ______________________________

____

Provide an illustration of your findings: ______________________________

____

Teacher Checklist:

	Completely	***Partially***	***No Evidence***
Student was able to identify the goal of the project	_____	_____	_____
Student was able to describe the problem and strategy used	_____	_____	_____
Student used the scientific method for problem solving	_____	_____	_____
Student was able to describe the solution to the problem	_____	_____	_____
Student clearly articulated the project conclusion and verified results	_____	_____	_____

Possible points: 10

Assessment Strategy: *Mathematics: Life Consumer Skills Checklist*

Strategy Description

This mathematics checklist assesses students' basic financial, consumer, and employment survival and practical life skills. This assessment is appropriate for students in the middle and secondary grades. Administration can be either individually or as a group. Time allotment, if skills are to be demonstrated, may take several class periods.

Questions to Ask

Does the student:

- Have mathematical knowledge and skills needed to deal successfully with basic money, job, and daily life experiences?

Assessment Preparation

- Plan performance-based, simulated daily life skill and vocational tasks in which students can demonstrate their skill level.
- Have practical life items available, such as job and consumer applications, sample checkbooks, credit forms, consumer advertisements, mortgage and tax forms, items for measuring (e.g., tape measures, scales, calculators, thermometer), menus, alarm clocks, utility bills, transportation data (e.g., bus/plane/train/taxi schedules, street maps, a global positioning system (GPS), gas charge receipts).

Implementation

✓ Provide students with real-life consumer tasks requiring mathematical problem solving.

✓ Identify students' ability to determine the information needed, the necessary components required, and the mathematical process(es) to be used.

✓ Observe the efficiency and accuracy of the skills they use to resolve the problem (see Figure 5–17 for a checklist of skills to monitor).

Special Considerations, Accommodations, Alternatives

- Presenting students with real-life situations in commonly used language, using pictures or authentic items, helps them to experience success (Ruffins, 2007).
- Application of authentic mathematical problem solving can facilitate proficiency and the ability to generalize.
- Grouping students of various skill levels help to promote problem-solving success.

Next Step

- *Mastered*—Challenge students with more complex, multistep, authentic problem solving.
- *Emerging*—Help students remember the order of mathematical processes required for problem solving by providing direct instruction of memory strategies/mnemonics, such as for solving algebraic equations (e.g., FOIL stands for "First, Outside, Inside, Last").
- *No skill yet*—Group students with various levels of skill and knowledge to help promote problem-solving success. Grouping helps to reinforce the more skilled students' learning while facilitating the learning of students who lack basic proficiency.

FIGURE 5–17 Checklist of Secondary Level Math Consumer Skills

	Proficient	Emergent	Lacks Skill
Community Living/Home Care Math Skills			
Can the student:			
Order items from a catalog (involving taxes and shipping costs)?			
Shop comparatively, using newspaper ads (e.g., comparing rents, cost of grocery items)?			
Use credit for purchases (involving costs of credit)?			
Compare costs of similar items at different stores (e.g., grocery, clothing, department, hardware)?			
Buy groceries in bulk to save money?			
Compute sales tax?			
Apply for consumer loans?			
Budget for and estimate expenses for food, rent, recreation, utilities, phone, transportation, clothing?			
Pay bills using cash, check, and/or bank debits?			
Check sales slips and exchange items at stores?			
Buy by installment and on sale?			
Explain the benefits of renting vs. buying a house?			
Calculate the costs of furnishing a residence?			
Compute closing costs and mortgage lending?			
Calculate property and real estate taxes?			
Calculate the costs of water, electricity, cable?			
Calculate the cost of telephone services?			
Estimate average monthly expenses?			
Explain the benefits of leasing vs. purchasing?			
Calculate the costs of furniture and appliances?			
Calculate the cost of purchasing homeowner's or rental insurance?			
Calculate the cost of home maintenance and home improvement?			
Calculate the cost of buying appliances and tools?			
Determine the measurements for purchasing wallpaper, windows?			
Calculate the tip in a restaurant, a hair salon, elsewhere?			
Health Care Math Skills			
Can the student determine:			
Costs and need for health and disability insurance?			
Differences between costs and benefits of various health plans?			
Cost of buying prescriptions?			
Cost of insurance deductibles and co-pays?			
How to use a thermometer?			
How to measure/dispense the correct prescription dose?			
How to count calories, cholesterol, fat?			
How to determine blood pressure and pulse rate?			
Transportation Math Skills			
Can the student determine:			
Miles per gallon of gasoline?			
Cost comparison of used vs. new cars?			
Cost of buying, leasing, down payments, and financing a car?			
How to use bus, train, and plane schedules?			
How to calculate a taxi fare?			
How to use and purchase a bus pass?			
Distance in miles between two points?			
How to read local, state, and national maps?			

CONTENT AREA ASSESSMENT

Assessment Strategy: *Content Area Skills Checklist*

Strategy Description

The checklist, a systematic means of recording the knowledge, skills, behavior, and/or attitude of individual students or whole classes, is a particularly handy assessment procedure for identifying and monitoring in an inclusive class setting. A checklist is an excellent source of record keeping; it is used to provide evidence that a skill has or has not been mastered, and provides a means of recording the date that the mastery has been achieved. Checklists are also useful when teachers are developing lesson plans and completing report cards, and when discussing progress with the student, parents, administrators, and case managers. This assessment is appropriate for all grade levels when modified accordingly. Administration can be individual or it can be used for monitoring groups. Allow approximately 15 to 20 minutes to assess each skill.

Questions to Ask

Does the student have:

- Basic knowledge in the content area subject?
- The ability to problem solve in the content area by using basic skills?

Assessment Preparation

- Prepare a list of skills or tasks to be mastered using curriculum standards or IEP goals.
- Develop a skills checklist for use with one student to monitor individual progress, or to observe, evaluate, and record the progress of multiple students during a group activity (refer to Figure 5–18).

Implementation

✓ Do a task analysis to identify the steps involved for specific assignments (e.g., each step in a science laboratory experiment), and list the steps in priority or successive order.

✓ Assess, track, and record progress using a rating system, such as mastered/emerging/no skills, or use categories that meet specific scoring needs to record the progress of individual students in checklist form.

✓ Use a class roster as a chart to monitor the progress of multiple students; tally the number or the degree of successful attempts at specific tasks. This can be accomplished while observing class activities; check off the degree and date of mastery for each skill.

Scoring

Score 1 point for each of the following components.

_____ Student demonstrated comprehension of the question/problem.
_____ Student completely addressed all aspects of the question/problem.
_____ Student accurately responded to the question/problem.
_____ Student explained the steps involved in the solution to the question/problem.
_____ Student provided a rationale or additional information.

Scoring Rubric

5: all five components checked
4: four components checked
3: three components checked
2: two components checked

1: one component checked

0: no component checked

Special Considerations, Accommodations, Alternatives

- Rather than rate as a yes or no, make a notation, including specific details, which provides information for later analysis.

FIGURE 5–18 Science Process Skills Checklist

Rate student's progress toward meeting his or her science IEP objectives using the rubrics rating scores listed below

Nov	Mar	June	
☐	☐	☐	**Observing** Using one of more of the five senses to gather information; may include use of instruments (e.g., hand lens)
☐	☐	☐	**Classifying** Grouping or ordering objects or events according to an established scheme, based on observations
☐	☐	☐	**Inferring** Developing ideas based on observations; requires evaluation and judgment based on past experiences
☐	☐	☐	**Predicting** Forming an idea of an expected result; based on inferences
☐	☐	☐	**Measuring** Comparing objects to arbitrary units that may or may not be standardized
☐	☐	☐	**Communicating** Giving or exchanging information verbally or in writing
☐	☐	☐	**Defining Operationally** Stating specific information about an object or a phenomenon based on experience with it
☐	☐	☐	**Hypothesizing** Stating a problem to be solved as a question that can be tested by an experiment
☐	☐	☐	**Making Models** Developing a physical or mental representation to explain an idea, object, or event
☐	☐	☐	**Estimating** Approximating or calculating quantity or value, based on judgment
☐	☐	☐	**Controlling Variables** Manipulating one factor that may affect the outcome of an event while other factors are held constant
☐	☐	☐	**Collecting Data** Gathering information about observations and measurements in a systematic way
☐	☐	☐	**Making a Graph** Converting numerical quantities into a diagram that shows the relationships among the quantities
☐	☐	☐	**Interpreting Data** Explaining the information presented in a table and/or using it to answer questions
☐	☐	☐	**Reading a Graph** Explaining the information presented in a graph and/or using it to answer questions
☐	☐	☐	**Reading a Diagram** Explaining the information presented in a diagram (including maps)

Next Step

- *Mastered*—Advance to next level while reinforcing learned skills, proceed to generalization and maintenance.
- *Emerging*—Provide students with strategies for retaining facts, such as using mnemonics (e.g., the order of the planets from the sun: "My Very Excited Mother Just Served Us Nuggets" [Mercury, Venus, Earth, Mars, Jupiter, Saturn, Uranus, Neptune]).
- *No skill yet*—Provide direct instruction, guided practice, and concrete examples.

Assessment Strategy: *Content Area: Concept Map Assessment*

Strategy Description

Concept mapping is a strategy used to probe the knowledge structures of learners and to assess changes in students' understanding of the subject. It is particularly well-suited for science and social studies concepts. Concept mapping is used to pretest students' prior concept knowledge before instruction, their understanding of the relationship among ideas during the instructional process, and as a summative evaluation following instruction. Therefore, it is an effective tool for planning and evaluating instruction. It can be used to promote both self-evaluation and peer evaluation as students can refer to the preestablished rubric criteria to determine the accuracy and adequacy of their contribution. This assessment can also evaluate students' ability to work cooperatively in groups, communicate and share ideas with others, and problem solve as they collaborate. Appropriate for students from kindergarten (with support) through the secondary school years and is generally a group activity. Allow approximately 20 to 40 minutes to assess this skill.

Questions to Ask

Based on grade level content area curriculum, is the student able to:

- Demonstrate understanding of concepts, interconnections, relationships?
- Construct a detailed and accurate map?
- Work cooperatively with peers to demonstrate knowledge?

Assessment Preparation

- Develop a list of concepts that are most important to understanding the central topic.
- Develop a rubric based on the level of explanation, complexity, and accuracy; base the rating on the correctness of the hierarchy and the inclusion of major cross links.

Implementation

✓ *Cluster concepts*—Have students group the concepts that seem most similar in nature and/or rank the concepts from "most general" to "most specific."

✓ *Position the central topic and begin linking concepts*—Have students write the central topic at the top of a blank sheet of paper, then write each of the remaining terms on very small self-adhesive notes to save erasing while rearranging the concepts and making meaning of the map. Start with a more inclusive concept to link to the central topic (see Figure 5–19).

✓ *Finish mapping all concepts*—Have students continue to construct the map by relating additional concepts from the list to concepts already on the map. Work from more inclusive terms to more specific terms until the concepts are mapped. As the map is developed, make horizontal rather than vertical branches when linking long strings of concepts.

Scoring

Concept maps are generally evaluated and scored using rubrics, either as pass/fail or to indicate specific achievement levels. Scoring should be based on the complexity of the conceptual relationships illustrated.

- *Number of relevant concepts*—Use when students are expected to provide the majority of relevant concepts to be mapped. Teachers provide only the overarching topic concept and possibly a few seed concepts to get students started. The number of relevant concepts is simply counted or the concepts can be weighted according to their degree of inclusiveness.
- *Number of valid propositions*—Determining propositions is important in the assessment of concept maps. The teacher should check each proposal for validity; to determine whether the relationship is scientifically correct and appropriate or does it illustrate a misconception or alternative conception? Propositions can be weighted equally or differently, according to the degree of importance ascribed to the relationship by the teacher.
- *Branching*—This parameter acknowledges the progressive differentiation of concepts. A branch is established when a concept at one level in the concept hierarchy is appropriately linked to two or more concepts at the next level. Again, the rubric can be designed so that instances of branching can be weighted equally or differently.
- *Number of appropriate cross links*—This parameter allows for assessing maps on the degree of integrative, meaningful connections between concepts in different vertical segments of the concept hierarchy.
- *Number of examples of specific concepts*—Students can include examples of specific concepts in their maps to facilitate the anchoring of concepts in their conceptual understanding or to assess whether they can identify types of objects and events that the concept label represents (Dorough & Rye, 1997).

Bonus Points

Depending on the goal of the lesson, students may earn extra points for creativity. Also, credit can be given for individual contributions and group interaction when working in cooperative groups. Additional points may be allotted when students demonstrate that they can generalize concepts and/or apply these concepts in real-world applications. Additional points should also be considered if the student demonstrates advanced skill for every hierarchical level in a concept map, indicating complexity of thinking; each time a concept branches into a new category; and for cross links and when branches or cross links are incorporated into the map at higher hierarchical levels.

Special Considerations, Accommodations, Alternatives

- Concept mapping is often a new skill for students, so it may be necessary to provide a visual model (e.g., on the blackboard) while verbally describing the step-by-step process. It may take months of regular practice for students to develop good maps (Martin, 2009).
- These maps are especially useful for students with low verbal proficiency, including English language learners (Nesbit & Adesope, 2006).
- Include concept maps in the students' portfolio, to allow progress monitoring over time.

Next Step

- *Mastered*—Encourage student to develop more concept words to make more complex and detailed maps (Peters & Stout, 2006).
- *Emerging*—Have students start by simply drawing concepts maps of familiar topics starting with three or four concepts.
- *No skill yet*—Provide explicit models and have students "talk their way" through their maps, working with a more proficient partner.

FIGURE 5–19 Sample Concept Map

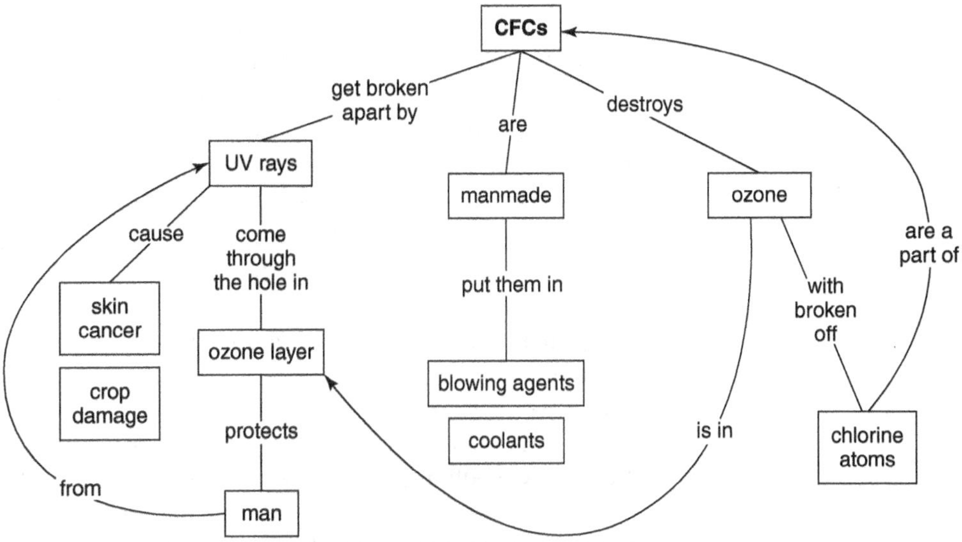

Source: "Mapping for Understanding," D. K. Dorough and J. A. Rye, January 1997, *The Science Teacher*, pp. 37–41. Reprinted with permission.

Assessment Strategy: *Content Area: Oral Interview*

Strategy Description

Oral interviews are effective procedures for evaluating the finished authentic product and for gaining insight into how students mentally process, organize, categorize, and sequence new concepts. The oral interview assesses students' ability to communicate about how they solve problems, to make decisions along the way, and to make connections with other learning during the problem-solving process (Yell, 1999). This assessment is appropriate for students at all grade levels as questions are based on skill level. Students are interviewed individually. Allow approximately 10 to 15 minutes to assess this skill.

Questions to Ask

Based on content area subject content, is the student able to:

- Describe the problem to be solved?
- Verbalize the steps involved in problem solving?
- Describe and justify conclusions/solutions?

Assessment Preparation

- Prepare for authentic assessment by having all needed materials easily available; however, since this is an oral interview assessment, have students tell what materials they will need to solve the problems presented and then the evaluator can gather them.
- Consider asking students to tell where they would locate needed materials and then have them gather these materials.

Implementation

✓ Have students "talk through" their work—describing what they are doing, how they are using materials, and their plan of action.

✓ Provide verbal questioning, as needed, to prompt students to provide sufficient detail. Avoid prompting unless absolutely necessary, and if necessary, less is best, as the goal of this assessment is to evaluate students' thought processes, their use of appropriate terms, and their analysis and problem-solving skills.

✓ Require students to describe their conclusion and, if appropriate, have them provide a judgment about the scientific quality of the information (Gargiulo & Metcalf, 2010).

✓ Evaluate the outcome and, more importantly, analyze the process students go through and the reasoning behind what they are doing, including their levels of thinking and reasoning ability.

✓ Interview students to gain their perspective and ability to describe their problem solving in detail and in sequential order using appropriate terms, at the conclusion of the problem-solving process (see Figure 5–20).

Special Considerations, Accommodations, Alternatives

- Using a think-aloud approach enables students to tell what they are doing and why. When the teacher follows up with open-ended questions, this can help clarify students' thought processes.

FIGURE 5–20 Content Area Subject Oral Interview Questions

Describe Your Project

- What are the project requirements? ______
- Why did you select this project? ______
- What is the design of your investigation? ______
- What did you do to prepare for your investigation? ______
- What steps are required to complete your project? ______
- What material or equipment did you use? ______
- What have you accomplished so far? ______
- What decisions did you make along the way? ______
- What connections were made along the way with prior learning? ______
- What do you expect to occur? ______
- What did you observe? ______
- Are you having any problem(s)? ______
- What do you think has caused the problem(s)? ______
- How did you solve the problem(s)? ______
- What kinds of results have you obtained? ______
- Where did you record your findings? ______
- What do you think would happen if . . .? ______
- What are your conclusions so far? ______
- What do you intend to do next? ______
- Describe the most important thing you learned or accomplished in your research. ______
- What do you like best about your project? ______
- If you could do anything differently, what would it be? ______
- What skills and knowledge from other subjects did you use to complete this project? ______
- What skills, concepts, or insights have you learned from completing this project? ______

Next Step

- *Mastered*—Advance to increasingly higher order thinking questions.
- *Emerging*—Ask open-ended or partially structured questions.
- *No skill yet*—Start with simple, closed-ended (yes/no) questions based on information that the student is likely to be able to answer correctly. Model how to respond to a question; provide picture cues or optional responses (e.g., answer bank) for the student to choose from when answering.

REFERENCES

AIMSweb. (2008). *Norms for math CBM: Correct digits.* San Antonio, TX: Harcourt Assessment, Inc.

Alper, S., & Mills, K. (2001). Nonstandardized assessment in inclusive school settings. In A. S. Alper, D. L. Ryndak, & C. N. Schloss (Eds.), *Alternate assessment of students with disabilities in inclusive settings* (pp. 54–74). Needham Heights, MA: Allyn & Bacon.

Cavanagh, S. (2007). Math anxiety confuses the equation for students. *Education Week, 26* (24), 12.

Crawford, D. B. (2000, April). *Making individualized educational programs (IEPs) easy: Using curriculum-based progress monitoring measures.* Paper presented at the Council for Exceptional Children Annual Convention, Vancouver, Canada.

Dorough, D. K., & Rye, J. (1997, January). Mapping for understanding. *The Science Teacher*, 37–41.

Fuchs, L. S., Fuchs, D., Hamlett, C. L., Walz, L., & Germann, G. (1993). Formative evaluation of academic progress: How much growth can we expect? *School Psychologist Review, 22,* 27–49.

Gargiulo, R., & Metcalf, D. (2010). *Teaching in today's inclusive classrooms: A universal design for learning approach.* Belmont, CA: Wadsworth.

Martin, D. (2009). *Elementary science methods: A constructivist approach* (5th ed.). Belmont, CA: Wadsworth.

Nesbit, J. C., & Adesope, O. O. (2006). Learning with concept and knowledge maps: A meta-analysis. *Review of Educational Research, 76*(3), 413–448.

Peters, J. M., & Stout, D. L. (2006). *Science in elementary education: Methods, concepts, and inquiries* (10th ed.). Upper Saddle River, NJ: Pearson.

Ruffins, P. (2007). A real fear. *Diverse Issues in Higher Education, 24*(2), 17–19.

Tindal, G. A., & Marston, D. B. (1990). *Classroom-based assessment: Evaluating instructional outcomes.* Columbus, OH: Merrill.

Yell, M. M. (1999). Multiple choice to multiple rubrics: One teacher's journey to assessment. *Social Education, 65*(6), 326–329.

Chapter 6

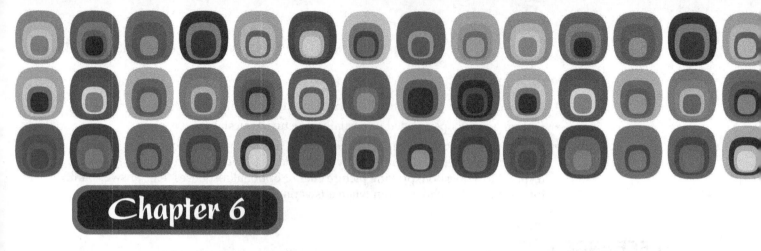

Assessment and Accommodations for Special Populations

INTRODUCTION

Legal, moral, and ethical standards clearly require that as professional educators, we administer fair, valid, and reliable evaluation measures to all our students. This can be particularly challenging with the current generation of students with diverse backgrounds, who come with various learning problems and work-study needs. Many of our students have cultural and linguistic differences; emotional, social, and behavior adjustment problems; and learning style diversity for which they may need special accommodations. This diversity requires that we, as teachers, are able to identify the need for accommodations and are able to provide these provisions appropriately.

Our classrooms are becoming more diverse every day with increasing numbers of children from various racial and ethnic minority groups. English language learners are a significant and growing portion of the school age population in the United States, with estimates between 1 and 7 to 1 and 11 of all kindergarten to grade 12 students (Yzquierdo, Blalock, & Torres-Velasquez, 2004). Researchers estimate that by 2030, the first language of 40% of our school-age population will not be English (National Symposium on Learning Disabilities in English Language Learners, 2004). Students who are English language learners are at high risk for being misdiagnosed and overrepresented when they are referred for evaluation to determine eligibility for special education classification and services (Gollnick & Chinn, 2009). These students may appear academically deficient or act inappropriately when, in reality, the problem is a language or cultural difference (Harry & Klingner, 2006). There seems to be a general lack of understanding in U.S. school systems regarding the influence of linguistic, cultural, and socioeconomic differences on student learning (Heward, 2009).

Besides those with cultural and linguistic differences, another population of students, those with emotional and behavioral disorders (EBDs), often require special test accommodations. Currently EBDs afflict about 1.3 to 4 million students in preschool to high school; and since these students are usually underserved, it is important to identify them as early as possible so that interventions can begin and possibly lessen the negative effects on the academic and social aspects of their education. These students, along with many others with various types of learning disabilities, require accommodations, modifications in assessment strategies, and/or learning environment adaptations. Test accommodations are not meant to give students an unfair advantage over the students who are not receiving them. They are designed to level the playing field between students with and those without special needs. This chapter will culminate with a focus on universal design which is intended to make assessments accessible to all students, to provide fair and equitable testing procedures.

ASSESSMENTS TO ACCOMMODATE ENGLISH LANGUAGE LEARNERS

Assessment Procedure: *Structured Family Interview*

Strategy Description

Students' life experiences vary, including differences in culture and ethnicity, language, educational and medical, social-emotional development, and family dynamics. Interviewing family members can provide important information—a fully contextualized account of the child's background and relevant life experiences.

Implementation

✓ Schedule a mutually convenient time for the interview meeting. When possible, holding the interview in the family home provides the opportunity to experience the student's family in a natural setting, to see the student's home and neighborhood environment, and to meet family members. It also may be more comfortable for the family; often the school setting can be intimidating.

✓ Ask open-ended questions that include the extent to which the significant others in the student's life, including peers, provide language assistance. This assistance might include modeling, expanding, restating, repeating, questioning, prompting, negotiating meaning, cueing, pausing, praising, and providing visual and other supports.

✓ Inquire about the student's previous language experience, the context of language learning, the academic learning opportunities, and the resources available to the student. It is also important to know the length of time the family has lived in the United States, the primary language spoken by family members and their level of proficiency in English, the native language of family members and the student, the cultural characteristics of the child and family, and how communication skills are progressing in the home environment (Twombly, 2001; Woods & McCormick, 2002). Family members can supply important information about how the child is learning and developing and also describe the child's language environment (see Figure 6–1).

✓ Interview the student to gain his or her personal perspective. In addition, analyze a conversation sample to determine the student's effectiveness as a communication partner in face-to-face conversation (see Figure 6–2).

Special Considerations, Accommodations, Alternatives

- Prior to scheduling the interview, determine whether an interpreter is needed.
- Encourage the parent to bring another family member or friend as an advocate for support and to help provide information.
- Realize that immigrant families, and others, may not have accurate medical or developmental records. Some families may prefer to complete a form rather than be interviewed, which also allows time to collect data, reflect, and then respond, often in a more comprehensive, accurate, and thoughtful manner.
- Be aware of and sensitive to cultural traditions (e.g., some cultures highly regard privacy and often these family members are not comfortable sharing personal issues with school personnel; some cultural traditions only allow the father, as head of family, to interact with school personnel).

FIGURE 6–1 Parent-Home English Language Learner Survey

What language did/does your child speak:

When beginning to talk?	English __	Other language ________
Most often at home?	English __	Other language ________
Most often with friends?	English __	Other language ________

What language do you use *most often* when speaking to your:

Child?	English __	Other language ________
Friends?	English __	Other language ________

What language do other family members in your home *usually* use when speaking to each other? English __ Other language ________

Family Member	Native Language	Language Used at Home	Second Language Fluency
Father	_____	________	None ___ Emerging ___ Mastery ___
Mother	_____	________	None ___ Emerging ___ Mastery ___
Siblings	_____	________	None ___ Emerging ___ Mastery ___
Others in home	_____	________	None ___ Emerging ___ Mastery ___
Peers	_____	________	None ___ Emerging ___ Mastery ___

Student's use of second language	None ________	Occasional ________	Frequent ________
	Speaking	Writing	Reading
Age began . . .	________	________	________

Student's English fluency
- ___ Uses basic nouns and verbs
- ___ Uses conjugated verbs, nouns, and adjectives
- ___ Speaks in full sentences uses form and structure inconsistently
- ___ Speaks fluently with good usage, form, and structure

Student's dominant language ________________ Language of preference __________

Language parents prefer for school instruction ______________________________

Student's school experience: ______________________________

Native language instruction___ Bilingual instruction ___ All English instruction ___

___ Bilingual aide ___ ESL teacher ___ Regular education teacher

FIGURE 6–2 Interview Guide for English Language Learners

Name ______________________ Date ______________________

F = Fluent **B = Broken** **U = Unable**

	Oral	Written
What is your name?	______	______
What is your address?	______	______
What is your telephone number?	______	______
What is your birth date?	______	______
How old are you?	______	______
How many people live in your house?	______	______
How many brothers and sisters do you have?	______	______
What country are you from?	______	______
Why did you come to America?	______	______
Did you go to school before coming to America?	______	______
What languages do you speak?	______	______
What is the first language you learned to speak?	______	______
What language do you speak most often?	______	______
What language is most spoken in your home?	______	______
What is your favorite subject in school?	______	______
Why do you like that subject?	______	______
Read a passage from a grade appropriate book.	______	______
Students who cannot read will be given a picture dictionary to identify the following:	______	______

Colors _____ Family members _____

Numbers _____ Classroom items _____

Assessment Procedure: *Language Disorders versus Language Differences*

Strategy Description

Teachers need to be aware that frequently students who are culturally and/or linguistically diverse, those who have not had the opportunity to become proficient in the English language, are misidentified as having an intrinsic learning problem (Amrein & Berliner, 2002; Pierce, 2002; Stiggins, 2002). Guidelines are helpful for distinguishing between language disorders and lack of language proficiency.

Implementation

✓ Check the student's background knowledge.

✓ Observe the student using language in a variety of settings.

✓ Consult with the ESL teacher, supplemental teachers, and school staff who regularly interact with the student regarding their knowledge of the child's language and learning (see Figure 6–3).
✓ Know the characteristics of a language learning disability.
✓ Consider whether there is the need to conduct the initial screenings of students with cultural or linguistic differences in both English and their native language.

FIGURE 6–3 Guidelines for Distinguishing Between Language Disorders and Differences

	Yes	No	Comments
Besides the referring teacher, have others (e.g., the remedial instructor, the ESL teacher, parents) noted similar problems?	______	______	__________
Are the problems evident across contexts (e.g., in the general education class, in the ESL class, in related arts classes, in the home)?	______	______	__________
Are problems evident in the student's first language (e.g., do native speakers have difficulty understanding the student)?	______	______	__________
Does the student have difficulty following directions in both English and the native language?	______	______	__________
Does the student continue to have difficulty reading in the native language despite effective instruction?	______	______	__________
Is the student's progress in English language acquisition significantly slower than age peers starting at the same level of language proficiency with comparable instruction?	______	______	__________
Can the difficulty be explained by cross-cultural differences (e.g., lack of eye contact as acultural tradition interpreted as inattention or behavioral defiance)?	______	______	__________
Could other factors (e.g., inconsistent school attendance or language variations) be causing the differences?	______	______	__________
Is there evidence of serious test anxiety, or is the student confused by the assessment process, since it may be the first time he or she has been tested in this country?	______	______	__________
Could procedural errors, related to administration or scoring, or a failure to provide necessary accommodations, test procedural or scoring error, or insufficient preparation cause the difficulty?	______	______	__________
Could bias in operation before, during, or after the assessment be a problem (e.g., using tests that are not normed for English language learners, using adaptations inappropriately, when the evaluator's low expectations influence the administration and interpretation of results)?	______	______	__________
Were research-based interventions (e.g., clinical teaching, remedial supports, curricular or teaching modifications) unable to close the achievement gap?	______	______	__________
Are assessment results consistent with the concerns of the student's teacher and parents?	______	______	__________

Source: Adapted from "Considerations in the Assessment of English Language Learners Referred to Special Education," by A. Ortiz and J. Yates, 2002, pp. 65–85, in *English Language Learners with Special Education Needs: Identification, Assessment, and Instruction,* edited by A. Artiles and A. Oritz, Center for Applied Linguistics and Delta Systems, McHenry, IL.

Special Considerations, Accommodations, Alternatives

Factors to consider when differentiating between a disorder and a difference include the following:

- Language spoken in the home
- Level of language proficiency
- Extent of ESL services already received
- Experiential and/or enrichment services received
- Level of parental involvement
- Amount of time and extent of services in an academic program for children who have had little or no formal schooling; the length of residency in the United States and prior school experience in the native country and in an English language school system
- Previous attempts to remediate performance, including supplemental aids or support services

Assessment Procedure: *Distinguishing Between Social and Academic Language Proficiency*

Strategy Description

There are two types of language proficiency and it is important to know whether your student's language proficiency is at the basic interpersonal communication skill (BICS) or at the cognitive academic language proficiency (CALP) level. Referring to the guideline for the expected age norms for the development of BICS or CALP is useful for determining whether the student is functioning within expectancy level. BICS is acquired naturally, without formal schooling; it is context-embedded, everyday language that occurs in conversation (e.g., "I drank milk for lunch."). CALP takes longer to acquire as it is the context-reduced language of academics ("Compare democracy and a dictatorship."). Whereas, BICS generally takes up to 2 years to acquire, CALP often takes from 5 to 7 years. English language learners often develop conversational English (BICS) so they may appear fluent and adequate for everyday communication. However, they often continue to struggle with CALP and have difficulty with academics (e.g., reading, writing, spelling, science, social studies, and other subject areas) where there is little context to support the language being heard or read.

Implementation

✓ Observe how English language learners interact at school with peers and adults, respond to class discussions, answer questions, follow class procedures and directions, and demonstrate comprehension of curriculum subject material.

✓ Compare these observations with BICS/CALP age norm guidelines (see Figure 6–4).

✓ Use information from observation and daily interaction with the student to note skill level according to the BICS checklist (see Figure 6–5).

Special Considerations, Accommodations, Alternatives

- It often takes longer for students to develop CALP due to several factors, including interrupted schooling, level of development of native language skills, and the emotional state of the child and family (Council for Exceptional Children [CEC], 2002).
- Many educators confuse the BICS–CALP gap with language learning disabilities. School language proficiency tests are often used to assess children's level of proficiency in English. Likewise, students who appear to be English proficient actually have not developed CALP and, thus, the use of standardized tests in English is biased against them. Therefore, when these standardized tests are administered, English language learners often score very low, are labeled as having language learning disabilities, and are inappropriately placed in special education.

FIGURE 6–4 Expected Age Norms for BICS and CALP Development

0 to 6 months	Responsive to sound, nonverbal gestures, facial expression, phonemes such as "da" and "ma," babbles
6 months to 1 year	Begins meaningful verbalization with one- to two-word utterances
1 to 2 years	Begins to construct short sentences, use of meaning words continues to expand, uses present tense and basic concept formation, repeats short phrases of adult speakers
2 to 3 years	Vocabulary growth continues, including the use of past tense and action verbs (*running*), able to supply basic personal data (name, age, gender) and academic concepts (numbers, colors, grouping), developing the basic pragmatics
3 to 4 years	Becomes more articulate and enjoys verbal communication, vocabulary is expanding, developing phonemic awareness, can provide more personal information, academic concepts include one-to-one correspondence, growth is evident in verbal reasoning skills
4 to 5 years	Increasing competence in phonemic awareness skills, uses irregular plurals in everyday speech and begins to use future tense, developing proficiency in question-answer skills
5 to 6 years	Uses future tense time markers consistently; can repeat up to 10-syllable sentences; vocabulary expanded to include basic terms used in social studies, science, and literature; has developed basic concept knowledge (space, time, numeration, etc.); growth in pragmatics which includes an understanding of nonverbal communication and taking turns; is able to retell simple story details in sequential order
6 to 7 years	Significant expansion in vocabulary, uses phonemes to formulate words, incorporates conditional tense, has mastered most preliminary reading skills, more appropriate use of irregular and past tense verbs, has developed sufficient written language skill to tell a story when spelling is not a factor, pragmatics skills have expanded to include introduction and termination skills and appropriate classroom/meeting behavior
7 to 9 years	Fundamental reading skills are mastered for word identification and comprehension, uses compound verb tenses
9 to 11 years	Basic communication skills, including reading and writing skills, are refined and used consistently, has developed spelling skills to include recognition of sight words and use of phonics skills
11 to 13 years	Development complete for basic BICS system, traditional tests of oral language or reading at the fifth- or sixth-grade level is used to measure CALP system development
13 years and up	Determination of the level of CALP development often includes traditional CALP measures, particularly reading. BICS is screened using writing skills, more formal oral assessment is used for those with any written language difficulty

Source: Adapted from *The Assessment of BICS/CALP: A Developmental Perspective*, by R. Anderson, 2000, http://home.earthlink.net/~psychron/homepage.htm.

FIGURE 6–5 BICS Acquisition Checklist

Does the student:

- ___ Demonstrate the ability to listen and comprehend and retain information sufficiently to maintain an intelligible communication?
- ___ Have the ability to provide basic personal information (e.g., name and age) at a more advanced level that includes knowledge of birthdays of all family members, extended family members' addresses and phone numbers, etc.?
- ___ Understand basic concepts that define space, time, numerocity, etc.?
- ___ Have at least minimal vocabulary skills that are growing as the age and education of the child increases?
- ___ Recognize how verbs and verb tenses work together?
- ___ Use verb tenses in words?
- ___ Have the ability to discriminate similar phonemes?
- ___ Have the abstract processing ability necessary to acquire and refine existing skills?
- ___ Demonstrate the retelling skills necessary to carry on a given conversation with appropriate verbal give and take?
- ___ Have question-asking skills?
- ___ Demonstrate pragmatic skills and the social understandings of language (e.g., turn-taking, maintaining topic, body language)?

Assessment Procedure: *Assessment of Language Proficiency*

Strategy Description

For students to be considered fluent in English, their level of authenticity and automatic control of both conversational and academic language should be comparable to that of their peers. Language proficiency assessment focuses on the particular situation and the type of communication mode in which the student demonstrates proficiency as well as the area of language use that is underdeveloped or deficient.

Implementation

- ✓ Assess students' receptive and expressive language skills in both English and their native language; involve them in conversations in various settings and contexts with different people.
- ✓ Assess students' academic language proficiency, including their ability to comprehend class-room discourse and lesson content, by having them explain what they learned from a lesson (see Figures 6–6 and 6–7).
- ✓ Assess students' narrative skills and their ability to organize and sequence information, by having them retell a story.
- ✓ Assess students' background and knowledge of vocabulary and grammatical structures by using a cloze or maze procedure.
- ✓ Determine students' language use in the home and community, language preference, and level of proficiency in the native language by interviewing parents or family members (refer to Figure 6–1).

Special Considerations, Accommodations, Alternatives

- It is important that assessments be administered by evaluators who are fluent in, or at least very familiar with, students' native language and culture. Generally the regional or state department of education has a list of certified educational diagnosticians and school psychologists who speak various languages and can be contacted to administer evaluations.

- Assessment should focus not only on the particular situations and types of communication modes in which students demonstrate proficiency, but also the area of language use that is underdeveloped or deficient.

FIGURE 6–6 Categories of Language Use Survey

Is the student able to use language to:

_____ Express feelings?

_____ Express anger?

_____ Apologize?

_____ Express joy, pleasure?

Is the student able to use language to express ideas about:

_____ How to do class projects?

_____ Nature, how the world functions?

_____ Using objects, toys, tools, etc.?

Is the student able to use language to engage in play by:

_____ Playing a role?

_____ Taking turns?

_____ Giving and following game rules?

Is the student able to use language to describe:

_____ When telling a story?

_____ When recounting past experiences?

_____ By retelling what was said?

_____ When telling about a picture or photo?

Is the student able to use language to ask for help when:

_____ Hurt?

_____ Trying to solve a problem?

_____ Working on a class project?

Is the student able to use language to:

_____ Solve a problem?

_____ Resolve a conflict with another child?

_____ Solve a problem occurring during a class project?

Is the student able to use language in private speech by:

_____ Playing with language?

_____ Rhyming words, chanting?

_____ Using puns?

Is the student able to use language to inquire by asking:

_____ For names of things?

_____ How something works?

_____ "Why" questions?

Source: Adapted from California Early Language Development Assessment Process: Categories of Language Use, by the National Clearinghouse for Bilingual Education (NCBE).

FIGURE 6–7 Student Oral Proficiency Rating Checklist

Comprehensive

Level 1 ___ Cannot understand even simple conversation

Level 2 ___ Has great difficulty following what is said. Can comprehend only "social conversation" spoken slowly and with frequent repetitions

Level 3 ___ Understands most of what is said at slower-than-normal speed with repetitions

Level 4 ___ Understands nearly everything at normal speed, although occasional repetition may be necessary

Level 5 ___ Understands everyday conversation and normal classroom discussions without difficulty

Fluency

Level 1 ___ Speech is so halting and fragmentary that conversation is virtually impossible

Level 2 ___ Usually hesitant; often forced into silence by language limitations

Level 3 ___ Speech in everyday communication and classroom discussion is often disrupted by the student's search for the correct manner of expression

Level 4 ___ Speech in everyday communication and classroom discussion is generally fluent, with occasional lapses while the student searches for the correct manner of expression

Level 5 ___ Speech in everyday conversation and in classroom discussions is fluent and effortless, approximating that of a native speaker

Vocabulary

Level 1 ___ Vocabulary limitations so extreme that conversation is virtually impossible

Level 2 ___ Misuse of words, very limited vocabulary, comprehension very difficult

Level 3 ___ Frequently uses the wrong words; conversation somewhat limited due to inadequate vocabulary

Level 4 ___ Occasionally uses inappropriate terms; must rephrase ideas due to inadequate vocabulary

Level 5 ___ Use of vocabulary and idioms approximates that of a native speaker

Pronunciation

Level 1 ___ Pronunciation problems are severe, speech is virtually unintelligible

Level 2 ___ Very hard to understand because of pronunciation problems, usually needs to repeat to be understood

Level 3 ___ Pronunciation problems necessitate listener concentration and occasionally lead to misunderstanding

Level 4 ___ Always intelligible, though one is conscious of a definite accent and occasional inappropriate intonation patterns

Level 5 ___ Pronunciation and intonation approximate that of a native speaker

Grammar

Level 1 ___ Errors in grammar and word order so severe they make speech unintelligible

Level 2 ___ Grammar and word order errors make comprehension difficult; must often rephrase or restrict what is said to basic patterns

Level 3 ___ Makes frequent errors of grammar and word order, which occasionally obscures meaning

Level 4 ___ Occasionally makes grammatical or word order errors, which do not obscure meaning

Level 5 ___ Grammatical usage and word order approximate a native speaker's

EMOTIONAL, SOCIAL, AND BEHAVIORAL ASSESSMENTS

Assessment Procedure: *Student Behavioral Checklist*

Strategy Description

Because students with emotional-social-behavioral problems are usually underserved, it is important to identify them as early as possible so that interventions can begin and possibly lessen or eliminate the negative impact on their academic and social development.

Implementation

- ✓ Gather relevant information about the student in both the social and instructional environment.
- ✓ Assimilate the data to create an overall picture of the concerns.
- ✓ Observe the student in various settings, at various times, and under a variety of circumstances. This includes structured and unstructured settings, different times of the day, in different classes and various situations, and over an extended period of time in order to observe incidents of the target behavior (see Figures 6–8 and 6–9).
- ✓ Identify what events or physical conditions existed before the behavior occurred, what appears to motivate or maintain the behavior, and whether a pattern exists.

FIGURE 6–8 Student Behavioral Skills Checklist

Behavioral Skill	Always	Most of the Time	Rarely	Never
On Time and Prepared				
Arrives to class on time				
Attends school regularly, rarely absent				
Returns all required papers and forms on time				
Brings necessary materials				
Completes homework				
Respects Peers				
Respects property of others				
Listens to peers				
Responds appropriately to peers				
Respects opinions of others				
Refrains from abusive language				
Respects Teacher and Staff				
Follows directions				
Listens to teacher and staff				
Accepts responsibility for actions				
Demonstrates Appropriate Character Traits				
Demonstrates positive character traits (e.g., kindness, trustworthy, honesty)				
Demonstrates productive character traits (e.g., patience, thoroughness, hard work)				
Demonstrates concern for others				
Demonstrates a Level of Concern for Learning				
Remains on task				
Allows others to remain on task				

✓ Identify how the student responds to the consequences of his or her behavior and whether the consequences maintain the challenging behaviors (e.g., what the student is "getting out of" the behavior, such as attention, avoidance).

Special Considerations, Accommodations, Alternatives

- It is important to observe whether problematic behavior is evident in more than one setting.
- Consideration needs to be given to the fact that the student's problems could be due to temporary developmental, situational, or environmental factors; cultural or linguistic differences; or the influences of other disabling conditions.
- The behaviors may have a medical cause. Allergies, infections, menstrual cycle effects, toothaches, chronic constipation, and other medical conditions may bring on challenging behaviors. Medication also can influence behavior.
- If the student is demonstrating more serious indicators (e.g., acting or reacting aggressively, being abusive, purposely destroying property, bullying, threatening, intimidating, blaming, failing to show empathy for others), referral should be made to the school's counselor, social worker, or psychologist.

FIGURE 6–9 Psycho-Social-Emotional Adjustment Checklist

The student:	Frequently	Often	Seldom
• Is impulsive			
• Gives excuses for inappropriate behavior			
• Constantly blames others for problems			
• Panics easily			
• Is highly distractible			
• Lies continually			
• Is fearful with adults			
• Is fearful of new situations			
• Is verbally hesitant			
• Is hyperactive			
• Has a short attention span			
• Is overactive			
• Is physical with others			
• Is intrusive			
• Is unable to focus on task			
• Procrastinates			
• Is very disorganized			
• Is inflexible			
• Is irresponsible			
• Uses poor judgment			
• Is in denial			
• Is unwilling to reason			
• Demonstrates social withdrawal			
• Is constantly self-critical			
• Bullies other children			
• Needs constant reassurance			
• Is despondent			
• Lacks motivation or indicates low energy levels			
• Shows inconsistent academic performance, ranging from very low to very high			
• Exhibits extreme and consistent attention-seeking behavior			

Assessment Procedure: *Functional Behavioral Assessment*

Strategy Description

Functional behavioral asessment (FBA) involves direct observation to analyze students' behavior in relation to social and physical aspects of the environment (Janney & Snell, 2008). The purpose of an FBA is to establish what behavioral supports are needed for students who exhibit a range of challenging behaviors, such as physical and verbal outbursts, property destruction, and disruptive behavior (e.g., temper tantrums, yelling). When a student's behavior does not respond to standard interventions, an FBA can provide additional information to assist in planning more effective interventions.

Implementation

- ✓ Gather relevant information using student, parent, former and current teacher interviews; questionnaires, direct observation, and rating scales to identify which events in the environment are linked to the specific problem behavior.
- ✓ Observe the student in natural and varied settings (e.g., in school, on the playground, riding the bus, in the community, at home) and over an extended period of time in order to observe incidents of the target behavior.
- ✓ Describe the problem behaviors, in concrete terms with examples, and include the age level or circumstances under which the behavior might be appropriate.
- ✓ Identify the events, times, and situations that predict when the challenging behaviors will and will not occur across the range of daily routines.
- ✓ Identify the onset, circumstances, and duration of the problem.
- ✓ Identify what events occurred or physical conditions exist that seem to influence the behavior (see Figure 6–10).
- ✓ Note patterns of good behavior and misbehavior and the student's skill level during periods of appropriate versus inappropriate behavior.
- ✓ Note student's role and the quality of interpersonal relations in class and in various school and out-of-school activities.
- ✓ Note student's coping styles, how he or she is supported or reinforced in the home and school setting, and incidence of self-motivation to change.
- ✓ Record what happens after the behavior occurs (see Figure 6–11).
- ✓ Note how the student responds to the consequences of the behavior. Identify whether the consequences appear to terminate or motivate/maintain the challenging behavior.

Special Considerations, Accommodations, Alternatives

- Many states have laws or regulations stipulating the need for a functional assessment before permitting significant behavioral interventions to occur.
- Consideration should be given to the student's developmental stage, family or personal crises, status with peers, implications of disability, cultural or linguistic differences, and health/medical situation.
- Whenever students' behavior is a risk to themselves or others, they should be referred to the school's counselor, social worker, or psychologist.

FIGURE 6–10 Functional Performance and Participaton Checklist

Does the child have difficulties in mobility—either access to or within the environment (e.g., hallways, classroom, gym, cafeteria, transportation, bathroom, field trips)?	**Y**	**N**
Does the child seem to be excessively fatigued (e.g., compared with other children)? If so, does this affect the child's attention or participation?	**Y**	**N**
Does the child display a lack of willingness or interest in participating in social/play activities (e.g., prefers to be or play alone at recess, tries to avoid cooperative activities)?	**Y**	**N**
Does the child have difficulty sitting calmly and attentively in class (e.g., cannot stay seated, displays excess or seemingly unnecessary movement, and is restless and fidgety)?	**Y**	**N**
Does the child need more supervision and adult assistance than peers to perform routine class activities (e.g., motor-planning issues, carrying out directions, working independently, and completing tasks in sequence)?	**Y**	**N**
Does the child have difficulty keeping up with peers in daily routine activities (e.g., tires easily, appears sleepy or disinterested, daydreams)?	**Y**	**N**
Does the child's decreased attention or inability to focus lead to behaviors of greatly increased or decreased physical activity (e.g., hyperactivity; repetitive movements; slumping in seat; leaning on walls, furniture, or other people or objects)?	**Y**	**N**
Does the child display significant clumsiness or awkwardness that is significantly greater than peers (e.g., lacks coordination and smoothness of movement)?	**Y**	**N**
Does the child act inappropriately or disrespectfully to adults or to peers (e.g., is critical, unkind, abusive, physically or verbally aggressive)?	**Y**	**N**
Do the difficulties seem to be getting worse (over the last 6 months), or do they worsen under situations of stress or excitement (e.g., loud or complex environments, new situations, specific times of the day)?	**Y**	**N**
Additional comments and explanations for all "yes" answers:	**Y**	**N**

FIGURE 6–11 Sample Form for Recording Behaviors

Student's name: ____________________

Date: ____________________ Time: ____________________

Location: ____________________

Behavior observed: ____________________

Significance of behavior: ____________________

What was happening before behavior: ____________________

Have these or similar behaviors been observed before? ____________________

under similar circumstances? ____________ different circumstances? ____________

What were the consequences of the behavior? ____________________

How did the student respond to the consequences of the behavior? ____________

Assessment Procedure: *Sociogram*

Strategy Description

Sociometric techniques, such as sociograms, are the most commonly used method of social skills assessment (Bukowski, Sippola, Hoza, & Newcomb, 2000). Sociograms are used to assess students' social status by graphically noting the manner and frequency of their social interactions. Specifically, sociograms track the number and types of overtures a student makes toward other students during a specified time period. This information can be used as a measure of students' current social interaction patterns. It is necessary to track interactions over an extended period of time in order to determine whether a pattern exists.

Implementation

- ✓ Proceed with the three-step process of the sociogram (see Figure 6–12). The first step is getting peer nominations. This involves asking all students in the class to identify their peer preferences (e.g., students are asked who they would pick to work with on a school project). Next, they are told to make a second choice (e.g., in case the first person is not available). The sociogram is developed by representing the peer nominations graphically or pictorially; data analysis consists of inspecting the sociogram to determine which students are class leaders, members of cliques, loners, or outcasts (Watkins & Schloss, 2001).
- ✓ Assess social skill development by observing and rating social interaction by using a checklist. At the same time of day for a period of 2 weeks, spend a few minutes observing the students in class and checking the level of social development for each student. After the 2-week period, total the checks for each student by adding down the column under each category, and then adding all the totals from left to right to get a grand total. Divide the total number in each social category by the grand total to get a percentage for that social level. The percentages can then be plotted on an individual social graph for each student (see Figure 6–13). This information is useful for determining how each child is functioning socially and whether developmental levels are age appropriate.
- ✓ Assess students' abilities to deal with interpersonal relationships by interviewing them about how they would react in a variety of social settings (see Figure 6–14).

FIGURE 6–12 Group Social Graph

Sociometric Matrix for Project Choices

	Bob	Tina	Josh	Theresa	Jose	Maria	Tim	Andre	Gina
Bob			1		2				
Tina				2				1	
Josh		1		2					
Theresa		1							
Jose									2
Maria			1					1	2
Tim	2		2					2	
Andre							2		
Gina			1				2	1	1
1st choice	0	2	3	0	0	0	0	3	1
2nd choice	1	0	1	2	1	0	2	1	2
Frequency Chosen	1	2	4	2	1	0	2	4	3
Ranking	5th	2nd	1st	4th	5th	6th	4th	1st	3rd

Source: Adapted from *Sociometric Matrix of Social Studies Choices. Informal Assessment in Education*, by G. R. Guerin and A. S. Maier. Copyright ©1983 Mayfield Publishing Company, Palo Alto, CA.

FIGURE 6–13 Social Skills Observation Checklist—Group or Individual

Student's Name	Unoccupied	Solitary	Onlooker	Parallel	Associative	Cooperative
*						
*						
*						
*						
*						
*						
*						
*						
Percent of time in a period/day						

Unoccupied: no social interaction
Solitary: plays alone, no communication with peers
Onlooker: mostly watches others socialize from a distance
Parallel: stands beside peers, may be involved in similar activity, no interaction or communication
Associative: interacts and communicates but not fully emerged as a participant
Cooperative: interacts in a purposeful, willing manner, communication is intentional, follows rules

FIGURE 6–14 Interpersonal Relationship Checklist

Directions: For each question, consider how you would respond in each of the four settings. Place a check in the box after you have considered that situation.

Conflict	**At Home**	**At School**	**In the Community**	**On the Job**
When a problem comes up, what do you usually do?				
What is the best thing to do when a problem comes up?				
When a problem comes up, what do you fear most?				
How do you cope with being afraid?				
Who would be a good person (or what would be a good place) to go to for more help when you are afraid?				
How do you handle the stress of problems?				
How is this working for you?				
When a problem comes up, do you feel sad, upset, or angry?				
What do you do when you feel sad?				
What do you do when you feel angry?				
What problems are you having now?				
How are you handling these problems?				
Is there someone you trust who is a good person to go to when you have a problem?				
Friends				
Who are your friends or people who you like a lot?				
How did you go about making these friends?				
Do you get along well with your friends and people you like?				
What do you like most about these people?				
What do you think they like most about you?				
Resolution				
What would you like to change about your social situation or interpersonal relationships?				
Do you think you can change these areas?				
Do you know how to change these areas?				
How motivated are you to change these areas by making changes yourself?				
Who can you ask or where can you go for help?				

Special Considerations, Accommodations, Alternatives

- Students with disabilities tend to experience more difficulty with social skills than their nondisabled peers. They also tend to have a higher incidence of social problems, are more isolated, and are more likely than their peers to experience loneliness. These students tend not to be as well accepted by their peers as they lack proficiency developing social relationships due to difficulty reading and processing social cues.
- Many students who have difficulty expressing themselves and behaving appropriately in social situations tend to be rejected by their peers. Often students with disabilities have social adjustment problems since they do not always have equal opportunities for full participation in educational and extracurricular activities at school (Pavri, 2001).

WORK-STUDY AND TEST-TAKING STRATEGIES

Assessment Procedure: *Study Skill Strategies*

Strategy Description

Study skills are support skills used to organize, store, locate, integrate, process, evaluate, and transfer oral and written information in the process of learning. Assessment is necessary to determine the level and types of skills students use to complete assignments, retain newly acquired curricular information, and prepare for tests.

Implementation

✓ Observe students during a study session, note work-study characteristics, including whether they are focusing on the task, how long they appear to be concentrating on the subject, whether they are using a specific study strategy, and how well they have prepared for the study session (e.g., having the appropriate materials). Note whether they use a visual, oral/auditory, or multisensory approach; whether they appear to have an organized system or study plan; and whether they are able to follow this plan (see Figures 6–15 and 6–16).

✓ Observe the environment in which students are studying. Are distractions kept to a minimum in the test preparation and test-taking environment? Is the test area quiet and well lit? Is the student studying with peers?

✓ Ask the student a series of open-ended questions, during and after the observation (see Figure 6–17).

Special Considerations, Accommodations, Alternatives

- Research indicates that students with mild disabilities often have documented deficiencies in study skills (Polloway, Patton, & Serna, 2009) These students require individualized study techniques and direct instruction to compensate for their particular learning and cognitive processing needs (Friend & Bursuck, 2009).

FIGURE 6–15 Work-Study Listening/Attention Skill Screening Assessment

Does the student:	**Always**	**Sometimes**	**Rarely**	**Never**
Filter out distractions?				
Comprehend verbal interaction?				
Apply meaning to verbal messages?				
Focus on directions, conversations, etc.?				
Shift attention from one task to another?				
Focus when a particular modality is used (e.g., visual, auditory, kinesthetic-tactile)?				
Maintain focus on relevant tasks and not have attention diminish at an unusually rapid rate?				
Identify the main idea of a class discussion?				
Make inferences or draw logical conclusions from discussions?				
Identify and discuss pertinent details from a listening situation?				
Recognize when the details of two discussions are similar?				
Concisely summarize information heard, presenting important information in correct sequence?				
Understand and use language concepts such as categorization, time, and quantity?				
Understand the underlying message in a lesson well enough to apply it to a new situation?				
Figure out solutions and predict outcomes from information heard?				
Understand information heard the first time it is presented?				
Understand the importance of good listening skills?				

FIGURE 6–16 Study Skills Inventory

Completed by: ______________________ **Student:** ______________________ **Date:** ______________

Place the appropriate number (1, 2, or 3) in the box next to each study subskill (1 = Mastered—regular, appropriate use of skill; 2 = Partially Mastered—needs some improvement; 3 = Not Mastered—infrequent use of skill).

Reading Rate
- ☐ Skimming
- ☐ Scanning
- ☐ Rapid reading
- ☐ Normal rate
- ☐ Study or careful reading
- ☐ Understands importance of reading rates

Note Taking/Outlining
- ☐ Uses heading/subheadings appropriately
- ☐ Takes brief and clear notes
- ☐ Records essential information
- ☐ Applies skill during writing activities
- ☐ Uses skill during lectures
- ☐ Develops organized outlines
- ☐ Follows consistent note-taking format
- ☐ Understands importance of note taking
- ☐ Understands importance of outlining

Oral Presentations
- ☐ Freely participates in oral presentations
- ☐ Oral presentations are well organized
- ☐ Uses gestures appropriately
- ☐ Speaks clearly
- ☐ Uses proper language when reporting orally
- ☐ Understands importance of oral reporting

Test Taking
- ☐ Studies for tests in an organized way
- ☐ Spends appropriate amount of time studying different topics covered on a test
- ☐ Organizes narrative responses appropriately
- ☐ Reads and understands directions before answering questions
- ☐ Proofreads responses and checks for errors
- ☐ Identifies and uses clue words in questions
- ☐ Properly records answers
- ☐ Saves difficult items until last
- ☐ Eliminates obviously wrong answers
- ☐ Corrects previous test-taking errors
- ☐ Avoids cramming for tests
- ☐ Systematically reviews completed tests to determine test-taking or test-studying errors
- ☐ Understands importance of test-taking skills

Time Management
- ☐ Completes tasks on time
- ☐ Plans and organizes daily activities and responsibilities effectively
- ☐ Plans and organizes weekly and monthly schedules
- ☐ Reorganizes priorities when necessary
- ☐ Meets scheduled deadlines
- ☐ Accurately perceives the amount of time required to complete tasks
- ☐ Adjusts time allotment to complete tasks
- ☐ Accepts responsibility for managing own time
- ☐ Understands importance of effective time management

Listening
- ☐ Attends to listening activities
- ☐ Applies meaning to verbal messages
- ☐ Filters out auditory distractions
- ☐ Comprehends verbal messages
- ☐ Understands importance of listening skills

Report Writing
- ☐ Organizes thoughts in writing
- ☐ Completes written reports from outline
- ☐ Includes only necessary information
- ☐ Uses proper sentence structure
- ☐ Uses proper punctuation
- ☐ Uses proper grammar and spelling
- ☐ Proofreads written assignments
- ☐ States clear introductory statement
- ☐ Includes clear concluding statements
- ☐ Understands importance of writing reports

Graphic Aids
- ☐ Attends to relevant elements in visual material
- ☐ Uses visuals appropriately in presentations
- ☐ Develops own graphic material
- ☐ Is not confused or distracted by visual material in presentations
- ☐ Understands importance of visual material

Library Usage
- ☐ Uses cataloging system (card or computerized) effectively
- ☐ Able to locate library materials
- ☐ Understands organizational layout of library
- ☐ Understands and uses services of media specialist
- ☐ Understands overall functions and purposes of a library
- ☐ Understands importance of library usage skills

Reference Materials
- ☐ Able to identify components of different reference materials
- ☐ Uses guide words appropriately
- ☐ Consults reference materials when necessary
- ☐ Uses materials appropriately to complete assignments
- ☐ Able to identify different types of reference materials and sources
- ☐ Understands importance of reference materials

FIGURE 6–16 (*Continued*)

Self-Management
- ☐ Monitors own behavior
- ☐ Changes own behavior as necessary
- ☐ Thinks before acting
- ☐ Responsible for own behavior
- ☐ Identifies behaviors that interfere with own learning
- ☐ Understands importance of self-management

Summary of Study Skill Proficiency
- ☐ Summarize in the chart below the number of Mastered (1), Partially Mastered (2), and Not Mastered (3) study subskills.
- ☐ The number next to each study skill represents the total number of subskills for each area.

Study Skill	Mastered	Partly Mastered	Not Mastered	Study Skill	Mastered	Partially Mastered	Not Mastered
Reading Rate—6				Test Taking—13			
Listening—5				Library Usage—6			
Note taking/ Outlining—9				Reference Materials—6			
Report Writing—10				Time Management—9			
Oral Presentations—6				Self-Management—6			
Graphic Aids—5							

Summary Comments:

Source: From *Teaching Students with Learning Problems to Use Study Skills: A Teacher's Guide*, by J. Hoover & J. Patton, 1995, Pro-Ed, Austin, TX. Copyright 1995 by Pro-Ed, Inc. Reprinted with permission.

FIGURE 6–17 Study Skills Survey

- How do you plan for and organize your study sessions? ____________________
- If you find that you do not understand something while studying, what do you do? ____________________
- What time of day is best for you to study? ____________________
- Where do you study? Is the place free of distractions and well lit? ____________________
- Are you able to stay focused on the task when studying? ____________________
- Do you feel you spend sufficient time studying? ____________________
- How do you keep track of your assignments? ____________________
- What conditions tend to cause you to become distracted? ____________________
- When you feel confused while studying, what do you do? ____________________
- Describe how you learn best (when you read, write, listen, draw pictures, or discuss)? ____________________
- How do you plan your time when you have to complete a big project? ____________________
- How do you keep track of your assignments and progress in class?____________________

Assessment Procedure: *Test Accommodations*

Strategy Description

Accommodations are changes in the way a student takes a test, which enables students to show what they know, without changing the actual test itself. The goal of accommodations is not to make a test easier, but to improve access, to give students a better opportunity to show what they know and can do. Besides accommodations, other ways to increase a student's access to assessments include teaching test-taking strategies, designing tests that are more accessible to a greater population of students, making sure that all students have opportunities to learn the content that is being assessed, and motivating students to do their best.

Implementation

✓ Provide accommodations only to students who, due to unique circumstances, need these test adaptations and modifications to demonstrate what they have mastered following instruction (see Figure 6–18).

✓ Use accommodations to enhance access without changing the skill or construct measured. Accommodations should be used on an as-needed basis only, be consistent with day-to-day instructional methods, and not be introduced during a test session, as students should be comfortable with their use.

✓ Provide presentation accommodations, which involves allowing access to test directions and content in alternate ways (e.g., items are read aloud).

✓ Provide response accommodations, which involves alternate methods of recording responses and includes either format alternatives, procedural changes, assistive devices, or a combination of these (e.g., marking answers in the test booklet, rather than on scantron sheets).

✓ Provide setting accommodations, which involves a change in location or the condition in which the assessment takes place (e.g., the use of a study carrel).

✓ Provide scheduling accommodations, which involves changes in when tests are administered, such as the day or time or order in which tests are administered (e.g., adjust subtest order).

✓ Provide time accommodations, which involves a change in the duration of the test, frequently an extension in the standard length of time allowed for test taking (e.g., double time allotted).

Special Considerations, Accommodations, Alternatives

- Familiarity with state policy on accommodations is essential. It is important to know that some accommodations are considered nonstandard or nonallowable. Each state has guidelines for the use of accommodations for accountability assessments (visit http://education.umn.edu/nceo/TopicAreas/Accommodations/StatesAccomm.htm for more information).
- Accommodations for English language learners should be determined by the teacher.
- Students with disabilities must have their accommodations documented on a current IEP or 504 Accommodation Plan.
- Examples of conditions in which students are likely to qualify for Section 504 accommodations include temporary disabilities (short-term hospitalizations or accidents), communicable diseases, allergies or asthma, environmental illness, attention disorders, and drug or alcohol addictions; however, the student must not be currently using illegal drugs.

Additional Resources

Academic Accommodations for Students with Learning Disabilities, *http://www.washington.edu/doit/Brochures/Academics/accomm_ld.html*

FIGURE 6–18 Assessment Accommodations Matrix

	ELL	LD	VI	AI	OD	ADD
Test presentation/directions are accommodated by the following:						
Tape record and replay directions/test questions		*	*			*
Read orally and reread test questions/content*	*	*	*			
Clarify, simplify, explain, translate directions/test questions	*	*				
Reread/restate in own words or native language*	*	*	*			*
Present using sign language or an interpreter	*		*			
Use a color overlay		*	*			
Use an amplification device				*		
Use a visual magnification device/enlarged print			*			
Allow page markers as a place marker		*	*		*	*
Allow student to make marks in test booklet		*	*			*
Turn pages for the student/assist in tracking items			*		*	*
Provide materials in braille			*			
Allow highlighting or color coding by teacher or student		*	*			*
Use sign language for directions and test questions/content				*		
Provide student with text talk converter*			*			
Provide a qualified translator to translate questions/content, orally or in writing*	*	*				
Provide enlarged test materials			*			
Order items according to level of difficulty		*				*
Provide a definition for unfamiliar, abstract words	*	*				
Provide fewer items on a page to avoid confusion		*	*			*
Test response is accommodated by the following:						
Use computational aids (e.g., calculator, multiplication table)		*	*		*	*
Use template, line/graph/grid paper, or graphic organizer for aligning work or recording answers		*	*		*	*
Allow writing in test booklet	*	*				*
Allow response in native language, interpreter records response in English	*					
Allow scribe to record response (e.g., oral, pointing, signing)	*	*	*		*	*
Allow pointing to the response	*	*	*		*	*
Allow oral responses	*	*	*		*	*
Use braille writer for recording responses			*			
Use a visual or audio device to record response		*	*	*	*	*
Use computer or word processor to record response		*	*		*	*
Use spell or grammar check, when appropriate	*	*				
Test setting is accommodated by the following:						
Provide individual, supervised test administration	*	*	*	*	*	*
Allow test taking in small group or different class setting	*	*	*	*	*	*
Provide distraction-free environment	*	*				*
Allow hospitalized or homebound student to take test in hospital/treatment setting or home with supervision	*	*	*	*	*	*
Provide adapted furniture and equipment		*	*	*	*	
Provide special lighting and/or acoustics		*	*	*		*
Allow student to move around, stand or lay down during testing, as needed		*			*	*
Provide a study carrel to work with minimal distractions	*	*				*
Provide an aide to assist with testing in a large-group setting	*	*	*	*	*	*

(*Continued*)

FIGURE 6–18 (*Continued*)

	ELL	LD	VI	AI	OD	ADD
Test scheduling is accommodated by the following:						
Plan during a specific time of the day		*				*
Change test schedule or order of tests		*	*	*	*	*
Break test into multiple sessions/over multiple days		*	*	*	*	*
Test timing is accommodated by the following:						
Allow extended time	*	*	*	*	*	*
Allow unlimited time		*	*	*	*	
Provide frequent breaks during test session		*			*	*

*Except reading or language arts tests

ELL: English language learner
LD: Learning disability
VI: Visually impaired (blind/low vision/partially sighted)
AI: Auditorily impaired (deaf/hard of hearing)
OD: Orthopedically impaired (physical disability)
ADD: Attention deficit disorder

Assessment Procedure: *Test-Taking Skill Assessment and Preparation Strategies*

Strategy Description

Teachers need to determine how "test wise" students are so that a plan can be developed to maximize their performance on evaluation measures. Students need to understand the mechanics of test taking, such as the need to carefully follow instructions and to check their work. They need to use appropriate test-taking strategies, including ways to address test items and make educated guesses. In addition, students should practice their test-taking skills to refine their abilities and to become more comfortable in testing situations.

Implementation

- ✓ Assess student's test preparation and test-taking skills (see Figure 6–19).
- ✓ Determine the student's knowledge of the test by asking the purpose, the general type, content, and approximate length of the scheduled test.
- ✓ Familiarize students with test directions, test format, how to avoid common mistakes, and how to use time effectively.
- ✓ Provide students with samples of previous tests to review so they can become familiar with a variety of test types and formats.
- ✓ Design some classroom tests using standardized test formats and administration guidelines so students can practice in simulated situations.
- ✓ Teach test-taking fundamental information (e.g., dealing with time limits, pacing, knowing that some tests penalize for incorrect answers so that it is better to leave blanks than to guess).
- ✓ Reduce test anxiety and build confidence in test-taking abilities; provide opportunities for discussions or support sessions to devise ways that students can manage test anxiety.
- ✓ Practice various forms of relaxation techniques.
- ✓ Ensure that test accommodations are written in students' IEP.
- ✓ Notify parents about the upcoming test dates and times so they can make sure their child is prepared (e.g., getting sufficient nourishment and sleep).

Special Considerations, Accommodations, Alternatives

- Many students, especially those with disabilities and recent immigrants, have test anxiety due to having no prior experience with test taking, a lack of test-taking strategies, or a history of poor test results.
- There are numerous factors that influence how well a student performs on a test, including mastery of the material covered, motivation and interest, self-confidence, anxiety, attention to detail, the ability to follow directions, and time factors (Technical Assistance Alliance for Parent Centers [Alliance], 2001).
- Sometimes, improving test-taking skills will help reduce the need for accommodations.

FIGURE 6–19 Test Preparation and Test-Taking Skills Checklist

Test Preparation Does the student:	**Yes**	**No**	**Comments**
• Set up a quiet, comfortable area conducive to study for tests?			
• Gather and organize all study materials before beginning to study?			
• Find out exactly what will be covered on the test?			
• Find out what kind of test it will be (essay, multiple choice, matching, etc.)?			
• Prioritize information and determine hierarchy of content to be studied?			
• Develop a study plan, deciding objectives for each projected study session?			
• Look up hard vocabulary to understand test content word meaning?			
• Skim chapter headings to recall the overall ideas in each chapter?			
• Reread chapter summaries?			
• Review all visual illustrations when studying?			
• Space studying over an extended period of time rather than cram for tests?			
• Systematically review previous tests to determine test-taking/studying errors?			
• Use test item formats for practice?			
• Review all practice items available?			
• Practice using answer sheets with different types of responses required?			
• Practice taking a test within time limits?			
Test Taking Does the student:			
• Carefully read all directions before beginning the test?			
• Follow directions carefully?			
• Budget time well?			
• Skim the test before beginning work?			
• Read the entire item and all answers?			
• Mark unknown questions and return to them later?			
• Answer easier questions first and persist to the end?			
• Apply memory strategies (e.g., mnemonics, keywords)?			
• Identify and carefully use clue words?			
• Use test-taking strategies (e.g., eliminate wrong answer)?			
• Make educated guesses?			
• Maintain a positive attitude when taking tests?			
• Carefully record answers, writing neatly and legibly?			
• Proofread answers and check for errors?			

Assessment Procedure: *Universally Designed Assessments*

Strategy Description

The term *universal design* refers to the effort to produce "optimal standard assessment conditions." Universally designed assessments (UDAs) are developed to allow participation for the widest possible range of students. The UDA is intended to meet the needs of all students in today's increasingly diverse population and to provide the least restrictive environment through design rather than accommodation. The UDA is intended to increase access but not to change the standard of performance or make tests easier, nor is it meant to replace needed accommodations or the need for alternative assessment for some students.

Implementation

- ✓ Define test content, clearly and precisely, and include what is to be tested so that irrelevant cognitive, sensory, emotional, and physical barriers can be removed (see Figure 6–20).
- ✓ Build accessibility into items from the beginning. To ensure test items are unbiased, have other teachers carefully review tests before administration.
- ✓ Design tests so that all needed accommodations can easily be used (e.g., all items can be brailled).
- ✓ Develop simple, clear instructions and procedures so that all students can easily follow the test-taking directions.
- ✓ Develop tests that have maximum readability and comprehensibility; use clear, plain language that reduces ambiguity and increases understanding.
- ✓ Develop tests that have maximum legibility; characteristics that ensure easy decipherability are applied to text, tables, figures and illustrations, and response formats (Thompson & Thurlow, 2002).

Special Considerations, Accommodations, Alternatives

- Tests that are developed using universal design, for inclusive assessment populations, provide students with equal opportunity for test taking.
- Refer to Universally Designed Assessments: Better Tests for Everyone!, *http://cehd.umn.edu/nceo/OnlinePubs/Policy14.htm*

FIGURE 6–20 Guidelines for Universally Designed Assessment

Plain Language Strategies	Description
Reduce excessive length	Reduce wordiness and remove irrelevant material.
Use common words	Eliminate unusual or low frequency words and replace with common words (e.g., replace *utilize* with *use*).
Avoid ambiguous words	For example, avoid using *crane,* because it could be a bird or a piece of heavy machinery.
Avoid irregularly spelled words	Examples of irregularly spelled words are *trough* and *feign*.
Avoid proper names	Replace proper names with simple common names such as first names.
Avoid inconsistent naming and graphic conventions	Avoid multiple names for the same concept. Be consistent in the use of typeface.
Avoid unclear signals about how to direct attention	Well-designed heading and graphic arrangement can convey information about the relative importance of information and order in which it should be considered.
Mark all questions	Give an obvious graphic signal (e.g., bullet, letter, number) to indicate separate questions.
Legibility Characteristics	**Description**
Contrast	Black type on matte pastel or off-white paper is most favorable for both legibility and eye strain.
Type size	Large type sizes are most effective for young students who are learning to read, students with visual difficulties, and individuals with eye fatigue issues. The legal size for large print text is 14 point.
Spacing	The amount of space between each character can affect legibility. Spacing needs to be wide between both letters and words. Fixed-space fonts seem to be more legible for some readers than proportional-spaced fonts.
Leading	Leading, the amount of vertical space between lines of type, must be enough to avoid type that looks blurry and has a muddy look. The amount needed varies with type size (e.g., 14-point type needs 3 to 6 points of leading).
Typeface	Standard typeface, using upper- and lowercase, is more readable than italic, slanted, small caps, or all caps.
Justification	Unjustified text (with staggered right margin) is easier to see and scan than justified text, especially for poor readers.
Line length	Optimal length is about 4 inches, or 8 to 10 words per line. This length avoids reader fatigue and difficulty locating the beginning of the next line, which causes readers to lose their place.
Blank space	A general rule is to allow text to occupy only about half of a page. Blank space anchors text on the paper and increases legibility.
Graphs and tables	Symbols used on graphs need to be highly discriminable. Labels should be placed directly next to plot lines so that information can be found quickly and not require short-term memory.
Illustrations	When used, an illustration should be directly next to the question for which it is needed. Because illustrations create numerous visual and distraction challenges, and may interfere with the use of some accommodations (such as magnifiers), they should be used only when they contain information being assessed.
Response formats	Response options should include larger circles (for bubble response tests), as well as multiple other forms of response.

Source: Adapted from *Universal Design Applied to Large-Scale Assessment,* by S. Thompson, C. Johnstone, and M. Thurlow, 2002, University of Minnesota, National Center on Educational Outcomes.

REFERENCES

Amrein, A. L., & Berliner, D. C. (2002). High-stakes testing, uncertainty, and student learning. *Education Policy Analysis Archives, 10*(18).

Bukowski, W. M., Sippola, L., Hoza, B., & Newcomb, A. F. (2000). Pages from a sociometric notebook: An analysis of nomination and rating scale measures of acceptance, rejection, and social preference. In A. H. N. Cillessen & W. M. Bukowski (Eds.), *Recent advances in the measurement of acceptance and rejection in the peer system* (pp. 11–26). San Francisco: Jossey-Bass.

Council for Exceptional Children (CEC). (2002). NABE recommendations regarding evaluation, eligibility and individual education programs. *Determining appropriate referrals of English language learners of special education: A self-assessment guide for principals.* Arlington, VA: Author.

Friend, M., & Bursuck, W. D. (2009). *Including students with special needs: A practical guide for classroom teachers* (5th ed.). Boston: Allyn & Bacon.

Gollnick, D. M. & Chinn, P. C. (2009). *Multicultural education in a pluralistic society* (8th ed.). Upper Sadde River, NJ: Merrill/Pearson.

Guerin, G. R., & Maier, A. S. (1983). *Sociometric matrix of social studies choices. Informal assessment in education.* Palo Alto, CA: Mayfield Publishing Company.

Harry, B. & Klingner, J. K. (2006). *Why are so many minority students in special education?: Understanding race and disability in schools.* New York: Teachers College Press.

Heward, W. L. (2009). *Exceptional children: An introduction to special education* (9th ed.). Upper Saddle River, NJ: Merrill/Prentice Hall.

Hoover, J. J. & Patton, J. R. (2007). *Teaching Study Skills to Students with Learning Problems: A Teacher's Guide for Meeting Diverse Needs* (2nd ed.). Austin, TX: Pro-Ed.

Janney, R., & Snell, M. E. (2008). *Teacher's guides to inclusive practices: Behavioral support* (2nd ed.). Baltimore: Paul H. Brookes.

National Symposium on Learning Disabilities in English Language Learners (2004). *Symposium Summary.* Washington, DC: U.S. Office of Special Education and Rehabiliation Services.

Ortiz, A. A., & Yates, J. R. (2002). Considerations in the assessment of English language learners referred to special education. In A. J. Artiles & A. A. Ortiz (Eds.), *English language learners with special education needs: Identification, assessment, and instruction* (pp. 65–85). McHenry, IL: Center for Applied Linguistics and Delta Systems.

Pavri, S. (2001). Loneliness in children with disabilities: How teachers can help. *Teaching Exceptional Children, 33*(6), 52–58.

Pierce, L. V. (2002). Performance-based assessment: Promoting achievement for English language learners. *Clearinghouse on Language and Linguistics News Bulletin, 26*(1), 1–7.

Polloway, E. A., Patton, J. R., & Serna, L. (2009). *Strategies for teaching learners with special needs* (9th ed.). Upper Saddle River: NJ: Merrill-Prentice Hall.

Stiggins, R. J. (2002). Assessment crisis: The absence of assessment FOR learning. *Phi Delta Kappan, 83*(10), 758–765.

Technical Assistance Alliance for Parent Centers (Alliance). (2001). *Evaluation: What does it mean for your child?* Minneapolis, MN: Pacer Center.

Thompson, S., & Thurlow, M. (2002). *Universally designed assessments: Better tests for everyone!* (Policy Directions 14). Minneapolis, MN: University of Minnesota, National Center on Educational Outcomes. Retrieved Feb. 15, 2009, from http://education .umn.edu/NCEO/OnlinePubs/Policy14.htm

Thompson, S. J., Johnstone, C. J., & Thurlow, M. L. (2002). *Universal design applied to large-scale assessment* (Synthesis Report 44). Minneapolis, MN: University of Minnesota, National Center on Educational Outcomes.

Twombly, E. (2001). Screening, assessment, curriculum planning and evaluation: Engaging parents in the process. *Zero to Three, 21*(4), 36–41.

Watkins, C. R., & Schloss, C. N. (2001). Assessment in the referral process. In A. S. Alper, D. L. Ryndak, & C. N. Schloss (Eds.), *Alternate assessment of students with disabilities in inclusive settings* (pp. 54–74). Needham Heights, MA: Allyn & Bacon.

Woods, J. J., & McCormick, K. M. (2002). Toward an integration of child- and family-centered practices in the assessment of preschool children: Welcoming the family. *Young Exceptional Children, 5*(3), 2–11.

Yzquierdo, Z. A., Blalock, G., & Torres-Velasquez, D. (2004). Language-appropriate assessments for determining eligibility of English language learners for special education services. *Assessment for Effective Intervention, 29*(2), 17–30.

Chapter 7

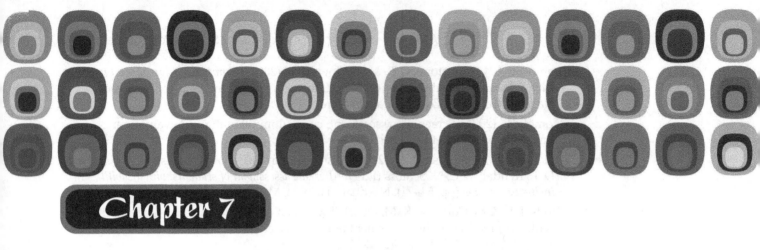

Scoring, Graphing, and Progress Monitoring

INTRODUCTION

Previous chapters have covered numerous types and methods of assessment ideal for identifying students' strength and areas in need of remediation. The content in this chapter is also critical for progress monitoring necessary so that students' individual profiles can be closely watched and critical interventions can be initiated quickly to avoid losing precious learning time. However, once the assessments have been administered and scored, the next step is to track students' performance, compare their current to previous achievement, graph their progress, rank their scores to monitor competencies, and compare current status to projected goals. Each of these provide a visual means of documenting whether instructional efforts have been effective. Also included in this chapter are clear guidelines for reporting this progress: communicating results to the student, family members, teachers, and school administration, as well as providing accountability to local, state, and federal officials using verbal and written forms of communication.

When reading about the various reporting systems discussed in this chapter, keep in mind the importance of including the student in the process of progress monitoring and developing reporting systems. Students who participate in the development of the major components of their educational program, such as rubrics, self and peer assessments, and personal contracts, feel empowered as they are actively involved in the learning process. Plotting their own graphs and recording their daily performance scores increases their investment in the academic program and is likely to improve motivation and interest. Providing students and their families with a copy of the rubric before instruction or test administration, helps them understand what is expected, the principle features, and the weight of the various dimensions so they will be aware of the criteria used to evaluate their work. Keeping students and their families informed and involved in the learning and assessment process, can ensure that everyone benefits.

SCORING PROCEDURES

Scoring Procedure: *Holistic Rubrics*

Strategy Description

A rubric is an established guideline or planned set of criteria that describes levels of performance; it outlines expectations so that an assignment or a performance can be judged.

Points or grades are awarded for specific levels of performance. Rubrics can provide clearer expectations and directions than the letter-grade system and are useful for charting students' progress toward attaining benchmarks, which are indicators or descriptors that represent nationally or locally agreed upon, minimally acceptable standards.

Although we will discuss several types of rubrics, the scoring rubric that uses only a single scale is a global, or holistic, rubric. In holistic scoring, points are awarded for the whole product or for performance based on an overall impression of a student's work. A single score or description of quality is based on clearly defined criteria—generally a scale ranging from 0 to 5 or 0 to 6. The criteria might range from no response, to a partial response with a strategy, to a complete response with a clear explanation (see Figure 7–1). The purpose of a holistic rubric is to (a) judge student work products with only one trait of performance, (b) get a quick snapshot of overall quality or achievement, and (c) judge the "impact" of a product or performance. Although holistic scoring lacks the depth of information contained in analytic scoring (which has multiple dimensions), it tends to be easier to design and score. The scoring rubric rating scales can be quantitative (numerical), qualitative (descriptive), or a combination of the two (see Figure 7–2).

Implementation

Steps for Developing a Rubric

✓ List the expected performance objectives for the learning activity. Typical performance objectives include the quality of the outcome; the organization, presentation, and comprehensiveness of content; the ability to focus and take a position; writing skills, including coherence, depth or elaboration, clarity, word choice, and sentence variety; accuracy of mechanics, grammar, and spelling; variety and number of reference sources.

✓ Review examples of student work to be sure all important performance objectives are included. Consider the following:

Appropriate developmental levels, which cover a range of disabilities and skills at the specific grade or age level

Culture, race, gender, or socioeconomic status

Skills that students have acquired and have been covered in class

✓ Add all the points from each trait to obtain a total score.

✓ Pilot test the rubric or checklist on actual samples of student work.

✓ Consider adapting previously developed rubrics to meet existing needs. This can be done by adding descriptors so that they are consistent with established school, district, state, and/or national curriculum standards or are based on grade and subject area standards. When modifying existing rubrics, consider the following options.

Change the wording of the various parts of the rubric, as needed.

Modify by changing or dropping scales on an analytical rubric.

Borrow scales from existing rubrics by mixing and matching.

Eliminate unnecessary or inappropriate criteria.

Adjust rubric criteria to adapt to grade level expectations.

Add more or remove categories.

Add a "no-response" category at the bottom of the scale.

Assigning Point Values

- The rubric scoring scale needs to be clearly written, free of educational jargon, and appropriate for the student's developmental level.
- Prioritize or assign more credit to one scale than to others (e.g., assign more credit for content than for grammar) by multiplying the prioritized scale by a number greater than 1. If content is twice as important as all the other areas, the score on that scale is multiplied by 2 before the scale scores are added to get a total score.

- Factors to consider when determining the points for a rubrics rating scale include the following:
  - Points (numbers) and/or words (e.g., *novice, intermediate, proficient*) can be used to evaluate the learning outcomes.
  - Points may vary according to the purpose or individual need.
  - Points should be specific, well defined, and clearly differentiated.
  - Larger scale ranges (i.e., more than 6 or 7 points) can make it more challenging to differentiate between points and to reach agreement among scorers (referred to as inter-rater reliability).
  - Smaller scale ranges (i.e., less than 4 points) can make it difficult to differentiate between students, yet can be used when the intent is to determine whether students' performance has exceeded, met, or failed to meet the outcome standard.
  - Scales of equal length should be used when the goal is to rate several different dimensions so that they are equally weighted when results are added.

FIGURE 7–1 Sample Holistic Rubric

Numerical Rating		
	Strong Command of Written Language	
6	• Opening and closing • Relates to single focus • Organized, logical progression • Variety of cohesive devices • Risks resulting in vivid responses	• Few, if any, errors in usage, sentence construction, and mechanics • Language adapted to audience and purpose • Strong voice
	Generally Strong Command of Written Language	
5	• Opening and closing • Relates to topic with single focus • Organized, logical progression • Appropriate and varied details • Strongly connected ideas	• Compositional risks • Papers may be flawed though complete and unified • Few errors in usage, mechanics, and sentence construction
	Command of Written Language	
4	• Opening and closing • Responses related to topic • Single, organized focus • Transition from idea to idea • Loosely connected ideas	• May have bare, unelaborated details • Some errors in usage with no consistent pattern • Few errors in sentence construction • Some errors in mechanics
	Partial Command of Written Language	
3	• May or may not have opening or closing • Has single focus • May drift or shift from focus • May be sparse in details	• Organizational flaws and lapses • Lack of transition • Patterns of errors in usage • Errors in sentence construction • Pattern of mechanical errors
	Limited Command of Written Language	
2	• May or may not have opening or closing • Some attempt of organization • May drift from primary focus	• Little elaboration of details • Severe usage problem • Numerous sentence construction errors • Numerous serious mechanical errors
	Very Poor Command of Written Language	
1	• Does not have opening or closing • Lacks coherence • Uncertain focus • Disorganized	• Numerous errors in usage • Grammatically incorrect sentences • Severe mechanical errors that detract from meaning

FIGURE 7–2 Quantitative versus Qualitative Scoring

Examples of Numerical Scores Based on Qualitative Criteria

Score	Criteria
1	No attempt made
2	Attempt made, incomplete or undeveloped task performance
3	Successful attempt made, adequate performance
4	Superior effort, excellent performance

Examples of Numerical Scores Based on Quantitative Criteria

Score	Criteria
1	0 responses correct
2	1 to 3 out of 10 responses correct
3	4 to 7 out of 10 responses correct
4	8 to 10 responses correct

Examples of Quantitative Score Hierarchies

Undeveloped, developing, fully developed
Not introduced, emerging, competent, superior performance
Novice, apprentice, proficient, distinguished
No evidence, minimal evidence, partial evidence, complete evidence
Poor, fair, good, very good, excellent

Scoring Procedure: *Analytic Rubrics*

Strategy Description

An analytic rubric has two or more separate scales that provide detailed analyses of students' strengths and areas needing improvement (see Figure 7–3). Analytic trait scoring is a scoring system that divides a product or performance into essential traits or dimensions so that each can be judged separately, thus providing an independent score for each criterion on the assessment scale. In analytic scoring, separate scores are given for various dimensions (referred to as traits) of students' performances or products. Although time consuming, analytic scoring may be more useful than holistic scoring as it provides detailed information for instructional planning and progress monitoring, as well as feedback for students.

Implementation

- ✓ Develop a continuum (scale) for describing the range of products/performances on each dimension and determine the criteria to be used for the evaluation scale (e.g., 4 points for excellent to 1 point for poor).
- ✓ Include a column to record the score for each dimension, as well as a row for the total score. Refer to Figure 7–4 for a guide to adapting an analytic rubric to a holistic rubric.
- ✓ Assign points for each dimension, such as overall organization, neatness, grammar, strategy solution, and self-assessment. Analytic scoring lends itself to providing descriptive feedback on complex assignments.

✓ Determine whether rating will be numerical (e.g., 1 to 5) or categorical (e.g., excellent/adequate/poor). Although categorical descriptors provide more detailed, definitive information, when numerical scores are totaled and averaged they can provide useful diagnostic information as well (see Figure 7–3).

✓ Score each area designated individually when scoring analytically, so that a poor performance in one area does not negatively affect the score in another designated area.

FIGURE 7–3 Sample Analytic Rubric

Content (20 pts) **Points earned:** ____________
Topic is narrowed.
Main idea is clear.
Main idea or theme is developed.
Details are tailored to the main idea.
Ideas are complete.
Reasons and examples are convincing.
Conclusion is clearly stated.
Evidence of writing is mature.

Structure/Organization (20 pts) **Points earned:** ____________
Ideas are sequenced (beginning, middle, end).
Writing follows assigned structure (expository narrative).
Sentences are varied (simple, compound, and complex).
Sentences are complete, fully developed.
Statements are logically supported.

Usage (20 pts) **Points earned:** ____________
Paragraphs contain topic sentences.
Correct style has been used.
Sentences are complete thoughts.
Transitions and conjunctions are used to connect ideas.
Conventional word endings are accurate.
Singular and plural possessives are correct.
Verb tense is appropriate.
Subject-verb agreement is correct.
Personal pronouns are used appropriately.
Homophones are used correctly.

Mechanics (20 pts) **Points earned:** ____________
Contractions are correctly used.
Spelling is accurate.
Punctuation is correct.
Capitalization is correct.
Numbers are used accurately.

Word Choice (20 pts) **Points earned:** ____________
Word choices are appropriate and varied.
Words are chosen to express purpose of writing.
Words are used that are descriptive.
Fluency is adequate to express ideas.

Total points possible: 100 **Total Points earned:** ____________

FIGURE 7–4 Analytic Rubric Modified to a Holistic Rubric

Writing Traits (Dimensions)	Above Average	Average	Below Average	Example Students' Score
Ideas and content (x2)	(10 pts)	(6 pts)	(2 pts)	6 pts
Organization	(5 pts)	(3 pts)	(1 pt)	(1 pt)
Voice	(5 pts)	(3 pts)	(1 pt)	(5 pts)
Word choice	(5 pts)	(3 pts)	(1 pt)	(3 pts)
Sentence fluency	(5 pts)	(3 pts)	(1 pt)	(5 pts)
Conventions	(5 pts)	(3 pts)	(1 pt)	(1 pt)
Presentation	(5 pts)	(3 pts)	(1 pt)	(1 pt)
			TOTAL:	22 pts
			AVERAGE:	3

Scoring Procedure: *Rating Scales*

Strategy Description

A rating scale, similar to a rubric, is used to evaluate students' knowledge, skills, and attitudes by placing a value on the performance observed. In other words, by assigning a numerical or descriptive rating that can be used and understood by those interpreting the ratings. They are used for scoring the degree of performance (e.g., mastered, emerging, no skill), provide more information than dichotomous scales (yes/no, pass/fail, good/poor), are detailed, and are versatile when converting to grades. Teachers can use these scales to rate students' level of proficiency, and for peer evaluations and student self-evaluations. They can be used to communicate a degree of competence for specific skills or to show progress over time.

There are three types of rating scales, those that (1) describe what the student can do, (2) specify the extent that dimensions were observed, and (3) rate the quality of the performance. The components of a primary trait rating scale include the listing of the dimensions to be rated (e.g., the student writes numbers accurately, regroups digits in the tens place), and the scale (referred to as a Likert scale) for rating each dimension (e.g., always, sometimes, never; excellent, good, fair, poor; mastered, emerging, not acquired).

Implementation

✓ Provide the student with directions to either circle or check a number on each scale that indicates the extent of the particular characteristic being rated (see Figure 7–5).

✓ Consider which of the following types of rating scales is most appropriate to use for a specific situation.

Semantic differential scales—See Figure 7–6 which uses opposite (or bipolar) adjectives rated along a continuum.

Graphic rating scales—See Figure 7–7 which rates along a graduated continuum with points separated by equal intervals.

Numerical or Likert scales—See Figure 7–8 which is used to rank each behavior, for example, the frequency of occurrence (always, often, sometimes, rarely, never) or the quality of performance (excellent = 1 to poor = 5).

Visual analog scales—See Figure 7–9 which is continuous and marked at any point along the scale.

FIGURE 7–5 Generic Rating Scale

Rater's name: ____________________
Presenter's name: ____________________ Date: ____________
Subject: ____________________ Topic: ____________________

Rate the presenter:	**Excellent**	**Good**	**Fair**	**Poor**
1. Followed assignment directions				
2. Included all required components				
3. Appeared to be organized				
4. Spoke in a loud and clear voice				
5. Established eye contact with audience				
6. Stood straight				
7. Avoided "umms" and "ahhs"				
8. Kept to the topic				
9. Involved the audience				
10. Maintained the audience's attention				
11. Allowed time for questions				
12. Finished within the allotted time limits				

List three things the presenter did well:

1. ____________________
2. ____________________
3. ____________________

FIGURE 7–6 Semantic Differential Scale

1. Interacts appropriately with other children.

   Always _____ _____ _____ _____ Never

2. Follows two-step directions.

   Always _____ _____ _____ _____ Never

3. Appropriately sits and listens during story time.

   Always _____ _____ _____ _____ Never

FIGURE 7–7 Graphic Rating Scale

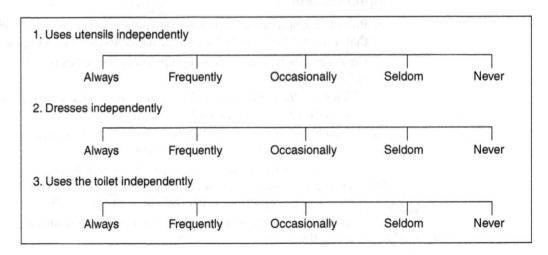

1. Uses utensils independently

   Always — Frequently — Occasionally — Seldom — Never

2. Dresses independently

   Always — Frequently — Occasionally — Seldom — Never

3. Uses the toilet independently

   Always — Frequently — Occasionally — Seldom — Never

FIGURE 7–8
Numerical Scale

1. To what degree does the child use utensils independently?
   1 2 3 4 5
2. To what degree does the child dress independently?
   1 2 3 4 5
3. To what degree does the child use the toilet independently?
   1 2 3 4 5

FIGURE 7–9 Visual Analog Scale

1. Uses utensils independently.

Skill Mastered ———————————————— Undeveloped

2. Dresses independently

Skill Mastered ———————————————— Undeveloped

3. Uses the toilet independently

Skill Mastered ———————————————— Undeveloped

Scoring Procedure: *Anchor Papers*

Strategy Description

Anchor papers are representative products, papers, and performances that guide and standardize the scoring of students' work in a school or district to ensure consistency. Students can be provided with copies of anchor papers to be used as models of exceptional, average, and poor papers (refer to Figure 7–10). Parents can be given sample models and tips for helping students meet the standards. A limitation of the use of anchor papers is that typically only one or two papers are used for any grade number. It is often difficult to match the wide diversity of responses against only one or two papers. It is critical to ensure repeatability and agreement between different scorers on grading the same response. This consistency of scoring between two or more independent scorers is referred to as inter-rater reliability. In order to achieve inter-rater reliability, there must be mutually agreed on elements of quality used as the basis for making judgments about, and the grading of, student performance so that scoring results do not vary from teacher to teacher (Arter & McTighe, 2001).

FIGURE 7–10
Examples of Anchor Papers

Level 1
My fraorite place is to be at texis because is has big dogs there and thyner a timber roof and my mom nd me She saw a indein there and She saw a cashle.

Level 3
My favorite place is the beach. I like to play in the water and sand. I go there with my Mom, Dad and brother. Sometimes my Nanny and Poppop come too. I like to go surfing in the oshin and make sand castles in the sand. I like it when the ice cream truck comes. My favorite kind of ice cream from it is the cookie sandwhich. My brother's favorote kind of ice creem from the truck is half vanilla half chocklite.

Implementation

✓ Rank students by determining overall quality of the work; sort work products into piles of excellent, good, fair, or poor work.

✓ Reread and reevaluate until the students' work is clearly ranked based on overall quality. Then convert to letter grades to fit district grading policies, (see Figure 7–11). Often, a breakdown is made between the final product's content (the actual message presented to the reader) and form (i.e., technical format, such as spelling, grammar, and punctuation).

✓ Give students a model of excellent work or examples of products that were rated at each level (i.e., from excellent to poor) with explanations as to how each work sample was rated. This provides students with clear expectations as well as examples to use when evaluating their own work and the work of others. When students understand what it takes to produce excellent papers, they are more likely to do so.

Inter-rater Reliability

✓ Inter-rater reliability training takes about half a day for most teachers using a holistic rubric and approximately one full day when using an analytic rubric.

✓ Arrange for group members using the rating scale (e.g., all fifth-grade teachers) to independently rate the same samples of work produced by students who are high achievers, average, and low achievers. Note the extent raters assign the same score to each piece of work.

✓ Compare ratings, discuss the rationale behind the ratings given, and arrive at a standard for each criterion or domain ranking.

✓ Recognize that when ratings are dissimilar or have no consensus, raters need to discuss the rationale for their scores, perhaps negotiate the differences to reach an understanding of the rating system, or involve an additional rater to evaluate the product. Rubric criteria may need further clarification to establish uniform scoring. Achieving consensus and consistency generally takes negotiation and practice.

Additional Resources

Teacher Treasures: Anchor Papers,
http://treasures.macmillanmh.com/utah/teachers/professional-development/anchor-papers

Grade 1: Prompt, Anchor Paper, Rubric,
http://www.sbsd.k12.ca.us/district/curriculum/AnchorPapers/Grade1/Grd1-1.pdf

FIGURE 7–11 Rating Scale Conversion to Grades

Point Criteria		Grade
40% or more are 5*, and . . .	10% or less are below 4, then . . .	student earns an A
10% or more are 5*, and . . .	30% or less are below 4, then . . .	student earns a B
20% or more are 4*, and . . .	10% or less are below 3, then . . .	student earns a C
10% or more are 4*, and . . .	30% or less are below 3, then . . .	student earns a D
all points are below 3 . . .	then . . .	student earns an F

(Based on a rating scale of 5 to 1)

Scoring Procedure: *Checklists*

Strategy Description

Checklists can be an efficient method of evaluating the level of skill mastery. Teachers can develop a checklist of skills, arranged in a consistent manner to systematically, quickly, and efficiently record whether specific skills or behaviors are or are not present (Arter & McTighe, 2001). The kind of checklist used depends on the type of information to be obtained. Curriculum checklists are generally based on curricular scope and sequence charts, and specific skills are checked off as mastered, emerging, or not mastered (refer to Figure 7–12). Behavioral checklists consist of specific problem behaviors or social skills that need to be monitored (refer to Figure 7–13). Formats may vary. Checklists can be used with an entire class or small groups, so that teachers can track multiple students on one form rather than maintain individual folders for each student being monitored. In this way, teachers can, at a glance, determine who does and does not need assistance with a specific skill or behavior, a determination that is useful for instructional planning and program evaluation. In contrast, checklists can be designed to monitor individual student's strengths and weaknesses.

Implementation

✓ Identify items to be observed and evaluated; checklists should be specific and have a realistic number of attainable goals.

✓ Determine criteria to evaluate performance; criteria should be limited for ease of rating and scoring.

✓ Indicators may include evidence of completion (e.g., x = completed, 0 = incomplete; yes or not yet), qualitative criteria (e.g., good/fair/poor), or relative level of proficiency (e.g., M = mastered, E = emerging, NS = no skill).

✓ Decide on indicators for identifying whether the performance or behavior has occurred (e.g., plus (+)/minus (−), mastered (M)/unmastered (unM), checkoffs (x)).

✓ Determine a hierarchy of skills; arrange in the order in which they would be observed.

✓ Keep checklists short and specific.

✓ Correlate items on the list directly to students' performance or behavior.

✓ Be consistent with word choice and format.

✓ Write items in objective, positive terms that highlight what students can do (e.g., "Student is able to solve two-digit subtraction equations not requiring regrouping.").

FIGURE 7–12 Self, Peer, and Teacher Checklist: Content Area Problem Solving

Problem: ____________________

___ Self-Assessment ___ Peer Assessment ___ Teacher Assessment

	Yes	Not Yet	Questions
1.	____	____	Can you explain the problem?
2.	____	____	Can you estimate a reasonable answer?
3.	____	____	Can you list steps to solve the problem?
4.	____	____	Can you think of another problem like it?
5.	____	____	Can you give an alternative solution?

Problem: ____________________
Operation to Use: ____________________
First Step: ____________________

FIGURE 7–13 Psycho-Social-Emotional Adjustment Checklist

The student:	Often	Occasionally	Rarely/Never
Is impulsive	_____	_____	_____
Gives excuses for inappropriate behavior	_____	_____	_____
Constantly blames others for problems	_____	_____	_____
Panics easily	_____	_____	_____
Is highly distractible	_____	_____	_____
Lies continually	_____	_____	_____
Is fearful with adults	_____	_____	_____
Is fearful of new situations	_____	_____	_____
Is verbally hesitant	_____	_____	_____
Is hyperactive	_____	_____	_____
Has a short attention span	_____	_____	_____
Is overactive	_____	_____	_____
Is physical with others	_____	_____	_____
Is intrusive	_____	_____	_____
Is unable to focus on task	_____	_____	_____
Procrastinates	_____	_____	_____
Is very disorganized	_____	_____	_____
Is inflexible	_____	_____	_____
Is irresponsible	_____	_____	_____
Uses poor judgment	_____	_____	_____
Is in denial	_____	_____	_____
Is unwilling to accept responsibility	_____	_____	_____
Demonstrates social withdrawal	_____	_____	_____
Is constantly self-critical	_____	_____	_____
Bullies other children	_____	_____	_____
Needs constant reassurance	_____	_____	_____

TRACKING AND CHARTING PROGRESS

Scoring Procedure: *Graphs*

Strategy Description

Graphing students' scores is a clear, illustrated method of monitoring their progress and is an integral part of using a curriculum-based measurement (CBM). It is a means for the teacher to track ongoing progress toward the projected year-end goal (e.g., adequate yearly progress [AYP] or the Individualized Education Program [IEP]) and, thus, to make instructional decisions. By carefully charting regular scores in each subject area, teachers will be alerted to the need to revise teaching methods, instructional strategies, or student accommodations in a timely manner. Use graphs to communicate student progress to parents, teachers, administrators, and multidisciplinary team members or other support staff. Students can quickly and easily track their own progress and see the relationship between their effort and progress in learning. This can motivate the student to beat their best score.

Implementation

- ✓ Start by determining the specific period of time that progress will be charted (e.g., 8 weeks, a marking period).
- ✓ Use a computer graphing program such as a CBM website to score online, which will provide a chart of performance.
- ✓ Use a program such as the University of Washington (UW) Slope Calculator, which can be downloaded at no cost at http://www.fluentreader.org. A spreadsheet is provided so teachers can automatically chart and calculate the weekly growth slope from baseline to the most recent CBM score by entering the student's baseline score and the desired rate of improvement.
- ✓ Construct a graph or template for students to create their own graph.

  Make a vertical axis to indicate student achievement (e.g., number of words read correctly per minute, number of correct letter sequences on a spelling probe) and the range of student scores (refer to sample, Figure 7–14).

  Make a horizontal axis to represent days or dates (e.g., Monday through Friday dates are listed to represent the school week).

  Provide demographic information about the student at the top of the graph (e.g., name, age, grade, teacher, academic area).

  Construct a table consisting of a data record of the student's scores at the bottom of the graph.

  Write the measurable objective on the graph.

Additional Resources

Graphing and Interpreting CBM Scores,
http://www.studentprogress.org/profdev/doc/graphing_interpreting_scores.pdf

FIGURE 7–14 Graphs

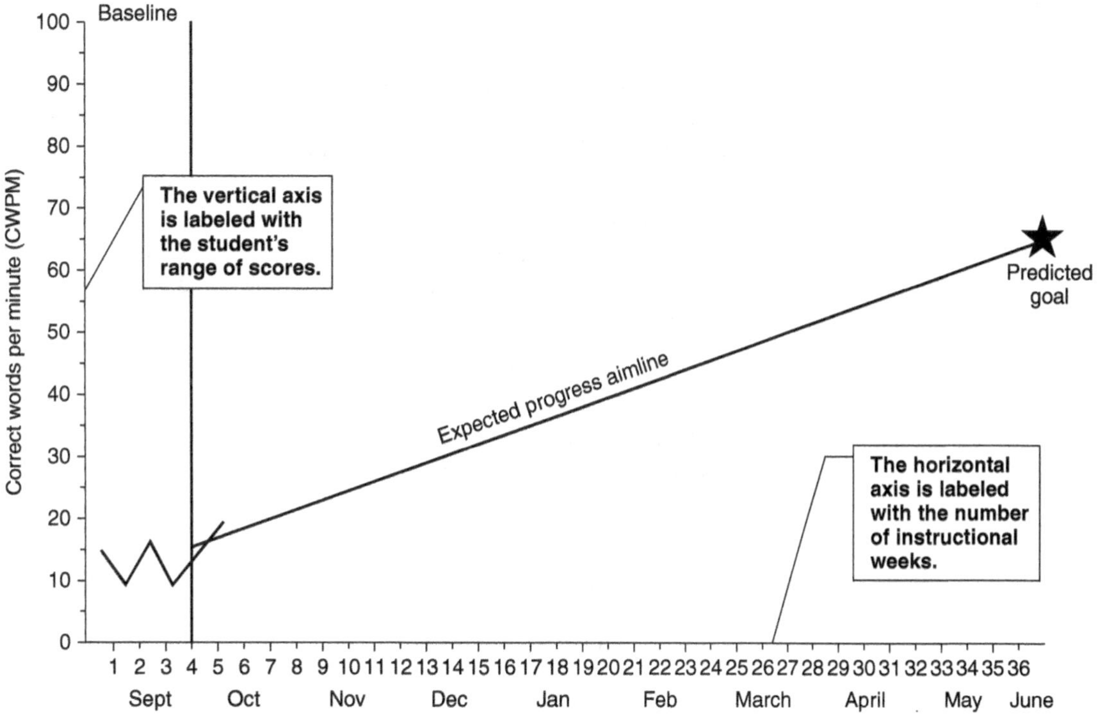

CREATING BASELINES, AIMLINES, AND GOALS

Scoring Procedure: *Creating the Baseline, Aimline, and Goal*

Strategy Description

The baseline represents the student's performance at the onset of the problem-solving process. The aimline represents the expected rate of academic growth for the student and is used to determine whether adequate progress is being made toward reaching the goal. Once the data is obtained, the aimline is drawn on the graph starting where current performance is noted (baseline) and extending to the desired performance for the specified date (long range goal (LRG)). When new data is plotted on the graph, a quick visual inspection of the position of the data informs the teacher of the student's progress in relation to the aimline. This provides an opportunity to revise the instructional plan immediately.

Implementation

Procedure for Creating the Baseline

- ✓ Administer three probes to the target student on three different days (e.g., Monday, Wednesday, and Friday).
- ✓ Score the probes. Proceed with best practice, which is to select the median (middle) score from the three baseline scores (the middle number when ranked from lowest to highest). This median score is used as the target student's baseline score.
- ✓ Record this baseline score on the graph (see sample, Figure 7–15).

Procedure for Creating an Aimline

- ✓ Determine the expected rate of improvement per week by multiplying the number of weeks (from the baseline to the LRG line) by the expected rate of growth per week which is based on published research and can be found in the tables for each subject area chapter.
- ✓ Determine the date for the long-range goal (LRG). This is generally a date at the end of the school year, or, for students receiving special education services, this is the date of the annual review of their IEP.
- ✓ Determine the total number of weeks from the baseline date to the LRG date. It takes 9 or more weeks after the baseline date to reliably determine the amount of true reading growth (Fuchs, Compton, Fuchs, & Bryant, 2006).
- ✓ To compute the LRG, count the number of weeks left in the school year or semester, multiply this number of weeks—from the baseline and the LRG date (e.g., 21)—by the expected rate of growth (e.g., two words per week) for a total. Add this total to the baseline median goal number and you will have the LRG, as shown in the following example.

  21 [weeks left in school year] × 2 [expected words per week] = 42;
  42 + 14 [baseline median] = 56 [LRG]

- ✓ Place the first X at the point of the target student's median baseline score. Then, place the second X at the now established LRG score number and established date.
- ✓ Draw a line between the baseline X point and the LRG X point to establish the aimline.
- ✓ Continue to collect data, score, and graph. When 9 to 12 data points have been plotted, begin drawing the trendline, which indicates the direction (trend or slope) of the observed behavior.

✓ Monitor the trendline closely to evaluate student progress and formulate instructional decisions. Follow the three–data point decision rule below:

When the three most recent data points lie below the aimline at any time, this indicates that the student's instructional program needs to be revised in an attempt to increase the rate of learning.

When the three successive data points are plotted above the aimline, the year-end performance goal needs to be increased to reflect the growth in learning rate.

When three successive data points cluster near (both above and below) the aimline, this may indicate that the student is progressing at the expected rate and no instructional modifications need to be made (refer to sample, Figure 7–16).

Compare Target Student to Peer Group

✓ Administer and then score the same three probes that were administered to each target student in the peer norming population. The norming population typically includes students who are average achievers in the class. However, if the target student is in special education classes, the norming population can be students with similar disabilities in the class or students with similar learning disabilities within the school district.

✓ Find the median score for each peer, and then find the total median score of the group of peers (generally three students) in the norming population. Use this number as the peer baseline score.

✓ Plot the median peer score on the graph with a wavy line starting at the baseline and ending at the LRG date.

Additional Resources

Special Connections: Creating Baselines and Aimlines,
http://www.specialconnections.ku.edu/cgi-bin/cgiwrap/specconn/main.php?cat=assessment&section=main&subsection=cbm/baselines

FIGURE 7–15 Baseline

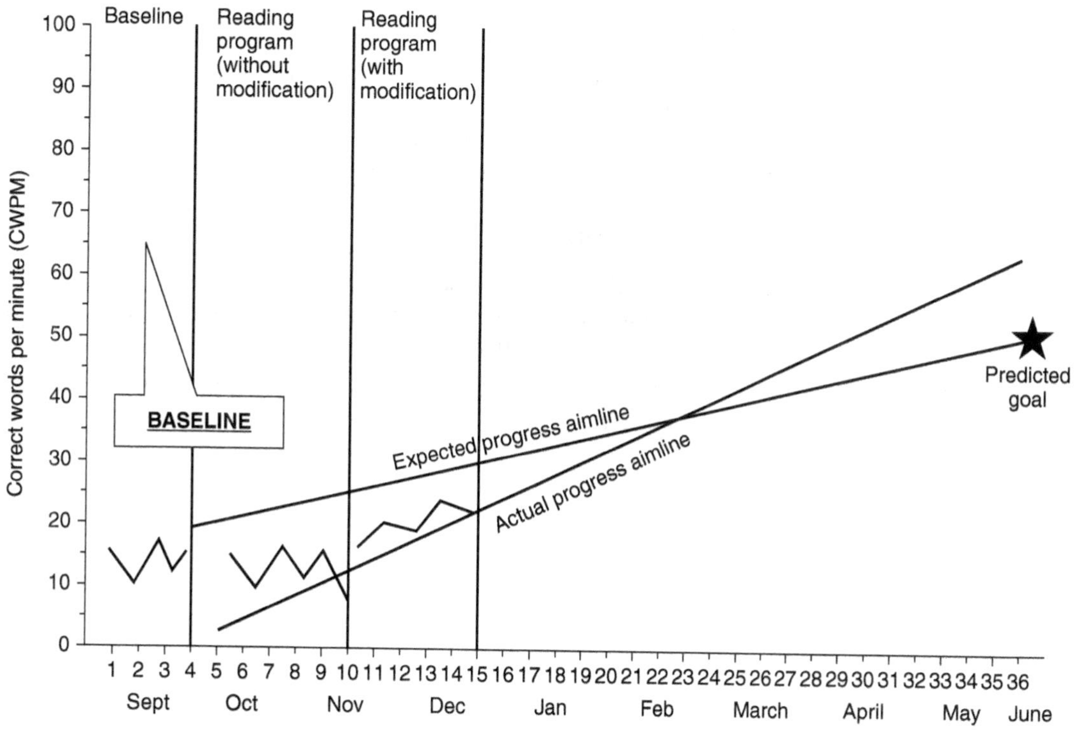

FIGURE 7–16 Aimline and Goal

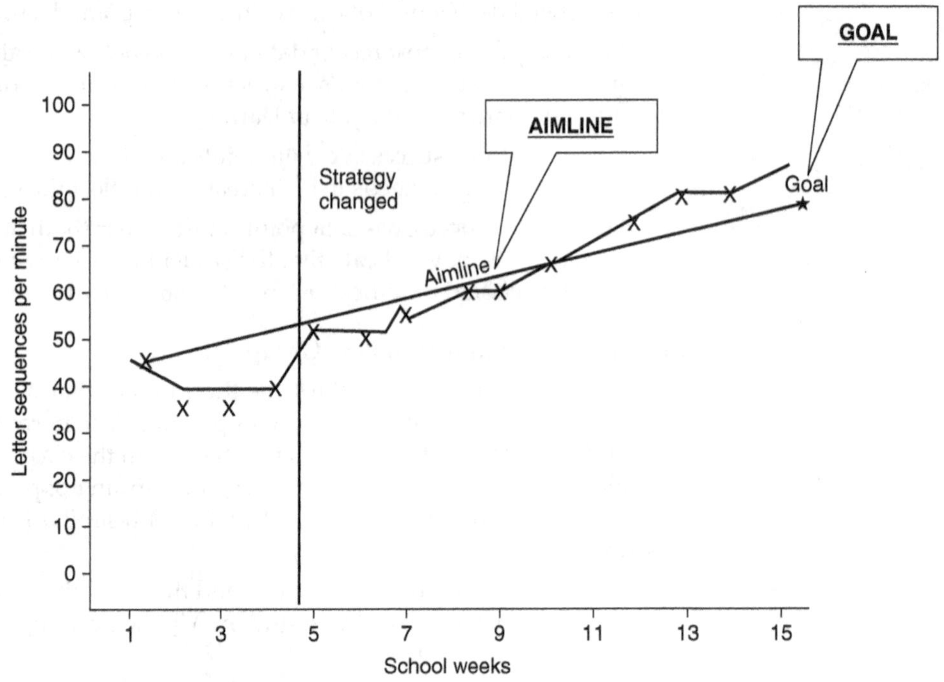

GRADING AND PROGRESS REPORTING SYSTEMS

Reporting Procedure: *Portfolio*

Strategy Description

Portfolios do not have to be graded, but they should document growth over time and demonstrate the process of improvement—both the increase in quality of the product and the quality of thinking that students exhibit. Some school programs require numerical or letter grades for reporting purposes, and portfolio data can be converted to letter grades or a point system.

Implementation

- ✓ Remember that a major benefit of the portfolio process is student participation. Have students participate in the decision-making process to reach consensus on the materials to be included in the portfolio and to help determine the evaluation criteria (see Figure 7–17).
- ✓ Establish a grading system that assigns specific points to criteria to be evaluated (see Figure 7–18).

FIGURE 7–17 Criteria for Grading a Portfolio

Portfolio Assessment

- Circle three criteria that could be used to assess a content area subject portfolio:

Accuracy	Evidence of understanding	Organization
Completeness	Form (Mechanics)	Reflectiveness
Creativity	Growth	Visual appeal

- Develop three subpoints that could explain each criterion more fully:

  Example: Evidence of understanding
  Knowledge of content
  Ability to problem solve
  Application of ideas

- Create a checklist to evaluate a portfolio.

Portfolio Checklist

Criteria and Subpoints	Does Not Meet Expectations 1	Meets Expectations 2	Exceeds Expectations 3	Total Score
☐				
*				
*				
*				
☐				
*				
*				
*				
☐				

FIGURE 7–18 Portfolio Criteria and Grading

Portfolio Criteria	***Possible Points***
Accuracy of content	15
Evidence of subject knowledge	15
All required information is included	15
Evidence of careful analysis, reflection, and attempts at improvement	15
Presentation is well organized, sequential, and clearly labeled	10
Presentation is creative with graphs, illustrations, etc., as required	10
Use of appropriate vocabulary and word usage	10
Correct sentence structure, spelling, and mechanics	10
Total Possible Points	100

Grade	***Point Range****
A+	95 to 100
A	90 to 94
B+	85 to 89
B	80 to 84
C+	75 to 79
C	70 to 74
D+	65 to 69
D	60 to 64
F	59 or less

* Resubmitted work may be reevaluated with additional point credit considered.

* Bonus points may be awarded for extra work or submitting in advance of assigned date.

Reporting Procedure: *Student Contracts*

Strategy Description

Personal contracts provide a method of evaluating concept knowledge in the content areas and a means of measuring work-study skills (e.g., note taking, organization, time management, research skills). Contracts between students and teachers can be an effective method for promoting students' commitment to a project and for teachers to monitor their progress. They are also effective in developing students' self-monitoring skills.

Implementation

- ✓ Get a commitment from the student and involve this child in the development of the contract.
- ✓ Determine the top priority of work projects to accomplish.
- ✓ List each step in the project (e.g., an item analysis or "to-do" list).
- ✓ Establish a realistic timeline; it may be necessary to identify deadlines for each item or a cluster of items on the list, rather than determine a final completion date. List the specific dates and provide a sign-off line for the student to check off and date as each item is completed.
- ✓ Draw a line for the commitment signature of the student and a line for the signature of the individual who will be monitoring progress toward the established goal; also include the date of the contract (see Figures 7–19 and 7–20).

FIGURE 7–19 Sample Assignment Contract

Assignment	Date to be Completed	Comments
• Read and outline Chapter 2.	______________	______________
• Highlight new vocabulary words.	______________	______________
• Make a list of the chief products produced in your state.	______________	______________
• Write a letter to your pen pal explaining the climate and cultural highlights of your state.	______________	______________
• In your journal, compare and contrast the seasonal differences between your state and a distant state of your choice.	______________	______________

______________	______________	______________	______________
Signed	Date	Witness	Date

FIGURE 7–20 Sample Research Project Contract

I agree to complete this project and to meet all deadlines as indicated below:

Research topic: ______________	Date project is due: ______________
Outline completed by: ______________	I will have an outline (plan) by: ______________
I will start working on ______________	By (date) I will have completed ______________
By (date) I will have ________ completed.	By (date) I will have completed ______________
I will have a progress report ready by: ___	My project will be completed by ______________

______________	______________	______________	______________
Signed	Date	Witness	Date

INTERPRETIVE CONFERENCE: REPORTING TEST RESULTS TO PARENTS

Reporting Procedure: *Interpretive Progress Reporting*

Strategy Description

Most school districts require progress reporting each marking period, which is accomplished by report cards, parent conferences, or both. Progress reporting not only keeps families informed but also facilitates regular communication and collaboration between home and school. It requires that teachers maintain a regular system of assessment, thereby proving a safeguard for ensuring that necessary programmatic and instructional modifications can be made in a timely manner. Families can also be kept informed of student progress through web pages, emails, and daily journals.

Implementation

✓ Develop a checklist that includes all subject areas, categories that are assessed and levels of proficiency (refer to sample, Figure 7–21).

✓ Begin by highlighting the student's strengths. This sets a more positive tone and helps parents hear less-positive information if they believe the teacher recognizes value in their child.

✓ Be sensitive when phrasing negative information. When stressed, parents can "read" the intent underlying a teacher's words more than the words themselves (see Figure 7–22).

✓ Encourage both parents to attend the progress reporting conference. If this is not possible, and in the case of single parents, suggest that the parent bring another family member or friend who can add support and be a secondary active listener.

✓ Be prepared: Have examples, graphs and charts, or other items to make the presentation explicit, especially when helping parents understand statistical terms (e.g., standard scores, percentiles, stanines).

✓ Be aware of body language: The teacher should lean forward, and if possible, sit beside the parent rather than behind a desk, which can appear foreboding or distant.

✓ Be sensitive to cultural and linguistic differences. Communicate with families in their primary language, and if needed, have a bilingual specialist as translator. Community members with the same cultural background who speak the same language may assist in communication.

✓ Be sure to explain terms that are not familiar to parents. Avoid educational jargon.

✓ Use active listening skills; attend to nonverbal communication such as facial expressions, shrugs, and eye contact. Do not overreact or become defensive if parents respond with grief, denial, shock, anger, or guilt. Be honest, clear, and supportive.

✓ Provide sufficient time for parents to respond without interrupting. A delay in their response may be interpreted as disinterest but may actually be due to the need for time to process the English language, the terms used, the concepts expressed, or to formulate a response.

✓ Encourage parents to ask questions. End the conference with a summary of the discussion, a clear understanding of what will occur next, and scheduled dates for follow-up discussions. Use a form to maintain a record of the issues discussed during the conference (see Figure 7–23).

Additional Resources

www.4teachers,
http://www.4teachers.org/testimony/sumner/index.shtml

FIGURE 7–21 Sample Classroom Progress Report

STUDENT: ______________________ DATE: __________ REPORT PERIOD: 1 ___ 2 ___ 3 ___ 4 ___

SUBJECT AREA	Excellent Progress	Satisfactory Progress	Needs Improvement	Average Grade	Comments
Reading/Literature					
Language Arts					
Mathematics					
Science					
Social Studies					
Physical Education					
Art					
Music					
Computer					

Assignments
(Classwork/Homework)

__ 1. Consistently well done
__ 2. Improvement shown
__ 3. Fails to complete homework
__ 4. Fails to complete class work
__ 5. Unprepared for class
__ 6. Needs to participate in class
__ 7. Unsatisfactory work quality
__ 8. Inconsistent work/effort
__ 9. Shows lack of preparation
__10. Make-up work incomplete
__11. Does not follow directions
__12. Shows lack of neatness
__13. Incomplete
__14. Carelessly completed

Assessments
(Tests, Quizzes, Projects)

__15. Improvement shown
__16. Unprepared for tests
__17. Consistently well done
__18. Unsatisfactory work
__19. Low quizzes/test scores
__20. Incomplete
__21. Lack of neatness, legibility
__22. Not turned in on time

Study Skills
(Behavior, Attitudes)

__23. Shows outstanding effort
__24. Does not accept responsibility
__25. Demonstrates strong organizational skills
__26. Demonstrates leadership skills
__27. Seeks/accepts help as needed
__28. Innovative/creative thinker
__29. Asks questions to improve understanding
__30. Sincere and trying to improve
__31. Does not ask questions/participate
__32. Works conscientiously, subject difficult
__33. Inappropriate classroom behavior
__34. Demonstrates lack of organization/study skills
__35. Does not work accurately/proofread
__36. Does not follow oral/written directions
__37. Shows initiative
__38. Works well in group
__39. Shows marginal effort
__40. Needs to use time wisely
__41. Does not accept criticism
__42. Missing assignments

Comments

Student Signature: ______________________ Date: ________
Teacher Signature: ______________________ Date: ________
Parent/Guardian Signature: ______________________

FIGURE 7–22
Professional Terminology

Examples of verbs that can be observed and measured

* write
* read
* spell
* name
* list
* label
* demonstrate
* participate
* construct
* summarize
* solve
* identify
* compare
* analyze
* differentiate

Examples of verbs that cannot be observed or measured

* understand
* know
* appreciate
* believe
* comprehend
* grasp
* instill
* foster
* enjoy

Words that promote a positive view of the student

* thorough
* shows commitment
* has a good grasp of . . .
* caring
* improved tremendously

Words and phrases that convey the student needs help

* could profit by . . .
* finds it difficult to . . .
* needs reinforcement in . . .
* requires . . .
* has trouble, at times, with . . .

Words to avoid or use with caution:

* unable
* can't
* won't
* always

Conditions under which the behavior is expected to occur

* Given a paragraph to read orally . . .
* Given a list of grade level vocabulary words . . .
* Given a two-step math problem involving measurement . . .
* With the use of a calculator . . .

Criteria level for acceptance performance

* Ratio-based mastery level; 7 out of every 10 attempts . . .
* Time-based mastery level; 5 answers within a 15-minute period . . .
* Percent-based mastery level: 80% of the time . . .

FIGURE 7–23 Sample Parent Conference Form

Parent Conference Checklist

Student: ________________ Parent/guardian: ________________ Date: ____________

Issues to share about the student's grades, work-study skills, disciplinary issues, and progress toward meeting IEP goals (include work samples, anecdotal records, etc.):

1. ______________________________
2. ______________________________
3. ______________________________

Areas to work on:

1. ______________________________
2. ______________________________
3. ______________________________

Reports from related service professionals:

Speech therapist	Counselor
Occupational therapist	Physical therapist

Adjustments in instructional, environmental, test accommodations: ____________
Adjustments in IEP goals and objectives: ____________
Next scheduled conference: ____________
Action to be taken, by whom, and date of accomplishment: ____________
Parent feedback/comments: ____________

WRITING AND REPORTING TEST RESULTS

Reporting Procedure: *Writing Progress Reports*

Strategy Description

It is important to be able to communicate test results, student progress, and general school information in both verbal and written forms. Written reports need to be comprehensive and direct yet understandable and compassionate. Although a verbal interpretation is generally provided in progress review meetings and eligibility for special education services conferences, a written report is often required for record keeping, and it provides details and documentation that can be reviewed after the conference session. The goal is to inform, that is, to provide a review of the student's specific strengths and weaknesses. Teachers must continually communicate with families. Other written formats used to notify parents of school updates include web pages, class newsletters, emails, and daily journals.

Implementation

- ✓ Write in clear behavioral terms, without educational jargon, and provide explicit examples.
- ✓ Use positive statements to constructively reframe problem areas (see Figure 7–24).
- ✓ Remember that students will likely read a teacher's comments. Negative comments can be counterproductive; they can reinforce an existing low self-esteem and limit confidence in students' academic and behavioral abilities (Hallahan, Kauffman, & Pullen, 2009).
- ✓ Recognize that parents may be illiterate in both English and their primary language. Although these documents are generally written at or above the 10th-grade level, the reading skills of many parents is closer to the third- or fourth-grade reading level. Ideally, written communication should be kept no higher than the fourth- to fifth-grade level in English or the family's language.
- ✓ Follow up on documents sent home but not returned to school. Documents may not be returned due to fear, confusion, or other family issues. Also, consider that parents may be illiterate in both English and their primary or second language and be unwilling to share this information.

Additional Resources

Teacher Service (create and post notes on the web),
http://schoolnotes.com/

FIGURE 7–24 Examples of Reframing

POSITIVE STATEMENTS FOR REPORTING TO PARENTS	
Uncoordinated, clumsy	needs to improve fine and gross motor control; increase coordination
Steals	needs to respect others' belongings
Inattentive	needs to be more focused, improve concentration
Rude	needs to be more respectful of others
Doesn't follow rules	needs to have own agenda
Talks excessively	needs to improve listening skills and socialize less in class
Lazy	needs to put forth more effort
Bully	needs to interact more cooperatively with peers

CONNECTING ASSESSMENT RESULTS TO PROGRAM PLANNING AND IEP DEVELOPMENT

Reporting Procedure: *Writing and Monitoring IEP Goals*

Strategy Description

Rather than rely on traditional grading systems that are inherently subjective, school personnel continue to recognize the value of monitoring progress toward IEP goals and objectives as a process by collecting work samples and using rubrics to measure growth. The IEP is another form of written progress reporting. This document is developed for each student who is classified as having a disability that impacts the individual's education. The components of the IEP should include the student's current educational status, the special services the student receives, the broad achievement goal for each area in which the student receives special services, the measure of progress toward the goal, and the identification of appropriate accommodation and modifications required to successfully meet program goals.

Implementation

- ✓ Determine the student's present level of academic achievement and functional performance.
- ✓ Identify the student's annual academic and functional goals (see Figure 7–25).
- ✓ Establish evaluation procedures and a schedule for assessing the identified goals (see Figure 7–26).
- ✓ Identify the special education, related services, and supplemental services the child will be receiving.
- ✓ Determine the amount of time the student is not included in general education classes.
- ✓ Identify the accommodations that the student requires to achieve success in the instructional program.

FIGURE 7–25 IEP Goal Form Template

Once the goal has been calculated, a long-range goal (LRG) can be written using the following formula.

In ________ (number of weeks until next IEP review) when presented with stories from Level ________ (level number in which the student currently reads 30–60 wpm) in ______________ (name of reading series) _________ (student's name) will read aloud _________ words correctly.

The following format can be used to write an IEP objective.

Each successive week, when presented with a random selection from Level ______ (same as for LRG) ______________ (name of reading series) __________ (student's name) will read aloud at an average increase* of _____ wpm.

* The average weekly increase is the aimline and can be obtained from calculating the numeric value of the aimline (see determining the trend [slope]).

FIGURE 7–26 Plotting IEP Progress: CBA Probe Graph

Eric continues to have difficulty with word recognition, which impacts his reading fluency and comprehension. As his teacher, you want to closely monitor his progress toward meeting the projected IEP reading goals so you can make necessary instructional adjustments, as needed. By graphing his biweekly CBA probe results, you are able to track and chart his skill development. This graph can be easily converted to a reporting system that meets IDEA-2004 mandates that parents receive regular progress reports.

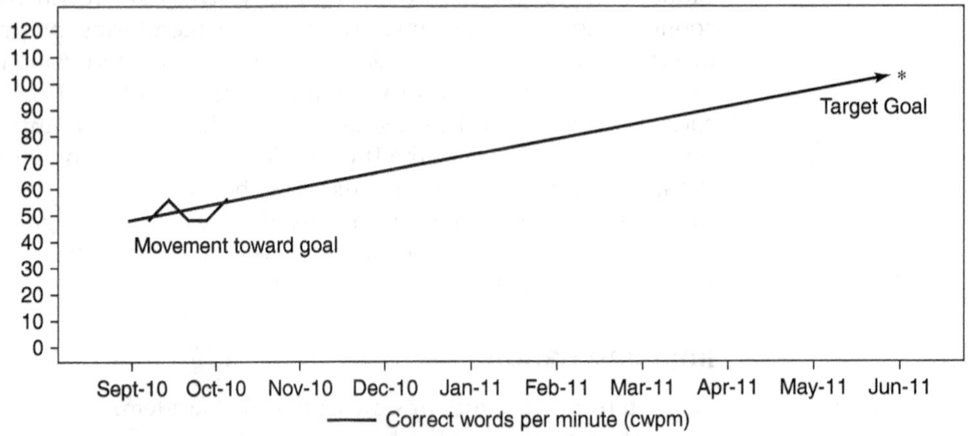

Present Levels of Academic Achievement and Functional Performance (9/15/10)

Eric, a student in your third-grade class, reads unrehearsed second-grade level material with 97% accuracy at a rate of 50 correct words per minute.

Progress Check Points

Progress Point 1: By November, Eric will read unrehearsed second-grade material with 97% accuracy at a rate of 65 correct words per minute.

Progress Point 2: By January, Eric will read unrehearsed second-grade material with 97% accuracy at a rate of 75 correct words per minute.

Progress Point 3: By March, Eric will read unrehearsed second-grade material with 97% accuracy at a rate of 90 correct words per minute.

Progress Point 4: By June, Eric will read unrehearsed second-grade material with 97% accuracy at a rate of 105 correct words per minute.

REFERENCES

Arter, J., & McTighe, J. (2001). *Scoring rubrics in the classroom: Using performance criteria for assessing and improving student performance*. Thousand Oaks, CA: Corwin Press.

Fuchs, D. F., Compton, D. L., Fuchs, L. S., & Bryant, J. D. (2006, February). *The prevention and identification of reading disability*. Paper presented at the Pacific Coast Research Conference, San Diego, CA.

Hallahan, D. P., Kauffman, J. K., & Pullen, P. C. (2009). *Exceptional learners: An introduction to special education* (11th ed). Boston: Allyn & Bacon.

Jenkins, J. R., Hudson, R. F., & Lee, S. H. (2007). Using CBM-reading assessment to monitor progress. *Perspectives on Language and Literacy, 33*(2). International Dyslexia Association.

Salend, S. J., & Garrick-Duhaney, L. M. (2002). Grading students in inclusive settings. *Teaching Exceptional Children, 34*(3), 8–15.

Index